FIXING
WASHINGTON
2016

TOM CHURCH

FIXING

WASHINGTON

2016

TOM CHURCH

PUBLISHED BY

FORTIS

A NONFICTION IMPRINT FROM ADDUCENT

WWW.ADDUCENT.CO

TITLES DISTRIBUTED IN

NORTH AMERICA

UNITED KINGDOM

WESTERN EUROPE

SOUTH AMERICA

AUSTRALIA

FIXING WASHINGTON | 2016
TOM CHURCH

ISBN 9781937592561 (hardback)

Published by Fortis (a nonfiction imprint from Adducent)
Jacksonville, Florida
www.Adducent.co

Published in the United States of America
Cover concept by Travis Getz of Getz Solutions.

Table of Contents

Dedication & Acknowledgments

Note from the Author (Disclaimer)

Introduction — 1

Chapter 1 - The Economy and Deficits — 10

Some Basic Definitions — 18

The Debt - Our Biggest Challenge — 28

Three Controversial Issues — 36

 #1 Income Inequality — 36

 #2 Inversions — 44

 #3 Student Loans — 47

The State of the Recovery — 48

The FIX — 51

Chapter 2 - National Defense — 66

First - A Little Perspective — 68

Defense Budgets — 72

Defense Strategy — 80

Leadership and Accountability — 92

Chapter 3 - Homeland Security — 100

Chapter 4 - Foreign Policy — 119

Global Leadership -- the Long View — 123

Treaties and Alliances — 126

Globalization and Trade — 134

Human Rights — 142

Geographic Perspectives — 145

 Israel and Palestine — 145

 Russia — 151

 China and the Pacific — 160

 Africa — 169

 Pakistan and India — 172

 The Greater Middle East — 175

 Iraq, Afghanistan, and Syria — 180

 Saudi Arabia and the Gulf Cooperative Council (GCC), Egypt, Jordan, and Turkey — 189

 Iran — 194

 Canada, South and Central America — 201

The Terrorist Threat — 202

Foreign Policy Summary — 205

Chapter 5 - Immigration   209
Chapter 6 - America's Veterans   218
Chapter 7 - The Environment and Energy   226
Chapter 8 - Our Youth, Our Future   240
Chapter 9 - Obamacare   254
Chapter 10 - Summary   263
About the Author   269
Endnotes   271

Dedication & Acknowledgments

This book is dedicated to:

- One Person: My daughter; that she and generations thereafter might live in a free, secure and prosperous America
- 50 million: The astounding number of k-12 children in public schools who qualify for subsidized or free school lunches; that your future may be brighter
- 150 million registered voters: Most of whom will vote in 2016, and most of whom think America is headed in the wrong direction. I am one of you, looking for that leader who can guide this nation to greatness again

The author would like to offer special thanks to my family members and close friends and classmates who have seen less of me over the past two years while I pursued the passion of writing this book. Thanks to Travis Getz of Getz Solutions for the cover concept, and for constructing the graphs in the Economy and Foreign Policy chapters from publicly available data sources. After many rejections, thanks also to Dennis Lowery of Adducent, Inc. for editing and publishing this book under their Fortis nonfiction imprint.

NOTE FROM THE AUTHOR (DISCLAIMER)

The author has made every attempt to endnote and/or give credit to ideas or writings that are reflected in this book. The author reads daily The Washington Post, weekly The Economist, occasionally catches a morning or evening talk-show, John Mauldin's Economic Newsletter, and other weekly publications. Any missing attribution is entirely unintentional.

The synthesized conclusions or recommendations in the book are strictly my own. By choice, no one was interviewed for this book, nor was a Foreword sought; the views expressed are just my opinions for how we address the significant problems this nation faces.

INTRODUCTION

In mid-summer 2015 the host of Meet the Press, Chuck Todd, noted that almost as many Americans identify as Independents (42%) as Democrats (27%) and Republicans (20%) *combined*; a growing trend toward Independents.

The message from that revelation should be pretty clear. The American people are increasingly disenchanted with gridlock in Washington and are breaking ranks with the established political parties and all the theatrics and spending surrounding the presidential election.

You saw it with the rise of outsiders like Bernie Sanders and Donald Trump, who offered new perspectives and appeal. It is only a matter of time before we have a viable 3rd Party candidate run and be elected president. Organizations such as Change the Rule and No Labels are leading the movement. All the dynamics are in place, from a grossly ineffective federal government to widespread unrest over income inequality and America's decline on the world stage. And much more.

In a 2014 Harris Poll the Congress got a 6% favorable rating; the lowest of any entity ranked. In a 2015 Rasmussen Report *63% of Americans stated they felt the 'country was headed in the wrong direction.'*

Both are startling numbers. Yet talking to many well-educated citizens we find that few understand a single element of foreign policy and can't articulate the difference between the federal deficit and debt.

Regardless of whether it's a Democrat or Republican who next enters the White House, the rancor between the two parties will continue and the nation's urgent business will languish. Although all the candidates will run a campaign based on 'changing Washington,' just as the current president did,

Absolutely nothing will really change.

The more polarizing the winner, the more contentious the ensuing four years will be. Just think, how long have we been trying to get meaningful tax reform or comprehensive immigration legislation?

2016 would be an ideal time for a strong Independent 3rd Party candidate who could bridge the partisan divide. We will hear, as we have in so many past elections, that 2016 will be perhaps the most important election in our lifetime. That hasn't proven correct yet, but the election of the president does set the stage for the national priorities for the next four (maybe eight) years. But each year the amount of unfinished business that is critical to this country's future continues to mount, largely unaddressed by our elected leaders.

Americans tend to focus on a short horizon. Maybe that is understandable when many of us worry about job security, our children, health care and saving for retirement, among many other things that consume our daily lives. But as we head to the polls, we should take heed of the serious longer-term challenges and trends that we, as a nation, must address. That can has been kicked down the road so many times on important issues that addressing them becomes all that more difficult the longer we wait.

While we were busy in Afghanistan and Iraq, we basically missed the emergence of China and, to some extent Putin in Russia. More recently, while we all intently watched the Iranian nuclear talks three significant events were all reported but went almost unnoticed by the larger public: The signing of the $400B oil deal between Russia and China, the formation of Chinese led Asian Infrastructure Investment Bank (AIIB) which many of our allies quickly joined, and a 60-minute report on China's virtual monopoly of Rare Earth elements that are vital to our military.

So here are a few of the most pressing issues, all of which the 2016 presidential candidates, and eventually the next president, will have to address:

- Our national debt has risen from over $5 trillion to over $ 18 trillion dollars over the last two Administrations. It is not sustainable.
- The appropriate role of the federal government should be debated. The separation and balance of powers envisioned by the framers of our Constitution are not functioning well. Congress is particularly dysfunctional.
- The fact that we spend multiple times more on our elderly as we do on our youth seems just wrong and is not sustainable either.
- Deteriorating infrastructure, education falling short of expectations, income inequality, antiquated tax laws, strained race relations, unmet immigration reforms, declining civility and empathy, and a tentative economic recovery all cry for action and leadership.
- America's technological advantage, both in the military and commercial sectors, is fast eroding.
- Russia, China, and Iran continue expansionist trends and suppression of their people and the media. The turmoil in the Middle East is growing worse with the emergence of

radical jihad. The failure of the Arab Spring, with an eventual Sunni-Shia civil war looking more probable, precipitated mostly by Iran. America is largely viewed, by both allies and adversaries, as weak and unreliable. What should America's role in the world be going forward? Do we trend toward isolation or regaining prominence as a world leader, and how does that exactly translate into a coherent foreign policy?

A couple of years ago I began to write some articles on national topics of interest to me, and as a means to become better informed on issues that I saw as important to our nation. Then in 2014 I took my daughter to see a One Direction concert at Washington Nationals stadium. I think I was one of only about twelve dads or other males among the 42,000 in the sold-out park who attended, and we all found the one concession stand that was selling beer. Proudly, I was the only one properly attired with earplugs. The concert was a turning point, however, and gave final impetus for this book, which was then in early stages. While most of the 42,000 attendees knew every detail about the band and every word to every song, I doubt that very few knew who the Vice President was, much less their elected officials. Not long after that concert, two items hit the press almost simultaneously that caught my attention. The first was that over 50% of our children in public schools are now eligible for subsidized lunches and the second, that a new Washington Nationals pitcher had signed a $210 million contract. I'm an unequivocal advocate of capitalism and free markets, but something struck me as strangely wrong with this picture, or at least out of balance. By the way, he is a great pitcher, but you get the point.

Thomas Jefferson once wrote: *"A well-informed citizenry is indispensable for the proper functioning of the republic."* That is the purpose of this book. To better inform voters on the critical issues that we as a nation face, so that each of you may be better prepared to critically analyze the positions of the Presidential candidates and vote in November 2016. Too many Americans, including many of my acquaintances, are overly consumed by narrow, short-term interests or wedded to a particular political party.

The urgency of action today argues for a much larger view of the world landscape, and a strong leader in the White House who is both pragmatic and able to work across the political aisle. Yes, demographics are changing as the country becomes grayer and less white, and a larger number are unmarried. There's room in America for all who choose to be responsible and productive citizens. As citizens, we all have a responsibility to vote. Like many of you, I am growing increasingly impatient with gridlock in Washington, and the inability of the Administration and Congress to work in support of our broader national interests.

I'm appalled that it's 2015 and we have events like those seen in Charleston or Chicago, that women still make less than men for doing the same job, that some still deny global warming in the face of overwhelming scientific evidence, and there seems wide dismay on the direction the country is heading. Outside of our soaring debt, apathy and the silent-majority who don't engage in the national discourse are our biggest internal threats. Our domestic prosperity and our foreign affairs are totally interlinked and complementary.

Sadly, for years our leaders have been focused on spending, rather than investing in our country's future. Rachel Maddow, MSNBC nightly talk-show host, had a trailer that went something like this:

> "We all have somewhat of an amazing inheritance in term of the infrastructure that our Grandparents and Great-grandparents thought to build, knowing that the benefits would rain down on us. WHAT ARE WE DOING?"

The quote is not exact, but the question she asks is exactly right. Probably like many who heard this on the radio, I answered "not much", or at least not nearly enough. Many younger Americans have no concept of what a Depression or World War would look like. And very little appreciation of the sacrifices made so that they might now enjoy the freedoms and liberties of living in America. While millions wait and hope to come to the U.S. someday, too many of our citizens take for granted the opportunities bestowed upon them by this great nation. The veterans from the Greatest Generation are all passing on now.

In his book, "The Rise and Fall of Great Powers," Paul Kennedy states. "In the largest sense of all, therefore, the only answer to the question debated by the public or whether the United States can preserve its existing position is no. For it simply has not been given to any one society to remain permanently ahead of the others, because that would imply a freezing of the differential pattern of growth rates, technological advance, and military developments which have existed since time immemorial."

Kennedy goes on to say that American statesmen can moderate this process by recognizing the broad trends and managing through policies for the long-term.[1]

Although others have espoused the same theory I don't entirely share this perspective. I think a fully engaged citizenry, and a properly functioning three branches of government (Legislative—Executive—Judicial), can ensure American primacy for a very long time into our nation's future. But we need a whole of nation approach that promotes innovation and technology, improves infrastructure, opportunity, and education, and that addresses our mounting debt. All while maintaining a robust military and deterrent capability. More than anything, it requires an informed and engaged citizenry.

According to Gallup, in 2002 about 60% of Americans thought that government would do the right thing most of the time; that figure is now about 19%. Every two years Harris conducts a poll of American confidence in our institutions. The most recent poll in 2014 shows the military leads with 55% of respondents expressing "A great Deal of Confidence", followed by small business. The numbers go down rapidly from there, with Congress and Wall Street at a less than 10% confidence factor, and the Press at 11%, as shown below. The election of 2014 was about anti-incumbency. 2016 will see two new candidates. Will anything change after the election or will it be gridlock as usual? How will you vote? How are you defining the issues most critical to our country's future?

CONFIDENCE IN LEADERS OF INSITUTIONS
2014 HARRIS POLL

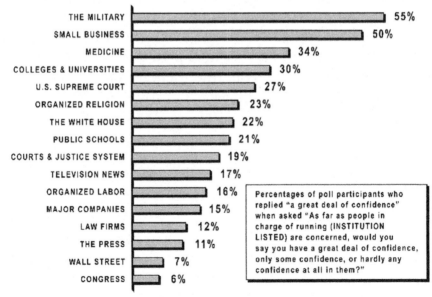

Institution	Percentage
THE MILITARY	55%
SMALL BUSINESS	50%
MEDICINE	34%
COLLEGES & UNIVERSITIES	30%
U.S. SUPREME COURT	27%
ORGANIZED RELIGION	23%
THE WHITE HOUSE	22%
PUBLIC SCHOOLS	21%
COURTS & JUSTICE SYSTEM	19%
TELEVISION NEWS	17%
ORGANIZED LABOR	16%
MAJOR COMPANIES	15%
LAW FIRMS	12%
THE PRESS	11%
WALL STREET	7%
CONGRESS	6%

Percentages of poll participants who replied "a great deal of confidence" when asked "As far as people in charge of running (INSTITUTION LISTED) are concerned, would you say you have a great deal of confidence, only some confidence, or hardly any confidence at all in them?"

While the next eight years carry with them great uncertainty and risk, there are some clear and recognizable trends. The national debt continues to soar and represents our greatest long-term national threat. The economic recovery is soft, with businesses increasingly using part-time workers and technology innovations set to replace as many as 40% of jobs by some estimates. Demographics will continue to change, with immigrants and their children making up a far greater percent of the population. The number of single-parent homes are increasing, and entitlement programs will be stressed to meet the demand of an aging population. Civic participation and civil behavior are in decline everywhere. Income disparity will get worse without concerted actions. *Congress is increasingly divided and can no longer get the job done, in my opinion.*

Clearer are the events on the international front where we see an emerging and increasingly assertive China more closely aligned with Putin and Russia. An emerging Shia and Shiite civil war post-Assad in Syria. The continued threat of the Islamic State of Iraq and Syria (ISIS) and radical jihad, and the most aggressive terrorist state in Iran, on an eventual path to a nuclear weapon and delivery capability. In China, the richest 50 members of the National People's Congress are worth nearly $95 billion.[2] In Russia the oligarchs and Putin control most of the wealth, with Putin's wealth alone estimated at $40 billion.

What should our foreign policy look like post-election? If anything we need a bipartisan Congress dedicated to solving these escalating issues. Instead, we will more likely see partisan fireworks and recriminations up to the election, and then well into the next term as nothing changes. Our nation deserves better, and the people should demand better! Foremost, we need a strong leader in the next president who can engage all of Congress, set critical national priorities, achieve great legislative success through compromise and engagement, and articulate a clear path for our foreign policy.

In 1980, Ronald Reagan asked Americans the question. "Are you better off than eight years ago?" Most answered "No" and voted that way. Ask yourself the same question. Do you think any Republican or Democrat elected in November 2016 to become our 45th President of the United States can change things in Washington? Our 44th president said he would, but couldn't. If you answered like I do, it points to why we need an independent running for the presidency. And we someday will. Sadly, the lyrics to the song below bear some truth.

IF A PRESIDENT GOES THROUGH THE WHITEHOUSE DOORS AND DOES WHAT HE SAYS HE'LL DO, WE'LL ALL BE DRINKING THAT FREE BUBBLEUP AND EATING THAT RAINBOW STEW.

--Merle Haggard's song, Rainbow Stew

CHAPTER 1

THE ECONOMY AND DEFICITS
OUR MOST SERIOUS CHALLENGE

"The fact that we are here today to debate raising America's debt limit is a sign of leadership failure. Increasing America's debt weakens us domestically and internationally. Washington is shifting the burden of bad choices today onto the backs of our children and grandchildren."
Then-Senator Barack Obama in March 2006

Obama has gone on as president to raise the debt limit six times and more than double the nation's debt from around $9 Trillion to over $18 Trillion, and growing.

"It's the Economy, Stupid!" We all remember that phrase from the first Clinton candidacy and the economy was pretty good in the Clinton years, due primarily to the technology boom, rather than any remarkable policy direction.

In the run up to the 2016 election, we can expect to hear much of the same regarding the lack of good job creation and wage stagnation, with each side blaming the other. In 2008, with the bankruptcy of Lehman Brothers, the U.S. entered a recession that officially lasted only until June 2009, but the lingering effects have continued much longer, impacting millions of Americans.

Finance reform that requires banks to hold more reserves and makes trading in derivatives more transparent has decreased the likelihood of another episodic financial breakdown like the last one, at least in the U.S., although risks remain. In 2015, you hear the welcome good news that the economy is picking up, wages are even seeing some uptick, and that deficits are declining and no longer the problem they once were. But that rhetoric masks the larger problems of the massive national and local debts that have accumulated over the past 16 years; Funding shortfalls in Medicare and Medicaid, projections of increased deficits again starting in 2016, an aging population reliant on Social Security, lack of good job creation and growing income inequality, to mention just a few.

From my perspective, reducing our national debt is the most compelling issue we face as a nation. The longer we wait, the more difficult the task and the more hardships we will create, not to mention the heavy burden we are passing on to the next generations. We can kick the can only so long – all bills come due at some point.

Like many Americans, I find the deluge of data hard to digest. Every time the Congressional Budget Office (CBO), Department of Labor (DOL) or Census Bureau issues a new report, or Pew releases a new survey, we are inundated with data about the debt, deficits, trade imbalance, income changes, Gross Domestic Product (GDP) projections, and other economic statistics. Trying to fit all the pieces together and understand the relationships is difficult. Most Americans I talk to may not comprehend the details of the huge budget mess we have created, but they share a pretty good understanding that, as a nation, we must balance our federal budget much like we must balance our personal checkbooks. They share a disquiet that while the recovery officially started in 2009, incomes have not kept pace for the middle-class; good jobs have not materialized as in most economic recoveries; that the well-off continue to prosper disproportionally, and that they are generally pessimistic about their own economic futures and those of their children and grandchildren. Those sentiments reflect the data that shows why a drop in oil prices did not produce the expected increase in consumer spending. They know that we are now six to seven years into an economic recovery that generally lasts eight years, and rarely over a decade.

Americans also share a strong belief that the political posturing and petty bickering in Washington are no longer acceptable, and that bipartisan congressional action is long overdue. We saw that sentiment clearly reflected in the 2014 mid-term elections. But then nothing really changed.

In my opinion, if we don't halt our burgeoning debt, then we are headed for an economic catastrophe, equal or worse than anything we have seen to date from some European countries. Aging demographics, robotic technology replacing workers, continuing impacts of globalization and the rise of new powers like China are all factors pressurizing our economy. Without action our bond rating, already once reduced, will erode further and our leadership role in the world will be further minimized, with increasing security risks. The standard of living for our children and grandchildren will be reduced (it is already projected to be less than my generation.)

If I'm painting a distressing picture, it is only because that seems to be where the evidence leads, and recent poll results show that the vast majority of the country agrees with this conclusion. But it doesn't have to be that way.

Americans have risen to challenges and threats in the past, and we have the resilience and capacity to do the same again. Both sides of the political aisle know what needs to be done, but lack the fortitude to pass the needed legislation, specifically because it will entail some uncomfortable compromise and likely cost votes, and maybe their seat in Congress. Wouldn't that be a shame!

We can get there, but I have deep reservations that our legislators in Congress will do so on their own accord. Of course, leadership on this issue starts with the president. As a highly respected sitting senator wrote in 2013, an assessment I agree with:

> *"If we don't make a major course correction with regard to the federal budget, a major course correction will be forced on us, sooner rather than later. The president and Congress have failed to inform the public about how damaging these events could be. Unemployment could reach 20%, the real gross domestic product could decline 10-15% and the bottom would fall out of the middle-class."*
> --Senator Tom Coburn (R—Oklahoma)

The uptick in the economy that we are enjoying in 2015, primarily the result of cheap oil for which our leaders can take little credit, is fragile on many fronts and may not last as long as many think. I hope I am mistaken.

Sorting through the many economic facts and figures can be frustrating, if not outright boring, so I have summarized a few for your consideration, accumulated from various General Accounting Office (GAO), Office of Management and Budget (OMB), CBO, and numerous other reports. This data changes with each economic update and is subject to projections based on a wide range of economic assumptions, how spending is accounted for, accounting provisions in the law, whether we are talking budget submission numbers or actual spending, etc.

In any case, and throughout this chapter, the exact numbers are really not so important. In fact, every number is wrong (more on this to come that will explain what I mean). What is important is the larger financial picture that they project. I am an eternal optimistic by disposition, but I don't like most of these figures, and the trends are even more troubling:

- **Our federal spending for 2014 was approximately 3.504T (Trillion) and we took in $3.021T in revenues.** Therefore, our 2014 deficit (the difference between what we take in and what we spend), was $483B (Billion), which is much improved over the 2012 figure of $1.08T, but any deficit still adds to the debt. You can see how deficits and the debt are trending over time in a chart that follows.

- In 1955, **household debt** was 49% of disposable income; by 2007 it was about 128%, then dropping to 112% by 2011. It is about 107% in 2015.

- Our **accumulated gross federal debt** in 2014 ended at around **$17.729T, and 2015 just shy of $19T**. This is the summation of all of our annual deficits and is the figure subject to the congressional cap legislation. I'll explain later how we got here. In the meantime, you may want to visit any number of websites that track our national debt (USDebt Clock.org is one) just to see the magnitude of the problem and how fast it is accumulating. Remember to thank our national leaders as you view the clock.

- **GDP** finished 2014 at about $17.251T a year. Therefore, our approximate Debt to GDP ratio is now over 100%! There are many analyses that show why this number is historically bad economic news. Another figure often used is the public debt to GDP ratio, which is about 75%. GDP is explained in more detail below.

- **State debt:** a report in 2011 estimated state debt at over $4.2T (not part of the federal debt), which included pension and health care liabilities. Many state pension funds are less than 50% funded as workers from Chicago to Jacksonville are finding out as their promised pension plans get cut. Teamsters truckers appear to be next in line for cuts. Chicago, with unfunded pension plan liabilities of over $20B, has seen the city's bond rating reduced to Junk status.

- **"The annual service (interest) on the debt was over $200B in 2010** and may reach close to **$1 Trillion by 2020** if action is not taken." This was lifted from a speech given by President Obama at George Washington University on April 13, 2011. In 2014 interest on the debt was $271B as shown below, and CBO now projects around $600B in interest debt in 2022, a high number that grows each year, and roughly the size of our entire defense budget. This is just in interest payments for which we get nothing in return! Just imagine what good things we could be doing with that money.

- **Medicare and Medicaid**: In 1965, the year Congress established Medicare and Medicaid, the cost represented 2.6% of the budget. In 2010, these expenditures consumed over 20%. In 2014, the figure was 24%. The unfunded liability of Medicare is around $37T by one recent estimate.

- **Fraud** for FEDEX it is about .3%. Fraud for Medicare is 10.5% and Medicaid is 8.4% - that's many billions of dollars - how come?[3]

- **Social Security**: When President Franklin Roosevelt first created Social Security in 1935 following the Depression, life expectancy was 61. He set the retirement age, intentionally, at 65: four years *after* life expectancy. By 1950, the average length of retirement was eight years. Full retirement age is now set at 67, but workers can retire as early as 62 with reduced benefits–the average age is 64.

Today's 65-year-olds can expect to live 19.2 more years, meaning they will likely draw on Social Security payments for about 20 years. The Social Security Trust Fund, which really exists on paper only, is expected to run out of money by 2033 by recent estimates. The unfunded liability for Social Security exceeds $15T. Annual spending on Medicare, Medicaid and Social Security combined are approaching 50% of the budget in 2014 (up from 27% in 1975). Today, Social Security supports about 55 million people; by 2035 that number is expected to be 91 million. In 1950, American had sixteen workers to each beneficiary. Today, three workers support every person claiming benefits. By 2035, that ratio will be 2:1. What does this all look like with medical advances on the horizon that might significantly increase lifespans?

- **Median income** in the U.S. from 2000 to 2010 declined by 7%, after adjusting for inflation.[4]

- **Income inequality:** In 1975 the top.01% of wage earners garnered about 2.5% of the nation's income, including capital gains, according to data collected by the University of California economist Emmanuel Saez. By 2008, that share had quadrupled and stood at 10.4%.[5] To be fair, the top 1% also pay 40% of income taxes.

- **Spending on our children:** in 1960 about 20% of the federal budget went to programs such as education and health that supported children under 18. That number is now around 10%. When we include Medicaid, 35% of the federal budget supports the elderly. Today, the federal government spends between $4 and $5 on elderly people for every $1 it spends on children, an astonishing figure.[6] To be objective again, most spending for children is done at the state and local levels.

- **Corporate taxes:** According to the NY Times, March 2011, General Electric paid no U.S. taxes in 2010 on $5.1B in U.S. sales ($14.2B worldwide). In fact, they filed a $3.2B tax credit. From 2009-2012, Apple shielded $74B in profits from U.S. laws through overseas subsidiaries.[7] According to various reports, U.S. multinational companies have accumulated almost $2T is offshore profits. One of the problems is that American firms pay corporate taxes, at 35%, which are among the highest rates in the world. More on that later.

- **Jobs:** we need between +100k to 150k/month just to handle the increase in population entering the workplace. We need a sustained +300k per month to reach the unemployment level that existed before the recession. In June 2014, we came close, with 288,000 new jobs created and hit 322,000 in November 2014. In April 2015, we created 223,000 jobs according to the DOL, and another 280,000 in May with signs of increasing wages. But are these good jobs? Are these numbers sustainable?

- **Digital revolution:** Over 40% of American jobs may be automated in next 20 years. What is the impact of that on the labor force, or on income disparity? Will new jobs appear as this revolution unfolds?

- **Dodd-Frank,** which sought to reform banking to avert the large failures that set off the recession, is both controversial and unclear that it will have the intended effect. On the one hand, it seems reasonable to better regulate the riskiest bank derivatives, but less clear to restrict the Fed's ability to respond to a crisis in a manner that it did in 2008-2009. Much risk remains in the banking industry.

- **Gender Wage disparity:** despite the Equal Pay Act of 1963, women are still paid (notionally) 77% of what a man makes. This figure is not adjusted for lesser working hours.

Still, Americans are fed up with any gender wage discrimination, and enhanced enforcement of existing laws, or better laws, are long overdue. Another missed opportunity for the current Administration and legislators.

One of the former mayors of New York's favorite quotes is *"In God we trust, everyone else send data."* And I may have just overwhelmed you with so much data regarding deficits and the debt, and should probably apologize for the possibly cryptic use of B for billions and T for trillions.

The data, nonetheless, is compelling. Sadly, we've known about this building fiscal crisis for a long time and lacked the will to implement the fixes. So now the fix is going to be more painful, whenever our legislators take on the task, or when a significant event forces the issue.

As you think about the U.S. debt it should affect how you intend to vote in 2016. You would be right to grow increasingly angry at the politicians who allowed this to happen. But you also need to have a very basic understanding of how our federal budget works. It's not as simple as I've made it in the charts and discussion below, but it frames the problem and paints the overall picture. Once again, every number is exactly wrong or right, depending on your source and assumptions. If you are not a numbers person, please bear with me as we go through this all-important chapter.

SOME BASIC DEFINITIONS

<u>Gross Domestic Product (GDP)</u> is measured several different ways, most commonly (as defined by Wikipedia) it is private consumption (C) + investment (I) + government expenditures (G) + Net Exports (exports – imports). When consumer demand (C) goes down, as it did with the recent recession, one theory is that more government spending (G) will prop up GDP until consumers re-enter the market. President Obama's stimulus actions were an effort to achieve just this effect and, although it did not produce the recovery hoped for, it did avert greater job losses and a much worse financial crisis. The following table shows these relationships, using approximate 2014 numbers.

2014 Budget Actuals (% of GDP)

Spending	Revenues	GDP	Deficit	Public Debt	Gross Debt	Debt (% GDP)
$3.50T	$3.02T	$17.25T	$.483B	$12.78T	$17.79T	74%/103%

There are many arguments over what spending is included in the numbers above. For example, should the Social Security Trust Fund be counted in the debt calculations? Including it and others get you to a different set of numbers. There is also a distinction regarding the debt figure. Of the $12.78T public debt held in 2014, $6.7T is from domestic investors (Federal Reserve, individuals, and mutual funds) and $6.1T from foreign investors (China, Japan). The gross debt figure includes the publically held debt and debt issued to other federal accounts, such as the Social Security Trust Fund). The latter figure, $17.79 at the end of 2014, is the one most often referred to, and also represents the congressional limits on the debt ceiling.

The Federal Budget: I don't care much for pie charts, but I'm not sure there is a better way to simply demonstrate the Federal Budget, so please bear with me again. The one below is re-created using OMB data and is greatly simplified. As shown, the budget_is broken into two parts: Mandatory Spending and Discretionary Spending. The total is what our government is spending each year.

- <u>Mandatory Spending</u> encompasses those entitlements that the government has an absolute requirement to fund. In 2014, that figure was about $2T or almost 60% of the budget. Examples of these include using 2014 figures: Social Security ($840B), Medicare ($509B), Medicaid ($301B), Interest on the Debt ($271B)

- <u>Discretionary Spending</u> is about $1.37T in 2014, of which roughly 1/2 for Department of Defense (DOD). The figures are shown below. After mandatory spending and Defense spending is accounted for, only around 22% of the budget is left to fund everything else.

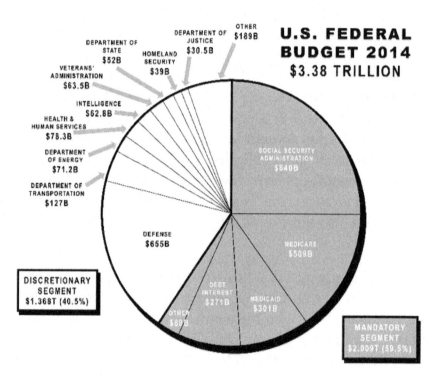

U.S. FEDERAL BUDGET 2014
$3.38 TRILLION

The lesson here for all Americans to understand is the ever-increasing piece of the federal budget going to mandatory programs and, frankly, the issue of how long we can sustain this trend. In 1962, the mandatory side of the ledger was 30% of the budget; in 2014 it is 60%. All this argues for balancing the budget and real tax reform, which we'll get to later.

Social Security and Medicare/Medicaid are the two biggest entitlement programs, so a little bit of background on each of these. If you are counting on Social Security in your retired years, you care about the health of this program. A lot of younger folks I talk to don't think it will be around when they retire and, without significant reform, they just might be correct.

Social Security refers to the Federal Old-Age, Survivors, and Disabled Insurance (OASDI) program. Social Security has had many amendments since legislation was first passed in 1935 that have adjusted rates, eligibility, retirement age, and benefits. The components of OASDI are listed below.

- Unemployment benefits and Temporary Assistance for Needy Families (TANF)–usually referred to as Welfare
- Health Insurance for Aged and Disabled (Medicare)
- Grants to States for Medical Assistance Programs (Medicaid)
- Others: State Children's Health Insurance Program (SCHIP); Supplemental Security Income (SSI); Federal Old-Age (Retirement), Survivors, and Disability Insurance (SSDI)

Social Security is funded by taxing both employer and employees. Current tax rates, for both employer and employee, are at 7.65% (6.2% FICA for Social Security and 1.45% for Medicare). The 6.2% FICA payments for Social Security are deposited into the

Social Security Trust Fund (SSTF). The Bush-era temporary 2% tax cut that reduced the employee rate from 6.2% to 4.2%, expired 1 Jan 2013, and was not renewed by the current Administration. The SSTF invests in fully backed government securities, which indirectly finances the federal debt. The SSTF is controversial in that respect, and also because it is off-budget, meaning the unfunded obligation of the fund (estimated at over $15T) does not contribute to the debt figures you often hear. Estimates are that as much as 40% of the elderly are kept above the poverty level through Social Security.

Unfortunately, and what most Americans don't know, is that the SSTF has no assets. Money received into it annually is paid out and the difference placed in the general treasury. This worked well for years when contributions to Social Security exceeded the payments that flowed out. But that ended in 2010 when outlays exceeded revenue and the SSTF began adding to the debt. As baby-boomers retire, this situation will grow worse every year and this is why you hear much talk as to when Social Security will run out of money. With no actual dollars in the SSTF some would argue it is out of money now.

Security Disability Insurance (SSDI) is often overlooked in the discussion on social programs. It was created in 1956, during the Eisenhower Administration, to help those over age 50 who were unable to work for their remaining lives, or terminally ill. After two years recipients are eligible for Medicare. It was reformed in 1984 and eligibility criteria relaxed, making it easier to qualify. Like other entitlement programs, spending on disability insurance has increased (tripled) since 1970, and in 2012 paid $135B to 8.8 million beneficiaries. Applications are up 30% since 2007. One of the drawbacks to this program is that it institutionalizes a disincentive to go back to work. Estimates are that 1 in 21 Americans age 25-64 now draw SSDI, and the percentage that re-enter the workforce is only around 5%, because recipients fear losing benefits and health coverage. Some programs have been tried to help the disabled return to productive work, with limited success. Payments come from the Social Security tax and average over $1000 a month. With baby-boomers reaching age 50 well before Social Security eligibility, applications will continue to increase and the SSDI Trust Fund, separate from Medicare, is set to run out of funds sometime in 2017 or 2018, according to recent projections. Fixing SSDI may require higher taxes, stricter criteria for entering or remaining in the program, or some combination of both. Like Social Security, addressing SSDI will be unpopular and contentious, but is ultimately unavoidable. So sooner is better.

Hopefully, I haven't lost you by this point.

All this discussion on our Federal Budget highlights the unsustainable mess we are in. And why action is needed to address entitlements and reduce deficits, both as a means to save these programs, but as a national security imperative as well.

Medicare is a federal health insurance program that provides hospital and medical care for certain disabled Americans and for the elderly, generally over age 65. Medicare Part A is paid for by payroll taxes deductions; the 1.45% described above, but rising to 2.35% for those with incomes over $200,000 ($250,000 for a family), and helps cover the costs of hospital stays to include meals, testing, etc. It can also cover costs of in-home health care and certain medical equipment. Part B is generally called Supplemental Medical Insurance (SMI) and helps pay for a range of services for the aged and disabled to include nursing and physician services, labs and X-rays, testing and out-patient procedures. Part B requires a monthly premium payment (which varies based on income, but averaged about $100/month in 2012), and is subject to an annual deductible. Parts C and D cover special needs plans and a prescription drug plan. Because it is so large, what Medicare considers a fair price for a medical procedure now directly influences what private insurers will pay, to include the recently passed Affordable Care Act (ACA.).

Medicaid is a federal-state social program that provides health and medical services for individuals and families with low income and inability to otherwise afford health care. Currently there are over 50 million recipients across the country. The federal government pays about 58% while the states pay about 42%. While oversight is at the federal level, states determine eligibility standards, type and scope of services, rates for payment and run their own respective Medicaid programs. There are a wide range of the 34 approved optional medical services (inpatient hospital, children's vaccines, lab and x-ray services for example) that states can provide to receive federal matching funds. Also, federal law requires that certain categories of citizens be covered, such as children under six and pregnant women whose family income is at or below 133% of the Federal Poverty Level (FPL), and have the flexibility to provide coverage to other similar, more broadly defined, groups. Medicaid is not paid to individuals, but to health care providers. As discussed in a later chapter, under the ACA, a.k.a Obamacare, Medicaid eligibility was to be expanded. But the Supreme Court held that states could not be forced to pay for this expansion, and 22 states as of May 2015 have declined to do so. The Administration has accused those states of denying Medicaid coverage to an estimated 5.7 million poor and uninsured, highlighting that the federal government would cover 90% of the additional costs. The states have a good counter argument, however, in that Medicaid costs are now consuming close to 20% of state budgets, up from 9% in 1989, and projected to keep rising.[8] Further, there is some healthy skepticism that the 90% marginal cost of this expansion would continue to be paid by the federal government in the future, as budgets tighten. With the 2015

Supreme Court decision now settled, you can optimistically expect to see more states expand Medicaid eligibility.

Annually, Medicare and Medicaid payments are around $810B (Federal) and another $125B (State) and increasing. Despite task forces and more aggressive enforcement by both the Departments of Justice (DOJ) and Health and Human Services (HHS), fraud across both programs still runs about 10%, or close to $100 billion annually. This a disturbing figure that would never be tolerated in the private sector.

Temporary Assistance for Needy Families (TANF), commonly referred to as Welfare, has seen a long history of evolution, but is now governed principally by President Clinton's 1996 Personal Responsibility and Work Opportunity Reconciliation Act. It is primarily executed by the states. It is one of many means-tested federal programs that provide benefits specifically to poor and low-income Americans. TANF requires states to implement criteria for job search and caps financial assistance at 60 months over a person's lifetime. In 2013, Congress reduced the timeline for receiving benefits from 73 to 25 weeks, so when you hear politicians debating an extension of welfare benefits, it applies to this very debate. Besides TANF, there are about 120 other welfare programs, including some of the better known as Earned Income Tax Credit, school lunch and breakfast programs, food stamps, and Head Start, to name a few. Some have proposed combining all of these into a single comprehensive program, eliminating much of the overlap. In early 2015 we had a media dust-up over a Kansas measure that would limit TANF expenditures on a range of luxury items; a similar Missouri proposal would have banned items such as sodas and steak. From a practical matter, I don't know how you would enforce such a provision or where you draw the line. Conversely, no one seems concerned about how retirees spend their Social Security checks.

Balance of Trade is simply the difference between net imports and net exports and impacts GDP, as we just saw. In 1975, the U.S. had a trade surplus of $12.4B, meaning we exported more goods and services than we imported. Every year since then we have had annual and growing trade deficits, which totaled $540B in 2012. Trade deficits account for the loss of jobs overseas, especially in the manufacturing area. It has been estimated that the trade deficit with China alone has caused the loss of 2.1 million U.S. jobs.[9] While some downplay the importance of trade deficits in the short-term since the impact tends to be cheaper consumer goods and lower inflation, trade deficits now approaching 40 years is cause for concern, and one element of the intense debate as we look at new trade treaties on the horizon.

Some factors go into this trade deficit calculation (oil prices is a notable example). But the resulting imbalance and loss of American jobs has now caused the Director of National Intelligence (DNI) to begin a National Intelligence Estimate (NIE) to assess the security implications of the loss of American manufacturing capacity and output. When the DNI and Central Intelligence Agency (CIA) start assessing impacts for security reasons, as they now do for U.S. trade imbalance, global warming, and the nation's debt, it's time to pay serious attention. Since 2001, when China joined the World Trade Organization (WTO), a move supported by both political parties, the United States has lost an average of 50,000 manufacturing jobs every month, according to multiple sources. Steel production is a good example. In the year before China joined the WTO, the United States, and China each produced about 100 million tons of steel a year. Fast forward to 2010 and China produced 880 million tons of steel compared to 81 tons for the U.S. producers, almost an 11 to 1 advantage. In the 20 January 2009 edition of the New York Times, it was reported that Chinese government subsidies for antibiotics so disrupted the global market that "many Western producers had to either move their facilities to

Asia or exit the business entirely." The U.S. is now heavily dependent on foreign sources of antibiotics and other critical healthcare materials. There are other examples such as the 60 Minutes TV NewsMagazine segment by Lesley Stahl in early 2015, highlighting Rare Earth elements. The top U.S. intelligence chief, General Clapper, has testified that Rare Earth elements are critical to our economy and defense industry. They need to be in concentrations that make mining economic, and right now China produces about 95% of Rare Earths, a virtual monopoly.

Trade deficits grew by 33%, to nearly half a trillion dollars according to a 2010 government report. Most of this resulting from a trade imbalance with China. In 2010, China shipped $365B in goods to America but bought only $92B of U.S. goods. The chart below shows the long and continuing history of our trade deficits.

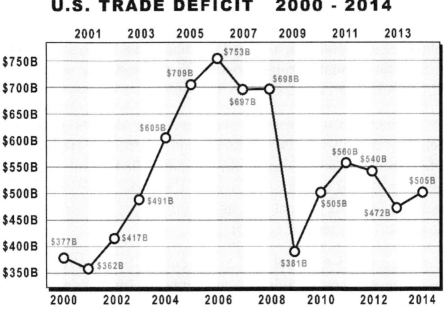

I'm no economist, and many of the best disagree, but there does appear to be an indirect relationship between trade deficits and federal deficits. Dollars and jobs flow out to some of the more than 80 countries we have trade deficits with, and then come back in the form of foreign investment. Trade is discussed more in the chapter on foreign policy.

THE DEBT – OUR BIGGEST CHALLENGE

This is probably the most important part of this chapter, and maybe the book. Understanding the magnitude and consequences of the skyrocketing national debt. Stay with me for just two more charts.

In 1991, having promised, "No new taxes" President George H. W. Bush (Bush 41) raised taxes as part of a fiscal reform package that was the right thing to do. It helped usher in the 1990s economic boom, but is generally credited with contributing to his loss in his 1992 re-election bid.

In 2001, the government actually had, not counting the off-balance sheet liabilities, a budget surplus and a manageable deficit. In fact, an annual surplus existed for the last four years of the Clinton Administration, starting in 1998.

Since 2001, however, we have run deficits every year, including 2009 when President Obama inherited a sizable $1.16T deficit from his predecessor. The annual deficits from 2002-2008 ran from $150B to $458B and were the result of fewer revenues resulting from tax cuts, as well as the funding of two wars following the events of September 11 2001.

Annual deficits all add to the cumulative federal debt that has to be serviced by interest payments. In total, President Bush basically doubled the federal debt from $5.73 to $10.63T in eight years and President Obama has almost doubled it again to nearly $19T with a year yet to go.

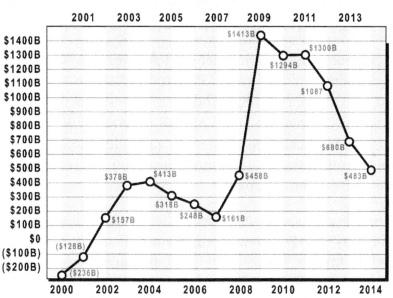

U.S. FEDERAL DEFICITS   2000 - 2014

The debt ceiling was raised by Presidents Reagan, Clinton, Bush, and Obama. Again, some hypocrisy: Obama voted against raising the debt limit in 2006. In 2007 and again in 2008 when the Senate voted to increase the limit by $850 billion and $800 billion respectively, he lacked the courage to vote at all. Then, when Senator Obama was a candidate in 2008, he criticized Bush for adding $4 Trillion to the debt, calling it irresponsible and unpatriotic. By the end of 2015 our national debt stood at close to $19T, roughly double the $10T when the current Administration took office. Both Presidents Bush and Obama raised, with congressional approval, the debt limit: Bush seven times and Obama now six. How times change!

The primary causes of the increased deficit: Revenues lost from tax cuts and the recession, two wars, rising entitlements, and $878B in stimulus spending. Although the charts for this book were prepared using 2014 data, the deficit figure for 2015 is now available and around $440B. This continues a downward trend, but still adds massively to our overall growing federal debt.

So today our national debt is just over 100% of gross GDP, often accepted as a trip wire for reduced GDP in the future. The interest on the debt alone, without serious action is projected, by CBO analysis, to reach around $600B by 2020, and $722B in the year 2024. As illustrated earlier, $722 billion dollars of interest payments would swallow up almost the entire discretionary budget, and the entire defense budget.

The budget deal cut in December 2013, orchestrated by Sen. Patty Murray (D—WA) and Congressman Paul Ryan (R—Wi.) was applauded for its success in gaining bipartisan support and eliminating the threat of sequestration. Unfortunately, it did nothing to reduce the climbing national debt. Essentially, it once again kicked the can down the road and avoided any hard choices. Jump ahead two years and on 2 November 2015, President Obama signed a two-year budget deal that avoids a government shutdown and raises once again the federal debt ceiling. This was concluded as Congressman Ryan took over the position as Speaker of the House, making him third in succession to the presidency. It deferred the Obamacare 'Cadillac tax' and opened up U.S. crude exports, but did absolutely nothing to address the real fiscal problems of the nation. Shown next is the staggering debt referenced at the beginning of this chapter, with a repeated recommendation that everyone go visit a website that captures the minute-by-minute changes. As mentioned, the latest figure is now close to $19T.

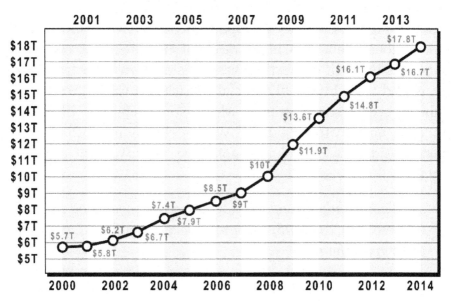

U.S. NATIONAL DEBT 2000 - 2014

Debt exceeding 100% of GDP, as previously mentioned, is only one of many warning signals. There is conventional thought that above this 100% figure, GDP slows by 1%, making a sustained recovery more difficult. Conversely, CBO has assessed that a 1% growth in GDP lowers the annual deficit by about $300B. So in the end we need to grow our way out of the deficit, but we will have to do so on both the spending and revenue sides of the budget. In my view, however, spending is the biggest driver, but we have to strike a balance. "Increasing taxation is the sign of a declining great power" it has been said,[10] and there is plenty of evidence that cutting taxes does increase revenues. After Reagan had cut the top tax rate from 70 to 28%, tax revenues grew from $517B in 1980 to $909B in 1988.[11] Others argue that the debt is just a symptom and that lack of demand and investment is the real disease. They contend that job creation and investment, particularly in infrastructure, should be our first priority. Of course, both sides are partially right.

It is interesting who we owe a debt to. When the figure was close to $17T we owed $1.1T to Japan, $1.3T to China and $2.6T to other countries. Contrary to popular belief, we owe less than 10% of our national debt to China. Most of this debt we owe back to ourselves through domestic investors and borrowing from pension plans and trust funds, like Social Security. If we fail to rein in the debt, it becomes a matter of when, not if, change will be forced upon us, and it will be painful. We are closing in on that time. The next president will probably not have the luxury of ducking the issue.

> *"People only accept change when they are faced with necessity, and only recognize necessity when a crisis is upon them."*
>
> --Jean Monet

Monetary versus Fiscal Policy is a dry subject, but also important to understand and there's a big distinction between them. Basically, fiscal policy deals with government spending and revenues. So the government, through budgets, impacts how much spending takes place and through taxation policies how much revenues it receives in. In difficult economic times that the nation has faced recently, the government can increase spending to help stimulate the economy, but creates deficits and accumulates debt by taking these actions. The law that requires cuts if federal spending targets aren't met, commonly referred to as sequestration, is an example of fiscal policy. As I hope I have demonstrated clearly by now, our fiscal policy is broken and our annual spending far outpaces our revenues into the Treasury, as it has for many years.

Monetary policy, on the other hand, deals with the supply of money, which is controlled primarily by the Central Bank (AKA the Federal Reserve Bank; AKA the Fed), to influence inflation and economic growth through interest rates and bank reserve requirements, and other measures.

Typically, the Fed buys short-term government bonds to lower interest rates and increase bank lending, at least in theory. When short-term interest rates approached zero, which is currently the case, the Fed next turned to purchasing longer-term bonds, a technique called Quantitative Easing (QE), to inject more liquidity into the markets, easing credit and stimulating growth. The idea is that banks, with new money available, would make lending easier and give the economy a needed boost.

QE has been going on in the U.S. since the recession in 2007. In QE1 the Fed purchased $1.7T in bonds; then in 2010 another $600B called QE2; and finally in 2012 the Fed began purchasing up to $85B in open-ended securities per month. QE began tapering off in December 2013 and ended in October 2014, with the Fed having added almost $3.5T to its books, well above its traditional security holdings. The results of QE are arguable. Some economists say it produced a modest impact on the economy while producing a bonanza for Wall Street.

Those of us old enough to remember the Carter presidency with 17% inflation and long gas lines are apprehensive of inflation. Inflation is highly regressive and mostly hurts those at the low end of the economic scale the most. Although how we calculate CPI, and thus inflation, has changed over the years, one school of thought is that inflation should run about 2%, and the Fed has indicated that sometime in late 2015 it would move to adjust inflation targets upward, a prospect that will depend on a range economic indicators. The problem is how does the Fed create inflation – just by raising interest rates? After six years of zero interest rates, some long-term bonds with negative yields, and a national debt over $18T, what would be the result? No one knows because we've never been in this precarious situation before, and no predictive model exists that we can rely on. Further, raising interest rates prematurely when the economy is still tepid could produce disastrous results, e.g. another recession, which is why the Fed has been so hesitant to act.

The Fed is not without controversy, with some even arguing that it should go away. I disagree and think the Fed, acting with great discretion, has served the nation well. The last time the Fed raised interest rates was back in 2006, until the modest increase in December 2015. Everyone is now closely watching the impact, to see if the raise was premature, or if a second round will soon follow. The Fed options now are limited, however, and they will need to inflate sooner, rather than later, while carefully monitoring the impact.

There is a lot of misinformation and misunderstanding surrounding the president's Bailout and Stimulus initiatives during the past recession. I think it is a good idea to quickly review both since we may see them again in a similar form come the next recession.

The Bailout (AKA the TARP - Trouble Asset Relief Plan) was actually started under President Bush and endorsed by then-candidate Obama. Statistics suggest that the president's Bailout was a measured success, an assessment that I agree with.

The Administration spent only about $422B of the $700B that was authorized. General Motors was on the verge of bankruptcy with accumulated losses of $70B between 2007 and 2008. The Auto Task Force forced plant and dealership closings and instituted a revised business model. Today, both Chrysler and GM have emerged from bankruptcy and are profitable again (although GM got back on the hot seat for faulty ignition switches that needlessly cost lives.) In 2011, the Treasury closed the books on the $12.5B Chrysler bailout, with a $1.3B loss. In 2013, the Treasury sold its remaining shares of GM, recovering approximately $38.5B on the $50B invested. In all, the Treasury will recoup all but about $15B of the $80B committed to the automotive companies.

The $245B invested in banks has mostly been recovered and a subsequent law that subjects banks to stress tests has somewhat reassured investors in the banking system. Unfortunately, the banks didn't lend to small business as they should have, and many folded.) Fannie Mae paid back the government $7.2B in March 2014, re-paying $121B, more than the $116B borrowed. Freddie Mac re-paid $71.3B, slightly more than it drew from the government.

By one recent Treasury account (the numbers are frequently adjusted), TARP will make a $15B profit when all the books are finally closed.

The Economic Stimulus (AKA The American Recovery and Reinvestment Act of 2009) was funded as an emergency measure to smooth out a particularly difficult economic cycle and was transformed by the Fed into a monetary policy that purchased government and corporate bonds, as we saw in the QE discussion above.

Of the $800B in the 2009 economic stimulus, only about $10B was effective according to one report,[12] and we all remember the debacle of Solyndra, the now-bankrupt solar panel maker that the president held up as a model. On the other hand, the CBO estimated that between three to four million jobs were saved by the Act (although we still lost eight million jobs, many of them from small businesses.)

In 2009, the year the recession officially ended, another $600B of stimulus was funded. Many economists think the stimulus was a failure, or at least fell well short of expectations. A minority think otherwise and believe that the government should have pumped more money into the economy, to include home mortgage restructuring. In any case, we certainly didn't take the austerity route some advocated. From 2008-2013, the annual deficits added $6T to the national debt, abetted by the Fed's monthly injection of cash into the economy.

THREE CONTROVERSIAL ISSUES

A lot of discussion has taken place leading up to the elections surrounding some issues that impact our economy or have budget implications, beyond just the burgeoning debt. Three of those are discussed below: Income Inequality, Inversions, Student loans.

#1 Income Inequality:

Much has been written about income inequality in America. President Obama has called income inequality "our greatest unfinished business." Americans largely agree as evidenced by multiple surveys. A Gallup poll in 2012 found that 46% found it extremely or very important for the government to enact policies to reduce the gap between rich and poor. The CIA, which measures and reports on 140 nations income inequality, lists the U.S. at 43rd (Sweden is best at 140).[13] Guess what – it's going to get worse and Occupy Wall Street (OWS) type demonstrations will be more contentious that the relatively calm encounters that started in September 2011.

In a free market society, hard work and education lead to success and tangible benefits like a higher income level. As the founder of the Container Store stated at an event I attended in Phoenix, free markets are responsible beyond any other factor for lifting so many of the world out of poverty. I am a big believer in free markets and individual freedoms, with government doing only what we can't do for ourselves.

Exactly why the inequality trend is increasing in America is complex, but several contributing factors are clear. More than two million jobs have been offshored through globalization and normalization of relations with China. Just as large department stores gobbled up the Mom & Pop stores, e-commerce now competes with both. The digital revolution is automating more and more jobs, displacing less skilled workers in a process called labor force polarization, driving income to the extremes (both up and down), and abetting income inequality. According to one report, up to 47% of American workers face a probability of having their jobs automated in the next 20 years, with uncertainty as to what new jobs will be created as this occurs.[14]

The recession and slow recovery further explain what we are seeing. Workforce participation and the workweek continues to shrink. A Federal Reserve report in 2014 showed that "only families at the very top of the income distribution saw widespread gains" between 2010 and 2013. [15] In other words, the recovery has disproportionately benefited the best-off as the stock market surged again and many jobs have shifted to lower paying service sector jobs and part-time employment. This is intuitive to most American's who have seen, and many personally experienced, wage stagnation and loss of skilled jobs over the past decade.

I've researched and there is no clear definition of the middle-class, so when you hear reports of a declining middle-class, ask yourself that very question. A good starting point is the middle 20%, or a family income range of $39k to $63k in 2014, which is close to the definition of the Pew Charitable Trust Fund, but doesn't account for federal subsidies and other policy considerations. In 2009, median income was $55, 589 and, after trending down for a few years has started back up and was at $53, 891 in 2014. That is still a 3% decline over a 5-year period, validation of the public's belief as expressed in polls.

According to the Pew Research Center, in 2008 53% of the population viewed themselves as middle-class. In 2014 that figure was down to 44%. A Pew report in 2012 shows increasing stress on those who consider themselves middle-class and a tendency to downward mobility. The White House Council of Economic Advisors (CEA) found that loss of productivity was the greatest driver of stagnating middle-class incomes, not inequality.[16] The Bureau of Labor Statistics reported that productivity increase in 2014 was a paltry.5%. There are lots of mixed signals and data in all that.

Taxes on capital gains and executive compensation are two additional contributing factors. Capital gains, which are taxed at rates below ordinary income, are a large source of income for the wealthy (reduced from 28% by Clinton to 20%, to 15% by Bush, and back to 20% under Obama.). This explains how Warren Buffet was able to say that his effective income tax rate was 17.4 %, and less than his receptionist. Still, keeping capital gains taxes below ordinary income fuels investment and creates jobs in a free market economy, so finding the right balance is the key.

Executive salaries are usually benchmarked to peer groups, even as company revenues and fortunes fade, which we saw clearly at Lehman Brothers, AIG, Countrywide Financial and AMGEN, just to name a few of the famous firms from the recession. It is estimated that from 1975 to 2007 the income that went to the richest one percent of Americans went from 5% to over 12%. In 2013, the top three percent of households earned 30.5% of all income, up almost 3% from 2010. According to the Bureau of Labor Statistics, Executive pay has increased 400% since 1970, while a typical non-supervisory employee has seen a 10% reduction.[17] A Harvard Business School study found that CEOs were paid on average 30 times what the average U.S. worker was and one study found that figure 300 to 1 for top CEOs.[18]

The Dodd-Frank Bill gave shareholders the right to vote on Executive Pay as well as their Golden Parachutes (compensation when top executives leave a company for whatever reason.) This tactic has been only marginally successful dealing with Fortune 500 companies; Wall Street generally prevails. Before we fall too far into the mode of criticizing CEO salaries, however, we should consider the extravagant salaries manifested in other fields such as some celebrities and sports figures who bear far less responsibility.

At least once a year Parade Magazine puts out an issue that's called an annual salary survey, titled "What People Earn" (April 2015 was the most recent.) Maybe I am in the minority here, but I find that issue offensive. What people earn has little relation to what makes them successful in life. I think the quote below stands the test of time.

> *"Money never made a man happy yet, nor will it. The more a man has, the more he wants. Instead of filling a vacuum, it makes one."*
> --Benjamin Franklin

Still, wealth accumulation and greed motivate so many to the detriment of a more fulfilling life, something Oscar Wilde might have had in mind when he spoke of the two greatest tragedies in life.

> *"There are only two tragedies in life: one is not getting what one wants, and the other is getting it."*
> --Oscar Wilde

A large contributing factor to income inequality is what I would call a cycle of poverty, a term that I am sure has been introduced elsewhere. There are some studies that show that those who come from stable middle-class families and received better (and early) education, moved on to college. And generally tended to marry someone of equal accomplishment, then having children later when incomes made that option more affordable. Those children in turn received great education opportunities and generally moved on to college as well, continuing the cycle. Education is clearly the key. This same cycle applies to those less educated.

Take as one example, that in 2013 60% of unwed mothers who had babies were high school dropouts as opposed to 9% who were college educated. There is a wide income gap between college education and high school diploma and even wider for high school dropouts. As reported by The Economist, the income gap between college educated and high school educated parents grew 400% between 1979 and 2012.[19]

Despite 120 or so social programs and clear evidence of the problem, these cycles continue and are receiving a lot of attention as the income gap between the skilled and unskilled widens. Still, the answers remain elusive. Presidential candidate Bernie Sanders proposed free college for all – nonsense. There's no free lunch and no free college – someone pays. There are no easy fixes, especially when you are looking at over $18T in national debt. Politicians are quick to seize the issue but weak on specifics on how the nation addresses the situation, beyond taxing the rich. That won't make a dent in the problem, nor address the ominous debt cloud.

Why It Matters!

With America having the largest income equality among developed nations (and growing), the most serious effect can be civil unrest as we saw in the OWS movement. In their book, Why Nations Fail, the authors conclude that poor nations got that way by being "extractive." Meaning one group benefited at the expense of the other. Great nations have promoted inclusivity.[20]

It matters because studies show a 25% wider gap of the test scores between rich and poor than existed 25 years ago, meaning that the more affluent will continue to see upward mobility opportunity, which is substantiated by higher average incomes tied to education and degrees. To assign actual numbers, a recent study showed an income gap of $58,000 for those with a college education and those without.[21] Another study confirms a 20-22% income below the median for high-school-only graduates, and many studies confirm that low-income children have less chance at advanced education and so the cycle of poverty persists.

Income inequality also matters because it narrows the tax base. In the U.S. the top 1% of earners pay over 40% of income taxes while around 40% pay no income tax at all. It also matters because it tends to drive divisive politics, like the Tea Party on the extreme right, or OWS and Senator Elizabeth Warren on the far left. It matters because America's international place in an increasingly interconnected world is dependent on our history and moral standing as a land of opportunity for all.

So everyone now highlights income inequality as a key issue for the 2016 election, but specifics on how to effectively address income inequality is complex. In truth, adjusted for inflation, it's not much different now than 25 years ago, but now it's highly politicized.

Much debate in 2014 was centered on raising the federal minimum wage to $10.10 per hour, although the President ultimately supported $9/hr. In February 2014 the non-partisan CBO estimated that increasing the federal minimum wage from $7.25 to $10.10 per hour would lift 900,000 above the official poverty line (although only 19% of the estimated $31B in additional earnings would accrue to those below the poverty line), and result in a loss of 500,000 jobs.

A Gallup poll found that 76% of Americans supported raising the minimum wage, but when asked if they would support a raise if the result were layoffs or loss of jobs, then 57% opposed the hike. A federal hike to $9/hr., while the right thing to do, is becoming less urgent as many states and localities are moving forward anyway, either by voter referendum or legislative action.

On 1 January 2014, twenty states raised the state minimum wage, and fifteen now have minimum wage indexed to inflation. Tax reform is another avenue to redress inequality, such as rolling back the residential real estate tax break that accrues to the wealthier Americans (a 2013 CBO survey reported that 30% of the residential tax break went to the wealthiest 1 %, and 73% to the wealthiest 20%).

My vote would be to raise the federal minimum wage to $10.10/hour now, and then peg it to inflation for five years, or something close. This should have minimal impact on the many Americans who rely on the Earned Income Tax Credit to reduce taxes.

States and cities that have raised the minimum wage, in many cases above $10.10, have not seen the negative economic impact that many feared. In the end, however, the minimum wage may come down to a state-by-state issue, to be determined by referendum or legislation and that's not such a bad thing as cost-of-living varies greatly by state and locale.

As part of tax reform, we need to revisit the capital gains tax and profit sharing with workers. As profits accrue to investors, who are taxed at a lower capital gains rate, the workers are largely left out.

Senator Warren has taken up the cause of the middle-class with much fanfare and support. She is half-right. Especially in the recent recession, but well before that, the saying that it takes money to make money has shown itself to be true. The better-off weathered the storm of the recession and benefited from a 75% increase in the stock market in the past five years, although that gain may be tentative. Those with debt and little savings lost jobs, and in many cases lost homes to foreclosure.

The census figure mentioned before showed a 7% drop in median household income between 2000 and 2010; from 2007, the year before the latest recession through 2013, the drop in median household income was 8%. But the long-term answers don't lie just in higher minimum wages or higher taxes on the rich, or more collective bargaining, or divisive political rhetoric. As Representative Cathy Rogers (R—WA) correctly stated in the response to the 2014 State of the Union address, "The real gap we face today is one of opportunity gap."

Yes, the tax code and entitlement programs are both in need of serious reform, and good places to start. The next most urgent task is to get our children in high-performing schools, starting in preschool, as we discuss in a later chapter. We won't fix the decline of the traditional family, sadly, but we can promote resiliency, character and perseverance as attainable goals for all. And as one journalist has succinctly stated, we need to rid ourselves of the nonsensical notion that "The poor are poor because the rich are rich... and the goal should be to make the poor richer which means jobs, education, and tax/regulation relief for employers."[22] I would add that it also argues for sensible policies that encourages work but also provides a safety net for the truly needy in our society.

While there will always be income disparity, America should not have the highest income inequality of Western nations, trending worse, as is currently the case. We can do better!

> *"An imbalance between the rich and the poor is the oldest and most fatal ailment of all republics"*
>
> --Plutarch

#2 Inversions:

> *"These companies are renouncing their American citizenship, turning their backs on this country, simply to boost their profits. They are taking advantage of all the good things that our government helps provide – educated workers, roads and bridges, a dependable court system, patent and copyright protections – and then running out on the bill"*
>
> --Senator Elizabeth Warren (D—MA) in Jul 1014.

Although existing for many years, tax inversions have been an especially hot topic for the past several years. It basically entails a U.S. company moving its headquarters to another country, through acquisition or merger, to avoid paying U.S. corporate taxes which, at 35%, is now among the highest in the developed world. The 35% corporate rate used to be around average but is now disproportionally high as globalization has expanded and other countries seek to attract new business by lowering rates. Ireland, for example, has a 12.5 % corporate tax rate and is a preferred destination for many companies. There are tax implications on interest payments as well, and no real metric exists on how many jobs are lost through inversions.

According to the Congressional Research Service (CRS), 47 companies have reincorporated overseas since 2003; two dozen of those since 2008. The current law requires that foreign shareholders own 20% of the merged company stock which, when passed in 2004, stopped inversions temporarily until new workarounds were developed. PayPal, for example, moved to Ireland in 2003, had been acquired by eBay (also out of Ireland) and now employs 2000. eBay, I should note, brought $9B back onshore and paid taxes owed [23] and spun-off PayPal. Some companies, like Carnival with headquarters in Miami, claim they never were U.S. corporations.

So it works basically like this: The U.S. taxes American firms on all income, whether earned in the U.S. or overseas, as opposed to most other wealthy nations who only tax in the country where the revenue was earned. (The latter is sometimes referred to as a territorial system.) U.S. multinationals, which incorporate overseas but leave most of their headquarters and leadership here, pay the lower tax rate of the host nation, but can defer paying taxes on profits to the IRS until they are repatriated when firms then must pay the difference between the country tax rate and the U.S. rate. In some respects, this situation is not much different than companies moving to states that are business friendly, which they do all the time.

Continued growth of tax code regulations is a contributing factor to the expansion of inversions, attributable to both political parties. Another contributing factor is that, since 2010, firms are not automatically thrown out of the S&P 500 Stock index when they move overseas, and thus lose value when index investors have to sell shares of delisted firms. One flare up in 2014 was drugmaker Pfizer's botched attempt to buy AstraZeneca and move to Britain. Then in late 2015 the greedy executives at Pfizer announced a deal with the Irish drug company Allergan that makes Botox, employing workarounds to avoid Treasury Department rules. Currently, about 45 large firms that include IBM, Apple, and General Electric account for 70% of the earnings stashed overseas, estimated by Moody's and others at about $2 Trillion. I mentioned this earlier and you may remember the headlines in 2011 which reported that GE paid no U.S. taxes in 2010. It instead got a $3.2 billion tax credit, while realizing $14 billion in profits; and it continues today. Walgreens, to the company's credit, withdrew plans to relocate to Switzerland (which would have saved them nearly a billion a year by one estimate) and saw their stock price quickly drop 14%.[24] But a number of inversions are ostensibly still on the table in late 2015, to include Burger King's intent to acquire Tim Horton's and relocate to Canada. With a large amount of tax savings now on the table, a new twist to the inversion problem is that foreign firms are starting to acquire American firms.

Like immigration and some other issues, this one should not be too difficult to solve, but actions by both Congress and the Administration to limit inversions have sometimes tended to make them more attractive. The answer may require several measures to make it more competitive and fair to continue to do business in the U.S. One would be to reform a dysfunctional corporate tax system to a lower capital rate (maybe 25% as proposed by Representative David Camp). Another is a tax holiday on repatriated funds (even though done before); I am intrigued by the proposal to use these funds for the underfunded Highway Trust Fund (I believe first proposed by Senator Rand Paul). And finally make the jump to a territorial system where taxes are paid to the country in which the revenue was earned, like most nations. The latter will be especially controversial given our national deficit and debt, but will largely diffuse the impetus for inversions and level the playing field. Once this step is done, our legislators can also move on enforcing stricter disclosure, tightening rules such as a tax on offshore cash held and other retained earnings, and possibly raising the 20% foreign ownership threshold to 50%, as already proposed by some in Congress.

#3 Student Loans:

This is a real head-scratcher! An estimated 20 million students attend college every year, and around 60%, or 12 million, take out loans to cover their education. In 2014, college graduates had loans averaging $26,000, graduate students $57,000, and the accumulated student debt is over $1.3 Trillion.[25]

Interest rates vary by undergraduate, graduate and parent loans, and are adjusted annually by Congress. Under current provisions enacted in 2010, known as the Obama Loan Forgiveness Program, borrowers pay back loan debt at varying interest rates, capped at 10% of their discretionary income, for 20 years. After that time, the loan is forgiven. The default rate is around 9% currently but has been as high as 20% in the past. This is a very oversimplified summary. Elizabeth Warren has made headlines by citing reports that the government will make tens of billions in profits off student loans in the next decade, but the author of the quoted study by Ms. Warren said the program is just as likely to lose money as turn a profit. Either way, the whole program has become problematic on several fronts.

The ever-rising cost of higher education has forced students to take out larger loans. I'll be less diplomatic; the cost of college is obscene! The high-interest repayments on loans hurt those starting out on new careers and tend to disproportionately hurt those at the lower income range. Who wants to pay off a college loan for 20 years? Finally, with an accumulated debt of over $1.3T, these loans have become a drag on the economy. While we certainly want to invest in higher education, I am not sure I am in full agreement with debt forgiveness as a sound domestic policy, but I certainly think loan rate reductions are called for, and the entire program should be re-visited.

Recent initiatives to make loan status more transparent to borrowers and simplify administration are good steps. Left up to me, I would notionally peg interest rates at inflation +1%, and I would link national service with a proportional reduction in loan principal, almost a reverse GI bill concept. There are some good ideas that should be explored to alleviate the burden of the 43 million or so who owe on student loans, and thereby ease the path to higher education as a national priority.

THE STATE OF THE RECOVERY

What caused the recession of 2008 is a combination of many factors: low interest rates, easy personal credit, Wall Street excesses, and risky home mortgages that were then re-packaged and sold, creating the housing bubble. Large foreign investments and inadequate bank cash ratios are often cited as other contributing causes.

Deficit spending, which has been going on for years, accompanied by accounting gimmicks, eventually eroded our economic strength to absorb the events that occurred. When the first domino fell (Lehman Brothers bankruptcy in Sep 2008, followed closely by AIG), the recession set in and the economy has sputtered, meaning a very slow recovery, through most of the intervening years until 2014. So, more simply stated, the weak economy and lowered tax rates produced an erosion of tax revenue, while entitlement programs, defense spending, new prescription drug benefits have all added to deficits and the debt. This is just federal debt and doesn't account for state and local debt and underfunded pension plans, some of which are being downsized to the dismay of retirees who were promised and counted on that income.

By the end of 2014 employment had fallen to 5.8 %, and the 4th quarter GDP growth exceeded 5% while adding 320,000 jobs in

November of 2014. The economic recovery has continued into 2015, with consumer spending up slightly, and oil prices falling, with 2015 GDP estimated at around 3.5%, a figure that fluctuates. However, uncertainty regarding foreign economies in China, Japan and the European Union (EU), and the bubble in the Chinese stock market should clearly dampen our enthusiasm, as it did in August 2015.

All this relatively good news, however, has done very little for the incomes of the middle-class. According to the 2014 Census Bureau report, 2013 median household income (at $51,939) is 8.3% *below* 2007 levels. Workforce participation has fallen about 3% since the recession, with multiple explanations to include those that have stopped looking and some aging-out, among others. Productivity gains since the recession are only about 1% annually, and only.5% in 2014. Many Americans are working multiple jobs just to keep pay parity. Unlike other recessions, the good jobs just aren't coming back. That same Census report showed a slight drop in the poverty rate, but that the same number of Americans, 45 million, are still at or below the poverty level, an absolutely staggering and shameful number for a nation as great as America. A third of all poor are children, as discussed in a later chapter. The Fed has reported that the net worth decline of the typical American family was almost 40% since the recession. The wage gap between men and women is remarkably unchanged, with women being paid 77% of what men make for the same job, unadjusted for working hour disparity! Although unemployment has ranged in the low 5% area in August 2015, underemployment is closer to 15% and over 40% of job growth since the recession has been in low-paying retail or food services industry.

Our manufacturing rebound has been disappointing overall, with many jobs giving way to technology or cheaper imports from overseas. The long-term unemployed, underemployed, part-time worker and minimum wage earners continue to view the recovery as weak, and their recurrent view that they are falling further behind, and skeptical of the future.

> *"We have to get back on a path that will allow us to pay down our debt.... Even after our economy recovers, our government will still be on track to spend more money than it takes in throughout this decade and beyond. That means we have to borrow from countries like China. That means more or your tax dollars each year will go toward paying the interest on all the loans that we keep taking out"*
> --President Obama 2011 (The Washington Post editorial by Ruth Marcus)

I certainly agree with the assessment, but the actions haven't followed the rhetoric. In December 2013, the Ryan-Murray deal that Congress agreed to over the 2014 budget ended a long stalemate between the parties. Although neither side was happy with all the provisions, at least a sequester was avoided and the federal agencies had some measure of certainty regarding their spending. Same thing for the deal that the president signed in November 2015. Unfortunately, these budgets were far from the bold step needed and did little to reduce deficits or the debt. All the difficult choices were avoided and the can was kicked down the road yet again.

There is certainly some good news that carries into 2016: falling oil prices, more job growth, and even some signs of wage increases. But, despite this good news, our economic recovery is still tentative, our economic power and standing the world continues to decline, our credit is weak and at risk, and business is uncertain as to what comes next as the national debt grows unchecked. In my view, the economic structure to sustain growth doesn't exist, with excessive regulations that squeeze small businesses and a burdensome tax code. Job growth of 300,000 a month and 5% GDP growth won't continue without change. The most recent CBO report on the Budget and Economic Outlook 2015 to 2025, at the time of this book, projects deficits rising again to over $900B by 2022 (only seven years from now), debt to over $24B in the same year, and the annual interest on the debt over $600B a year (from $229B in 2014.) Those numbers are absolutely frightening and unsustainable, and all Americans should be greatly concerned for what they portend. Couple those numbers with the economic slowdown in China and the recent devaluation of the yuan, the continuing economic challenges in the EU, our own developing credit bubble and growing personal debt, the strong dollar that inhibits U.S. exports and a nervous stock market, and the call for action appears all the more compelling. With interest rates close to 0%, the Fed has little maneuvering room to deal with the next recession. The wake-up call is loud and clear, but is anyone listening?

THE FIX

If you've stayed with me so far, through all the gloomy budget figures, you might not suspect that I really am an eternal optimist. But we have some work to do. This is the difficult part, and why many politicians try to remain vague or skirt the issues altogether, since addressing the problems will require trade-offs and some sacrifice. But not to the extreme if done correctly.

I already alluded to my strong belief that no Administration and/or Congress can implement into law the dramatic changes that are so urgently needed. Partisan bickering and posturing and concerns about the impact on the 2016 election, or future midterms, will prevent the kind of comprehensive and effective actions that must be taken. The rhetoric that 'we'll deal with that after the election' holds no water. Think about *the premise—that our ineffective Congress is incapable of enacting the needed legislation!*

There is a recent history of attempts to legislate fixes to our spending and deficit problems as many might remember. The Gramm-Rudman- Hollings Balanced Budget Act of 1985 calculated allowable deficit levels toward the eventual elimination of the deficit. If federal budgets exceeded those limits, automatic cuts were exercised, called, sequestration. Ultimately this law was declared unconstitutional based on how the cuts were determined, and was replaced by the Budget Enforcement Act of 1990, which replaced sequestration with a system known as PAYGO, meaning that you pay for what you legislate, as you go.

In 2010, the Simpson-Bowles National Commission on Fiscal Responsibility and Reform reported out with a series of recommendations to address the deficit. It was not supported by the Administration (which chartered the report) or Congress, both of whom walked away from the opportunity. Senator Lindsey Graham of S.C. is correct in saying we need to go dust off Simpson-Bowles. Erskine Bowles, a Democrat, stated, "If it had been President Clinton he would have said, God, I created this, this is wonderful. It was all my idea." [26] Still looking for a solution, Congress passed the Budget Control Act of 2011, which was signed by the President and, once again, imposed sequestration if spending limits were exceeded.

To quote President Obama again from his 13 April 2011 address to the nation:

"So here's the truth. Around two-thirds of our budget is spent on Medicare, Medicaid, Social Security and national security. Programs like unemployment insurance, student loans, veteran's benefits and tax credits for working families take up

about 20%. What's left, after interest on the debt, is just 12% for everything else. That's 12 percent for all of our other national priorities like education and clean energy; medical research and transportation; food safety and keeping our air and water clean."

That's a great speech, and those are all pretty accurate observations; unfortunately, virtually nothing has been done to address this serious situation, either by the Administration or Congress, and it stands to get much worse! Tax reform has not been meaningfully pursued, nor has entitlement reform of a welfare system that comes very close to discouraging work, underfunds re-training, and remains a drag on the economy.

President Obama has also stated, "More importantly, the cost of Medicare, Medicaid, and Social Security will continue to skyrocket. I refuse to pass this problem on to another generation of Americans."[27]

Unfortunately, he has done exactly that, along with an $18+ Trillion-dollar federal debt. Once upon a time the president was willing to raise the Medicare age thresholds and change the Social Security cost-of-living formula, and House Speaker John Boehner was willing to find $800B in increased revenues. That time long has passed.

Evidence the bold attempt by Congressman David Camp (R-Mi.) in early 2014 to introduce meaningful tax reform that he had been working on for years. It would have accomplished much of what Simpson-Bowles recommended by lowering individual and corporate taxes, eliminating many deductions and imposing a surcharge on income over $450,000, among many other provisions. It too went nowhere.

Hence my conclusion that reform can't be achieved the old fashion way, by bold and bipartisan passage of comprehensive legislation. Not now and not after the 2016 elections, when nothing will really change. Washington can't be fixed by conventional processes.

So What Can We Do?

I propose two concurrent National Commissions, very much along the lines of the National Commission on Fiscal Responsibility and Reform (Simpson-Bowles), but with the statutory authority of the Base Closure and Realignment (BRAC) process.

Military installations tend to bring millions of dollars of revenue and good jobs to the surrounding community, so there is great pushback from legislators and constituents when the prospect of a military base closure arises. Well-paid lobbyists are in full throttle for the highly charged and vaguely transparent process that ensues around BRAC. Congress created the BRAC process in 1988 and designed it to overcome these difficult constituency issues. It required the president to approve the commission's recommendations without modification, and then for the Congress to either reject the proposals within 45 days of the report, or they became law. I agree with Senator John McCain in that I really don't much care for commissions in a perfect world, but I am convinced this approach will be the only way we can aggressively and authoritatively implement changes needed to address some of our nation's overwhelming fiscal problems. So here goes.

Commission on Social Security, Medicare, and Medicaid Reform

As we've seen, there is no SSTF with real assets. As former OMB director under President Clinton once stated, balances in the SSTF are only a bookkeeping device – there are no real assets that can be drawn from it. So when we hear that Social Security is solvent until 2033, that would assume that there are real assets in the fund, and not that all of the $2.6T+ that should be in the SSTF hadn't been spent by the government. Social Security is essentially a pay-as-you-go system.

In an MSNBC interview, Senator Harry Reid stated that *"Social Security does not add a single penny... to the budget problem. Never has, and for the next 30 years, it won't do that."*[28] Nothing could possibly be more misleading to the American public. For 30 years, Social Security took in more revenue than it paid out, providing a nice cushion for the Treasury. That all changed in 2010.

The trust fund is really an intragovernmental debt, or part of the public debt figure. The unfunded liability of Social Security and Medicare exceeds $80 Trillion by most estimates, which is unpayable and ensures the system as we know it won't endure.

In 2014, Social Security and Medicare alone made up 40% of the entire federal expenditure. By around 2035, there will be 77 million older Americans compared to 47 million today, and only two workers for each beneficiary, which should give you a feel for the huge pressure on the programs, both now and in the future. No issue is more emotional or volatile. There is a general belief, among many beneficiaries and others, that the Social Security payments are entitlements and that retirees are simply getting back what was paid into the system from their taxes and employer-matching withholding. The Supreme Court has ruled otherwise and numerous studies by the Urban Institute and others show that beneficiaries generally receive several multiples of what they contributed. Many of the recommendations of the Simpson-Bowles report need to be enacted, like getting more aggressive in going after Medicaid and Medicare fraud, and phasing in new retirement ages and means tests while grandfathering those now receiving, or those soon to be receiving Social Security benefits.

Making gradual structural changes to entitlement programs will be highly controversial, but without such changes the long-term future of these programs is entirely at risk.

Here are some specifics I would personally like to see enacted as part of Social Security reform:

1. Put all trust funds on an accrual basis, with real assets as opposed to government IOUs, so we have a sustainable path ahead for these important programs. This would take many years, probably a generation, to implement, and be highly controversial.

2. Follow a template suggested by former Senator Joe Lieberman: phase in new retirement ages (I would be more assertive than his proposal), reform the premium and benefits structure, reform Medigap policies. I like a model that phases in one year older for every four years and automatically adjusts so that Medicare kicks in, for full payment, 10-15 years before notional life expectancy.

3. Another template is that proposed by former Senator Coburn, who is also a doctor. He advocated some of the same measures as Senator Lieberman, but would also include further means testing (reduced payments for the wealthiest individuals), and freezing the Medicare reimbursement rates for doctors for 10 years. The latter is now overcome by the bipartisan legislation in April 2015 that overhauled how doctors are paid and stopped a potential 21% reduction in billing payments. Coburn would also increase funding for investigating fraud and abuse to tackle the 10% Medicare Fraud. His proposal and phase-in would also have the average American on Medicare for 10 years, which greatly exceeds the time span envisioned when Medicare was originally created, and half the current 20-

year span. Somewhere in the middle is probably a workable balance.

4. As a means to fix Social Security for the next generation, my idea is that we should also consider requiring taxes on earned income above $118,500 (the 2015 cap) up to, $500,000, or maybe even higher.

5. Finally, all working Americans should be provided a regular status update on their Social Security, Medicare and SSDI benefits, as well as the cost of these programs.

Ironically, many reforms being suggested by both sides have their roots in legislation endorsed by some members of the other party. Just as we will see with Obamacare and immigration reform; these include Medicare exchanges, tax credits, and premium support. None of the fixes that ultimately result will be popular, but they will preserve the system.

As former Senator Bob Kerry (D-Neb.) stated "AARP (the American Association of Retired People) has made a decision to make it almost impossible to fix the program. If they tag you as someone who wants to cut benefits, you're dead in the water."[29] That statement, correctly or incorrectly, nevertheless highlights the challenge and why an up-down vote on a Commission Report would be not only a logical approach, but possibly the only practical approach.

Without reform, Medicare as we know it will end – it's only a matter of when and what replaces it. I would like to see auto-IRA considered as part of this commission; that would help address the low savings for retirement dilemma. But the requirements and management of these IRAs would be subject to much debate, and it may be a bridge too far. The suggestions that I've made above are not prescriptive, just a starting point. The Commission would be doing the hard work of getting the details right, and hopefully Congress and the president would follow with their support.

Commission on Comprehensive Tax and Accounting Reform

Here are some ideas for this Commission:

- First on accounting: we need to do away with the treatment of off-budget expenditures. Everything, from emergency and contingency spending for war to Freddie and Fannie and student loans, needs to be on-budget, and transparent to the nation and our creditors. All these expenditures add to our debt. We should budget proactively and accrue reserves for natural emergencies.
- Move to chained consumer price index, which is a more appropriate way to measure inflation and index benefits.
- Personal Tax Reform: It has been 1986 since President Reagan and Congress last passed meaningful tax reform. The Simpson-Bowles commission noted that over a trillion dollars in potential annual revenues were lost due to loopholes, 7% of GDP by some estimates and that the solutions had many attractive features to both political parties. Largest among these is the mortgage tax deduction (which notionally benefits the top 30% of wage earners primarily), 401k savings plans and employer deduction for employee health insurance. I don't agree with all of the recommendations of Simpson-Bowles. For example, Obamacare requires employers to offer health care to full-time workers, called the employer mandate, but the thresholds have changed and implementation delayed. The impact of requiring employers to provide coverage and then also eliminating the tax deduction would need to be carefully studied. Still, there is a benefit in a gradual implementation

in many of the recommendations of Simpson-Bowles. I personally would not favor abolishing the 401k, but I would prefer that it be after-tax or ROTH only. I also think the mortgage interest deduction for one primary residence should remain (up to a dollar limit), but not for second homes or investment properties. I also know we need to change capital gains and restructure and simplify the tax code, promote small businesses, and encourage savings. A bolder action by any Commission might be to close the law (or loophole if you prefer) that allows firms to deduct interest payments on debt from taxable income. Although it will not fix the downward trend in marriage or out of wedlock birth rate, there is still a marriage penalty in the tax code that needs to be addressed. How to do that without penalizing our large single population will be the challenge. Various studies suggest that a 1% tax increase would reduce GDP by 3% in the following ten quarters.[30] By contrast, other studies suggest that fundamental tax reform could add 1% to annual GDP. Balancing all these considerations, and many more would fall to the commission. We would all have to compromise on what recommendations ultimately result.

- Corporate tax reform: $2T in cash of U.S. companies is sitting overseas because of the burden of U.S. taxation. There is a range of solutions mentioned in the inversions discussion that encompasses a combination of lower corporate tax rates, tougher criteria for moving offshore, a second (and last) tax holiday, and moving to a territorial tax system. As globalization expands, corporate concerns with growing parity in overseas pay scales and overall security considerations may weigh in the balance of many future inversion decisions, especially if tax rates can be reduced to some more competitive level, maybe around 20-25%. The overseas profits need to be repatriated. Additionally, U.S.

companies reportedly have around another $2T in cash that they are not investing, waiting for more certainty in the economic picture. Finally, any tax reform must deal with the excessive regulations that are stifling businesses, especially the small businesses that are the engine of our economy. Small businesses account for 50% of the U.S. workforce and have generated 65% of new jobs since 1995.[31] Legislation has been reintroduced, called the REINS Act, which would give Congress the final say on any regulation whose impact exceeds $100M (passed twice before in the Republican-controlled House.) It's not a bad start, but I would prefer a broader approach that addresses the masses of regulations impacting businesses. In 2010, the Small Business Administration released a report estimating that the overall impact of burdensome federal regulations cost the economy $1.75T annually. Wow!

- Finally, although radical ideas such as a flat tax and value-added tax (VAT) would be controversial, the Commission might be bold enough to try the latter (a flat tax is a non-starter.) Properly implemented it could significantly lower individual and corporate tax rates, preserve the progressive taxation system that protects those at the lower income scale and be revenue-neutral or better. A shift to a consumption tax would help address both income inequality and deficit issues. But it, also, may be a bridge too far. So I would personally favor something like four categories of progressive tax brackets: 10%, 25%, 35% and 50% for very high-income earners.

We desperately need both of these commissions, and the ideas presented above are just starting points for the difficult tasks and decisions that they would face. There are also other initiatives that should be undertaken.

First, we need a new Budget Enforcement Act, possibly patterned after the Budget Enforcement Act of 1990 which incorporated spending caps and the provision known as pay-as-you-go (Pay-Go) already mentioned. Pay-Go simply required that any increase in the annual deficit be offset by savings elsewhere in the budget. The 2010 Dominici-Rivlin Debt Reduction Task Force introduced a Save-Go provision, not unlike Pay-Go, as well as the other recommendations that would have Congress create a 3-pronged mechanism for hitting targets with automatic enforcement mechanisms if targets were not achieved. How exactly future legislation might be constructed would be hotly debated, but it is clear that we should take the lessons from the 1985 Gramm-Rudman-Hollings effort, the Budget Enforcement Act of 1990, and the Budget Control Act of 2011 to pass legislation that enforces discretionary and non-discretionary targets and encompasses both spending and revenues. Almost every state now has legislation requiring a balanced budget, and there is increasing interest in a constitutional amendment to drive the federal budget the same direction. Both Simpson and Bowles continue to suggest ways to reduce the debt, modifying and updating their original proposals.

Secondly, President Obama has spoken of the "need to win the future." Besides fixing our debt problem, that statement to me means robust funding for Infrastructure, Education, and Science & Technology. As a nation, we are overspending on consumption today and marginalizing investment for the future. Unless we address our debt problem in a serious way, this trend will continue, and will contribute to our 'losing the future' for successive generations. Simpson-Bowles offered some suggestions for this in the form of a Transportation Trust Fund and a Cut-and-Invest committee.

The 2013 report by the American Society of Civil Engineers (ASCE) gave D grades to our Dams, Drinking Water, Energy Sector,

Roads, Schools, Transit and more. In their 2011 report, ASCE estimated that the deteriorating surface transportation infrastructure "would cost the economy more than 876,000 jobs and suppress the growth of GDP by $897B by the year 2020." Similar results for Water/Wastewater, Energy, and Airports/Inland Waterways and Marine Ports, which totaled a $3.1T impact to the economy, and recommending roughly $100B a year in additional investment. Infrastructure investment, or lack thereof, was again a hot topic following the Amtrak derailment in May of 2015. In late 2015 the Congress finally passed a $300B+ multi-year transportation bill that is insufficient to meet our infrastructure challenges, and using dubious methods of financing that includes selling off national petroleum reserves and raiding earnings on the Fed's bond portfolio. Surely we can do better.

There were encouraging discussions, as previously mentioned, surrounding using repatriated corporate taxes to replenish the underfunded Highway Trust Fund. In early 2015 Senators, Paul and Boxer introduced a plan that would allow offshore companies to pay offshore taxes due at a rate of 6.5% (versus 35%) over the next five years. Add to that a much needed federal gas excise hike of around 18 cents/gallon to the Fund (essentially doubling the figure that has not changed since 1993), to take advantage of the unique opportunity we now have with oil and gas prices down. Even though states tax gas at an average of 50 cents/gallon, I would propose to rebate 5 cents of the 18 cent hike to states for improvments of existing infrastructure, where the need is greatest. Hopefully, enlightened legislation such as this will be passed and incorporated into an overall tax reform commission effort. With that investment, our nation's infrastructure could be well on the way to recovery, not to mention the thousands of good jobs that would be created.

Thirdly, and especially difficult, will be an effort to streamline and improve the 120+ overlapping and inefficient welfare programs (beyond Social Security and Medicare) that are administered by multiple departments and agencies. By any measure, the welfare state in America is expanding both in terms of beneficiaries and cost. Entitlement transfers are increasing, yet the poverty level remains at roughly 15%, the same as it was in 1983, and half the children in public schools are considered poor. What's the problem? Something is out of balance when the federal government (e.g. taxpayers) funds $680 Billion (2011 figures) on these programs which include Medicaid, Welfare payments, Supplemental Nutrition Assistance Program (SNAP) and many others, plus the state and local expenses on top of that. The current Administration has added $190B to these numbers. As the CATO Institute points out, this $680 billion represents $18,530 for every person and child designated as poor, or $44,500 for a family of three. But the poverty line for a family of three in 2012 was $19,090 so you would think poverty would be declining or almost nonexistent? With that kind of outlays and subsidized health care, incentivizing hard work becomes problematic.

We need a comprehensive revision to the 1996 Personal Responsibility and Work Responsibility Act that would address and streamline many, if not all, of these often redundant and apparently ineffective programs into something digestible, transparent, and that reflects our heritage and ethos as a self-respecting and hardworking nation. We can do that and still provide for those most in need; in fact, do it far more efficiently, while saving taxpayer dollars.

Finally, we need to revitalize the manufacturing sector of the country. We have lost nearly 850,000 relatively well-paying jobs in the manufacturing sector alone post-NAFTA. The loss from 1970 when we had 17.8 million to 11.9 million in 2012 is more telling, caused by automation, globalization and opening relations with China (a million manufacturing jobs lost to China between 2000 and 2007 alone.) The clothing industry went from 1.3 million employees to 150,000.[32] Once vibrant rust belt cities such as Detroit, Gary, and Pittsburgh suffered as jobs went overseas or, in some cases, shifted to the southeast. The theory of globalization is that everything will even out and all countries will benefit from a more efficient system with lower consumer prices. Many disagree. Economic strategist Clyde Prestowitz argues that we need a government-industry high-level industrial policy that focuses on high-value-added industries, which would replicate the success of the semiconductor rebound in the late 80's.[33] Value-added is a term that basically defines the difference between the manufacturing sector's inputs and final output. Manufacturing value-added today represents about 12% of GDP and has declined steadily since 2000. Looking at the change in value-added from 2005 to 2013, the U.S. is up 5% and China is up 140%.[34] Some economists have warned that unless steps are taken, up to 50% of the value-added of the U.S. economy is at risk of disappearing. Another Wow! If that happened, the U.S. trade deficit would top $1T."[35] If America has a well-defined manufacturing plan, I am not aware of it, but clearly it is urgently needed. We can't default to the unintended consequences of trade agreements and globalization.

So, what are the chances? Likely not much if we vote in another Republican or Democrat. I was encouraged by Rep. Camp's proposal that he had worked on for many years, but it was pronounced Dead-On-Arrival (DOA) shortly after the legislation was introduced. Apparently, something this consequential couldn't risk being tied to the 2014 mid-term elections. Now, we are in the ramp up to the 2016 presidential election, and no comprehensive change has any chance of succeeding in the near-term. Next, we'll be worried about the 2018 mid-term elections. As the population ages, no one wants to take on entitlement reform, even if grandfathering is an entering argument. So after the election, it will be back to business as usual, with partisan bickering and finger pointing. The only question is whether the new president will get a 100-day grace period or not. I seriously doubt that any sitting Democrat or Republican would take the risk of leading the charge on these reforms because of the probable political fallout.

Which all gets back to my assertion at the beginning of this chapter, that America's economic prosperity and future security is at critical risk by our failure to deal with mounting problems, especially our extraordinary and rising debt. And my conclusion that these reforms can't be dealt with in this political climate, and why we need to go the Commission route. I just hope Congress, with their impressive 6% approval rating, agrees.

CHAPTER 2

NATIONAL DEFENSE

The previous chapter showed that spending on our national defense is a large portion of the discretionary side of our annual budget. Despite cuts and force downsizing, some still think it is too much, and that it is rife with bureaucratic waste. Precisely because it is discretionary, and because it represents a significant investment, it is a frequent target for reductions, especially in the challenging fiscal environment we now find ourselves in. Most of this section deals with the DOD, generally referred to as the 'Pentagon', which constitutes the bulk of our military and defense spending. There are some interesting facts following, for consideration, as we discuss the issues surrounding what I am terming National Defense and the Defense Budget. Some of the data may be a few years old, but the issues and trends raised are still very relevant.

- The $691B spent on defense in 2010 (includes the Afghanistan and Iraqi wars) is more than double the (inflation-adjusted) $316B spent in 2001.[36] However, it can be argued that today's defense expenditure is a relatively modest 4.6% of GDP, especially considering multiple wars since 2011. (For example Defense spending in war years from 1940 to 2000 has averaged 13.3% of GDP and 5.7% of GDP in years of peace.[37] In 2014, the Defense Budget had dropped to $655B.

- In 1955, Defense spending was 62 percent of annual outlays; by 2012 it was 19% as funding moved to entitlement programs.
- A 2011 study commissioned by the Army identified $32B in funding for equipment since 1995 that was never built; this is for the Army only![38]
- 90% of all commercial goods travel by sea, making protection of the sea lanes as critical as ever. However, the size of the U.S. Navy has shrunk from 594 ships in 1987 to 288 ships as of the end of December 2014.
- In the 111th Congress, only 25% of the Senate and 21.6% of the House members had served in the military, steadily declining from a peak of 78% and 74% respectively.[39]
- While the military All-Volunteer Force (AVF) has been a great success, there is a growing disassociation from those who serve and those who are served, starting with our elected leaders.

"Since 9/11, a near doubling of the Pentagon's modernization accounts – more than $700B over 10 years in new spending on procurement, research & development – has resulted in relatively modest gains in actual military capability."
--Secretary of Defense Gates speech May 2011

Most of the recent news and topical debate surrounding the Defense Department revolves around a few topics broadly categorized as:

1. Defense Budgets, to include discussions of the AVF and the Industrial Base.
2. Defense Strategy, to include the size of the force and the ongoing War on Terror.

3. Issues of Service leadership and accountability.
4. The border defense establishment: the National Security Agency (NSA) and CIA, specifically.

Because there are so many intersections between our Defense Policy, Homeland Security Policy, and Foreign Policy, I've covered topics where I think they best fit, realizing the subjectivity in many cases. China and the terror threat, for examples, are covered in multiple chapters.

FIRST - A LITTLE PERSPECTIVE

Section 8 of the United States Constitution directs the federal government "to provide for the common defense... to raise and support armies... and to provide and maintain a navy."

Our nation has fought many wars since the War of Independence (1775-1783) and the first articles of the Constitution, which were adopted in 1787. It serves us all well to remember the many battles since, and those who served in the Civil War (1861-1865), World War I (1917-1918), World War II (1939-1945), Korean War (1950-1953), Vietnam War (1955-1975), the Cold War (1945-1991), Persian Gulf War (1991-1992), the War on Terror (2001-present). Not to mention the many lesser conflicts such as Grenada, Panama, Haiti and others around the world.

Tens of thousands of Americans have been wounded or perished fighting so we can preserve our free way of life and prosper. Parents, wives, husbands and children have all been left without a loved one who gave the ultimate sacrifice, or returned seriously wounded. Here is an abbreviated chart of the casualties (this doesn't include over 35,000 missing.)[40]

War or Conflict	Total Americans Dead or Wounded
Civil War	646,392
WWI	320,518
WWII	1,076,245
Korean War	128,650
Vietnam War	211,454
Gulf War	1.231
War on Terror (to date)	47,017

At $655B, the U.S. spends more on Defense than the next eight countries combined, a list that includes China and Russia. So why the huge defense budget?

As we reflect on that question, it is informative to recall some of the great sacrifices that our sailors, soldiers, marines, and airmen have made over the years, illustrative of why we maintain a strong and ready military. There are so many great stories of heroes and heroics, of famous battles won, that it is doing a great injustice to mention only a few. But because only 1% of our population now serves in uniform, it is especially important that we understand the framework and history of our military forces, their service and sacrifice, and why the world looks to the U.S. to lead in maintaining global security and order. An earlier version of this book contained summaries of some of our greatest battles and ordeals, from the Battle of Midway to the Bataan Death March. If I were a high school history teacher I would require that each student watch the History Channel documentaries about our military history for one hour every couple of weeks, and write a report. Too many people today do not truly comprehend and appreciate the sacrifices of our forefathers and those who have served and continue to serve our country.

In March 2014, we lost one such hero, Retired Rear Admiral Jeremiah Denton. He was a prisoner of war in Vietnam for 7 and ½ years and is remembered for blinking the word t-o-r-t-u-r-e on camera. He later served as a Senator from South Carolina. Among our many national heroes of wars gone by, a grateful nation remembers Jeremiah Denton, as do his seven children and 22 grandchildren. That same year we said farewell to Chester Nez, the last of original 29 Navajo Indian code talkers who developed an unbreakable code and then went on to risk their lives on the battlefields of WWII. April 2014 was also the 10-year anniversary of the death of Corporal Patrick Tillman, USA, a professional football player with the Arizona Cardinals who rejected a multi-million contract to join the Army and serve on the front lines. In doing so, he reminds us of the greats of yesteryear like Warren Spahn, Ted Williams and Rocky Blier whose own professional careers were interrupted by military service.[41]

In 2015, we played taps for another hero, Alex Vraciu. He was the son of a Romanian immigrant and WWII ace who shot down six Japanese enemy planes in eight minutes during what was called the Great Marianas Turkey Shoot. The valiant veterans of what Tom Brokaw called "The Greatest Generation" are now dying at a rate of between 600 and 1000 a day by one source. As time goes by, soon our remaining veterans of the Korean and Vietnam conflicts will pass away, as well. As will, in decades to come, the men and women who have served in our War on Terror.

There are far too many to mention that would qualify as heroes. But all that have served and sacrificed for our country should be acknowledged. They and the men and women that serve today deserve our appreciation and support.

> *"In my opinion, any future defense secretary who advises the president to again send a big American land army into Asia or into the Middle East or Africa should have his head examined."*
> --Secretary of Defense Robert Gates at West Point,
> 2/10/2011

That comment by then Secretary of Defense Robert Gates as he was nearing the end of his long career of service and distinguished tenure running the Pentagon, is very understandable. He felt personally accountable to the troops he sent into battle and had grown weary of fighting two wars and signing condolence letters every day to families who had lost loved ones. Like with any war, and Vietnam particularly comes to mind, the country, too, has grown tired. And while I empathize with Secretary Gates, history suggests that we will fight again, someday, even as we try to bring Iraq and Afghanistan to something that may resemble closure.

There is an old Latin adage from around the 5th century: "Si vin pacem, para bellum." Which translated means, "if you want peace, prepare for war." In modern day parlance, that means to stay focused, strong and prepared, particularly in times of relative peace. I would be hard pressed to argue that the world is a peaceful place in 2015, or our own nation particularly secure in any sense.

So how do we view the Defense Department in the coming 2016 election?

Clearly the size of the force will shrink. The Army has already begun downsizing the active force by over 100.000 and the U.S. Marine Corps is scheduled to cut 20,000 at the same time to a new level of 182,100 active members. In theory, you would like to think that the threat and the Defense strategy drives the size and composition of the force, which in turns drives the corresponding budgets.

Senator John McCain, who now chairs the Senate Armed Services Committee, wants a strategy-driven defense budget and has held many hearings early in his tenure. But having been in this business a long time, I can attest that the budget absolutely drives the process and we fit the strategy and the risk around the topline funds available. Good on Senator McCain for taking on the challenge and I hope he is successful. In the meantime, since budgets rule, let's look at that first.

DEFENSE BUDGETS

> *"Our national debt is our biggest national security threat."*
>
> --CJCS Mike Mullen at a Tribute to the Troops
> breakfast in 2010

One of the top challenges for any Secretary of Defense over the next decade will be managing the defense topline without jeopardizing our national security. As already noted, defense budgets have doubled in real terms in the last decade, counting the war efforts. And as President Obama noted in his address of April 13, 2011, commenting on our national debt trend, "By the end of this decade, the interest we owe on our debt could rise to nearly $1 Trillion. Just the interest payments."

As mentioned previously, interest payments at $1T would exceed the entire defense budget and then some. Since that statement projections have improved somewhat. In January 2015 CBO estimated that the interest on the debt would be $722B by 2024, a still staggering number that offers no consolation. Compare that number to the chart in Chapter 1.

It is, nevertheless, clear that defense spending will have to take some cuts as we wind down our commitments in the Middle East. When Congress passed the Budget Control Act (BCA) in 2011, one provision was to cut deficits by $1.2 Trillion over 10 years. Each year that the budget fell short of that goal the difference would be automatically cut equally between discretionary and mandatory programs by a process called sequestration. The CBO has estimated that defense budgets would be 2.7% of GDP in ten years, well below norms, based on this process alone. Just as Social Security and

Medicaid were exempt, so too were military pay and benefits. For defense, that means that cuts would be applied primarily to readiness and acquisition programs. Cuts of the size required by the BCA would have to involve personnel (military, civilian, and contractors), force structure, and large procurement programs. All this must be done while managing the industrial base, the readiness of the fighting force, critical acquisition programs that modernize or replace existing legacy platforms and new combat systems that pace the threat.

As one author has stated "Wisely, both Panetta and his predecessor, Robert Gates, have declared that any budget cuts must be informed by a well-crafted strategy... a crucial test will be how it addresses these rapidly growing risks to our security."[42] Nice words – hard to implement!

As Secretary Gates stated in 2010, nearing the end of his tenure, my *"greatest fear is that in tough economic times people will see the defense budget as the place to solve the nation's deficit problems."* Practically speaking, the only real way to measurably cut defense in the short-term is to cut personnel, military, civilian and contractors. The active military force, particularly the Army and Marine Corps, are already reducing end strength, as aleady mentioned. The Navy and Air Force previously downsized their force levels. Although the cost of military healthcare is often criticized as a driver of defense spending and does need reform, especially in the area of co-payments, the overlooked fact is that personnel and health costs have comprised that same budget share roughly 1/3 for the past 30 years.[43]

One point that virtually all agree on is that the overly generous military retirement system needs reform, but only as part of larger debt reduction initiatives, and not targeted against those that have been serving in combat the past decade and more. The

2016 Defense Bill started this process, but left more work to be done. Likewise, the federal civilian workforce is reducing, but not fast nor deep enough, and suffers from grade creep (meaning that work is re-classified at increased levels, resulting in more and more personnel serving at higher grades.) Many of us were amazed during the furloughs in 2013 that 800,000 Defense workers, determined non-essential, were told not to report to work. By contrast, Department of Homeland Security (DHS) declared almost all of its workforce as essential, and had all report to work.

Different analysts will throw out various numbers, such as the gap between private and federal pay widening, but the CBO is arguably a very good, unbiased source. Its 2012 report found that overall the federal workforce is paid 2% higher than their civilian counterparts and have 16% higher benefits. This dispels the rhetoric on both sides that federal workers earn nearly double the total compensation of private sector workers (as some analysts contend), as well as the contention that the approximate 13% pay gap between federal and civilian is widening as some union representatives would have you believe. The CBO analysis is close enough, and should end that debate.

In the meantime, any proactive Secretary of Defense interested in reform should start with the bloated bureaucracy at the Pentagon, which is ten times the size it was when we won WWII![44] As Senator McCain and others have pointed out, we won WWII with two regional combatant commands; now they have proliferated with large staffs, and the same for the number of Defense Agencies. The services have had to grow ridiculously large staffs to address volumes of issues and questions from congressional members and staff and the Joint Staff, in an escalating cycle that has been somewhat humorously referred to as a 'self-licking ice cream cone.' And, by the way, there is virtually no expedient way to rid the federal government of poor performing workers, despite what the Merit System Protection Board, the American Federation of Government Employees and other unions might state (another critical area needing reform).

In 2011, the DOD spent over $77B on its civilian workforce.[45] In my opinion, 95 percent of federal workers do a fabulous job, but the other 5% wouldn't survive a week in the private sector, and shouldn't be coddled with taxpayer dollars.

Another primary concern for any Secretary of Defense must be preserving the nation's fragile industrial base. When President Eisenhower warned of the dangers of the military-industrial complex over 50 years ago, the DOD budget represented over half of the entire federal budget, well below the current levels, so the picture has changed markedly. Fortunately, the industrial base challenge appears to be known to the defense leaders, even if not yet fully embraced as an emergent and priority issue by all, in either the Pentagon or the Congress.

Former Deputy Secretary Bill Lynn, speaking in New York on 11 May 2011 recalled the defense cutbacks in 1993, when then Secretary of Defense William Perry called industry leaders to the Pentagon for a meeting that later became known as, The Last Supper letting them know that industry consolidation would be inevitable due to reduced spending—and that happened. In 2014 and 2015 we saw that very same merger & acquisition activity, especially in the service sector. As Lynn further said "Our defense industrial base has emerged in the past three generations as a strategic national asset—an asset that is not a birthright and cannot be taken for granted. Thousands of firms —some big, others small— equip our military. These firms, their suppliers, and their supplier's suppliers are the links in a chain that, if broken, can have an outsize impact on our military capability."

There have been many studies and many annual reports to Congress, all highlighting the fragile nature of our industrial base. Once marginalized or eroded, it is not a capability that can be quickly reconstituted. Just as the size of our active force needs to reflect how we view the military component to our nation's security and vital interests, protecting the core (and now fragile) industrial base needs to be a central component of that discussion, and a primary consideration in all budget deliberations.

Finally, acquisition reform seems to continually elude the Pentagon, with cost overruns and schedule delays more the norm than the exception for the larger acquisition programs. The Army study referenced at the beginning of this chapter, that identified $32B[46] in spending on items that were never built, comes as no surprise. The Navy spent over $700M on a remote mine hunting system that never worked and the newest aircraft carrier is $6B over budget. How many hard working Americans paid taxes for years to accumulate that kind of money? Did anyone get fired? I don't think so. In years past, the late Senator William Proxmire (D—WI) produced a monthly Golden Fleece Award, which the Defense Department won many times. The outstanding Senator from Oklahoma who recently retired, Senator Tom Coburn, produced an annual report on waste and was one of the architects of reforming earmarks in congressional appropriations. His November 2012 "Department of Everything" report is sadly revealing. Among other things, Senator Coburn highlighted how the Army spent almost $300M on a blimp and the Air Force $432M on planes, none of which produced items that will ever be used.[47]

Many reports, studies, realignment of responsibility and other attempts haven't done much to effectively reform the military procurement system. It is interesting that the individual who from October 2011 to December 2013 was the acquisition chief at the Pentagon, Ashton Carter, is now the Secretary of Defense. In March

2014, Congress directed the Pentagon and industry to look at how to stop the bleeding: $300B in cost overruns in the top 100 programs, and nearly $50 billion in canceled programs over the past decade."[48] The Joint Strike Fighter (F-35) alone is about $160 billion over budget. All these overruns and cancelations have been a bonanza for the big defense giants who continue to post solid profits and pay dividends, but catastrophic for taxpayers and warfighters.

What's wrong with this picture?

I would concede that, with declining and uncertain budgets levels, coupled with the continuing threat of sequestration, it is virtually impossible for any acquisition professionals at the Pentagon, or in industry, to deliver a sophisticated combat program on cost and schedule. There is plenty of blame to share. Congress, which is quick to criticize, is every bit a part of this problem as is the Pentagon, or the mega-defense contractors.

> *"A good Navy is not a provocation to war. It is the surest guaranty of peace."*
>> --President Theodore Roosevelt

Affording the All-Volunteer Force and the 1%: In 2013 we recognized the 40th anniversary of the AVF. It has been a resounding success, but not without some significant downsides, or unintended consequences. First of all, we are creating a system where fewer and fewer Americans will have served in the Armed Forces. I noted in the introduction the rapid decline in the number of members of Congress who are veterans, now less than 20%. Of the 44 U.S. Presidents, who also serve as Commander-in-Chief, 26 were war veterans and only 16 never served in uniform, a list that includes only Bill Clinton and Barrack Obama in recent times. As many observers have pointed out, less than 1% of Americans have been defending the other 99% for over 10 years. One retired General and former CIA Director David Petraeus states: "In World War II, 11.2% of the nation served in four years. During Vietnam, 4.3% served in twelve years. Since 2001, only.045% of the population has served in the Global War on Terror."[49] It is easy, as also pointed out, to fight wars with "other people's kids."[50] The Iraq War Resolution of 2002 passed the Senate 77 -23, including 'Yes' votes by Democratic Senators Kerry, Clinton, and Biden, but only one—Senator Tim Johnson (D—SD) had a child who actually was soon to fight in that conflict.

It's also easier when you finance that war with money you don't have.

It is very fortunate that, through the ongoing wars in the Middle East, the military has not become disconnected from the people it serves, even as most remain relatively untouched by the war. Most Americans, it now seems, understand that the military is an instrument of civilian policy, not the maker of policy. Recent Harris Polls and Pew surveys continue to reflect high American confidence in the military.

Another downside to the AVF besides limited participation, is the cost, a fact now coming into increased focus as defense budgets tighten. As Loren Thompson of the Lexington Institute pointed out back in 2009, "the average cost of each warfighter has increased 45% over the past dozen years—from $55,000 to $80,000. When health care costs are added to this baseline, the current cost of each warfighter, including a set-aside for retirement, rises above $100,000 annually." [51] Those number have surely increased in the intervening years. Another one of the challenges in maintaining the AVF is the declining percentage of the population who have a propensity to enlist, and who are eligible. A somewhat dated 2007 study found that "only 4.7 million of the 31 million 17-

24 year-olds' population are eligible to enlist." [52] Disqualifiers included medical/physical problems (35%), drug use (18%), criminal record (5%), and low test scores 9%). More recent studies show those who serve come disproportionately from military families or from the south. Still, very few (including the author) are advocating a return to conscription, so sustaining a robust AVF is critical to our national interest. At the same time, it is disconcerting that the gap is growing between those who serve honorably and sacrifice on our behalf, and those who take little notice and often take for granted that service, with no comprehension of the inherent sacrifice. It's a worrisome problem.

I think the nation should embrace a healthy discussion of a template for national service of some sort, to give all Americans an opportunity to serve their country. Retired General Stan McChrystal and others are leading such efforts with various proposals to expand service after high school, whether it be military, Peace Corps or some other form of service. I like the idea of volunteers in our toughest schools, discussed in a later chapter. The concept of National Service has been around for some time and I think now deserves real consideration. Two years with pay is not too much to ask and, properly instituted, could better prepare our youth for follow-on job opportunities. I think National Service could also be used to help offset college loan principal, as proposed in the previous chapter.

At the end of the day, however, we need to come to grips with the role that we want the nation's military, and America itself, to play in this ever-more dangerous world, recognize our many commitments to allies, and then make the necessary investment. While the U.S. defense budget is relatively flat, the Chinese defense budget has seen double-digit growth every year over the past decade.[53]

Many have reported on the declining technology edge that the U.S. possesses vis-a-vis our potential adversaries. America remains the strongest military in the world, but the technological advantage is slipping away and preeminence in space and cyberspace especially vulnerable as competitors catch up. For this reason, the Pentagon is aggressively pursuing game-changing technology, as it must. A great American and late Senator, Scoop Jackson of Washington, believed that the defense of the nation was the first job of government. There is no benchmark of GDP that makes sense to shoot for in terms of topline for the defense budget; better that our elected leaders sort this out and arrive at a budget that ensures America remains engaged internationally, technically superior, unchallenged militarily, and provides a credible deterrent force throughout the world.

> *"The richest nation on earth can afford whatever it needs for defense"*
> --Senator Scoop Jackson, 1960, campaigning for
> John F. Kennedy

DEFENSE STRATEGY

The mission of the DOD has been, and remains, to keep the nation safe by deterring war, influencing world events and, when necessary, defeating the enemy on the battlefield. In the course of our nation's history, the military has been called on many times to protect our freedom, at great cost and loss of life. "Freedom is not free" is as true as statement today as ever in our history. As President George Washington said in his first annual address, "the most effectual means of preserving peace is to be prepared for war," as the Latin adage I mentioned previously, si vin pacem, para bellum, suggests.

The Pentagon publishes a comprehensive National Defense Strategy, which derives from the National Security Strategy, and informs the National Military Strategy. While the documents evolve over time and with different administrations, I would suggest four overarching missions for the Defense Department for the foreseeable future. *This is solely my view*, as someone who served for many years, unfettered by any official document or another body of work. Many will see these missions from a different perspective and there is, in fact, much synergy with our foreign policy:

1. Promote peace and freedom through active presence and engagement, but be prepared to fight and win against our enemies whenever called upon.
2. Contain the proliferation of Weapons of Mass Destruction.
3. Deter and defeat ideological extremism.
4. Focus on the increasingly critical Western Pacific region.

Promoting peace and freedom, and winning our nation's battles, is what the DOD does every day. Whether on the battlefield in Afghanistan or the Horn of Africa, patrolling the Malaccan straits or providing humanitarian assistance to the Philippines, it is the most visible of DOD missions.

We are bound by many treaties and partnerships throughout the world, and our troops are stationed worldwide. We have large geographic commands that provide forces and expertise to the regions under their respective jurisdictions. Being forward and present makes a difference, particularly as access and overflight issues often constrain our engagement.

How capable our Armed Forces remain, and how prepared we are to fight and win, is directly dependent on the budget authority provided, preserving a robust AVF, enlightened priorities, visionary leadership, and the oversight of an engaged and supportive Congress. All this, in turn, rests on a strong national economy and a shrinking national debt (a matter of great concern).

Containing the proliferation of Weapons of Mass Destruction. Deterrence is a second fundamental mission of our defense establishment and takes many forms. For almost a half-century of the Cold War, deterrence was focused on the Soviet Union. Today, deterrence is focused on a range of potential adversaries, such as Iran, to include non-state actors (jihadists.) Deterrence has both a defensive and offensive component. Certainly our nuclear arsenal is fundamental to our credible deterrence from attack. So too are our conventional forces, our special operations forces, and our forward presence around the globe signaling our national resolve and commitment to free international commerce.

While there is no universally agreed upon definition of Weapons of Mass Destruction (WMD), the term commonly used now is Chemical, Biological, Radiological, Nuclear, and Explosive (CBRNE), which includes both nuclear weapons and chemical, biological and radiological gasses. Control of proliferation of CBRNE weapons is a critical responsibility of our interagency effort (multiple departments that includes Homeland Security, Defense, State, FBI, CIA, etc.)

There are multiple treaties that govern and control these weapons, to include the Biological Weapons Convention (since 1975) and the most recent Strategic Arms Reduction Treaty with Russia in 2010, which further limits nuclear warheads and launchers. Nine countries admit to having nuclear weapons (the U.S., Russia, China, France, India, Pakistan, Britain, North Korea and Israel). Currently, it is estimated that China has 240 operational, strategic nuclear warheads, Russia 2400 and the U.S. approximately 2000.[54]

Disarming Syria of chemical weapons and attempting to halt the enriched uranium program in Iran are two examples of recent initiatives; the latter the subject of completed negotiations in July 2015 and explained more in the foreign policy chapter. Much more remains to be done, with non-state actors possibly posing the greatest threat, and biological agents possibly the worst case scenario. A strong and modernized nuclear arsenal is a top priority for DOD, starting with the timely replacement of the Ohio-class submarine fleet for the Navy.

Deter and Defeat Ideological extremism. To start this discussion, here are some points for your consideration, some dated, but still relevant:

- "Our initial investigation has concluded that there are between 400 and 500 radical Islamic centers in the U.S. In these places, they preach an extreme vision of Islam that says America and the West are the enemies. They espouse violence, hatred and the need for terrorism."[55]
- The Islamic Saudi Academy in Alexandria, Virginia continued to use textbooks that teach hatred of everyone not of their specific brand of faith.[56] The Center for Islamic Pluralism quotes a former Treasury Department General Counsel, to a Senate subcommittee that (Saudi) spending on these schools exceeds $75B.[57]
- In February 2008, FBI Director Robert Mueller told the House Permanent Select Committee on Intelligence that the Muslim Brotherhood, the Islamic group whose ideology has inspired terrorists such as Osama bin Laden, are in the United States and have supported terrorism here and abroad.[58]
- 15% of U.S. Muslims under 30 (and 6% of the overall U.S. Muslim population) believe that suicide bombings in defense of Islam "can often or sometimes be justified." Only 26% of

the overall Muslim population survey feel the U.S. led War on Terrorism is a sincere effort. This data from a Pew Research Center report in May 2011.

The ongoing, and probably generational war against radical terrorists and jihadists permeates our national budgets, foreign policy, homeland security considerations, and more. Where to place it in this book became somewhat arbitrary; the same could be said for cybersecurity and other issues: It is covered here and since we have been involved in overseas combat missions for over a decade, but we discuss this also in our foreign policy chapter. Today there are an estimated 3.5 million Muslims in the U.S. and the growth by 2030 is expected to be about 9 million, a 151% increase, based on the 2011 Pew Research report. Additionally, the same Pew report estimates the birth rate of Muslims will be more than double the rate of non-Muslims. In 2009, there were approximately 115,000 Muslim immigrants to the U.S., a figure also expected to continue to grow significantly.

Not everyone will like the quotes and facts presented above because they tend to generalize Muslims and obscure the fact that a large majority of Muslims are law-abiding citizens and patriotic, well assimilated into the mainstream of American society, and espouse neither violence nor jihad. Linking terrorism to religion is also an anathema to all Americans who don't like linking politics to religion, even when the data might support some linkage. As I read in one editorial, "But the unavoidable fact is that, however, much violent terror reflects a distortion of the tenets of Islam, it is not only practiced by adherents of the religion but practiced in its name."[59] Indeed, the 9/11 Commission concluded just this: "The enemy is not Islam, the great world faith, but a perversion of Islam. The enemy goes beyond al-Qaeda to include the radical ideological movement, inspired in part by al-Qaeda, that has spawned other terrorist groups and violence. Thus, our strategy must match our means to two ends: dismantling the al-Qaeda network and, in the long-term, prevailing over the ideology that contributes to Islamic terrorism."[60]

In this respect, our current President is probably correct in not linking radical jihad to Islam, something that King Abdullah of Jordan has said he agrees with. That's good enough for me. In 2014, ISIS became the most visible and threatening group of international terrorists, claiming a caliphate, a strict Islamic State headed by a descendant of Muhammed. They are extreme in their intolerance of women's education, other racial minorities, and other religions.

We have been fighting terrorists well before the attack of 11 September 2001. In the Philippines for example, government forces (with U.S. support) have been fighting multiple Islamist extreme groups for over four decades. Even in the early 1900s General "Blackjack" Pershing was fighting the Moro insurrection in the Philippines, with some interesting surviving lore on how he stopped the attacks. In 1984, possibly in response to the October 1983 Beirut barracks bombings in which 241 Americans were killed (220 marines, 18 sailors, 3 soldiers), the Reagan Administration began using the term War on Terrorism as part of proposed legislation to freeze assets of terrorist groups.[61] In the 1983 Beirut attack, much like the 2012 attack on the Benghazi diplomatic mission on Sep. 11, 2012, no senior Administration official was fired, or even found accountable. In 1986, the World Islamic Front for Jihad against Jews and Crusaders (WIFJAJC), sponsored by Osama bin Laden and which later evolved into al-Qaeda, began forming a large base of operations in Afghanistan, the same year that the Taliban seized power.[62] Following the bombings of U.S. embassies in Tanzania and Kenya, Reagan's successor, Bill Clinton, began a campaign against suspected WIFJAJC, to include a pharmaceutical plant suspected of producing chemical weapons. Clinton also started the highly controversial program of rendition usually linked to George Bush, whereby suspected terrorists were flown to 3rd party countries for harsh interrogation by the CIA, although the 2014 Senate report on enhanced CIA interrogation techniques failed to point this out, one of many shortcomings of this report. The attempted attack on the Los Angeles airport and the bombing of the USS Cole are two other events that preceded the 9/11 attacks.

> *"Thanks to the sacrifice of our men and women in uniform, the war in Iraq is over, the war in Afghanistan is winding down, al-Qaeda has been decimated and Osama bin Laden is dead."*
> --President Obama, Green Bay, WI Nov. 2012

So, who is the enemy and who are we fighting. As one former NSA director stated, "As many critics have pointed out, terrorism is not the enemy. It is a tactic."[63] Likewise, Islam is not the enemy, it is a religion. More generally it is an ideology based on a perverted interpretation of the religion, but one that is proliferating and gaining adherents. Despite the killing of bin Laden and the assessment by the current President, on more than 30 occasions citing the demise of al-Qaeda, the war against al-Qaeda affiliates is far from over. [64] We now face even greater threats with the emergence of ISIS.

Although bin Laden's successor, Ayman al-Zawahiri, lacks the leadership and governance ability of his predecessor, al-Qaeda affiliates are growing after some stagnation following the Arab Spring. The Benghazi, Libya attack on 11 April 2012 where four were killed (including Ambassador Chris Stevens) and ten were injured, was directly linked to a pre-meditated attack by an Islamic militia. On 21 September 2013 al-Qaeda's Somalia affiliate, al-Shabaab, attacked the Westgate shopping center in Nairobi, killing 67 and injuring hundreds more. In Yemen, AQAP continues to flourish, despite the loss of some key members to drone attacks; it reportedly continues to publish the online magazine, <u>Inspire</u>. Iraq is in disarray with Iraqi forces fighting with Iranian militia against ISIS, which has moved into Syria and continues to fight and expand its territory in Iraq, and in May of 2015 captured the key town of Ramadi, although it was re-captured late last year. There are many factions of fighters, from the Shiite militia called Hezbollah Brigades to the Kurdistan Worker's Party (PKK) to the radical Sunni – ISIS. ISIS, as we have seen, has brutally murdered fellow Sunni tribesmen who have been uncooperative and beheaded westerners and many other nonbelievers. In late 2014 and early 2015 they burned alive a Jordanian pilot and then beheaded twenty Egyptian Christians. Their tactics have been so brutal that al-Qaeda's leader, al-Zawahiri, with whom they compete for the minds of jihadists, has distanced himself from the group and many of the other radical militias are following suit.

A 2008 RAND Corporation Study for "Defeating Terrorist Groups," presented to the U.S. House of Representatives, recommended that "the U.S. military should generally resist being drawn into combat operations in Muslim countries where its presence is likely to increase terrorist recruitment." While there may be some merit to the argument that U.S. presence in Muslim countries is a catalyst for jihadist recruitment, as it clearly was following the Abu Ghraib prison debacle, conduct of harsh interrogation techniques and years of drone strikes—often killing innocent civilians. (and more recently an American and Italian hostage, for which our president has apologized) this line of reasoning suggests that we abandon our Islamic friends in Iraq and Afghanistan, with the likely consequences in Afghanistan that we now see in Iraq.

For the near-term, America needs to stay engaged in the Middle East. As Colin Powell allegedly said on the eve of our invasion of Iraq, sometimes called the Pottery Barn rule, 'You break it, you own it.' Well we did break it, and helped set off the chain of events that now engulf the region, so we need to ensure that as we retrench we leave those countries in a position to sustain and win the fight. That's far from the situation as of this writing. So here are a few suggestions for the continuing battle against the jihadist movement:

- Retain some presence and engagement in Afghanistan (2-3 bases) and Iraq as a stabilizing force. Do not take kinetic forces off the table realizing, however that this is exactly what ISIS wants – U.S. troops back on the ground.

- Continue to grow the coalition in the Middle East, as many countries from Turkey to Pakistan to Jordan and Egypt now see the threat from radical jihadists (from the Taliban to ISIS).

- Continue ongoing efforts to close the detainee facility at Guantanamo, Cuba, through all reasonable, means possible and on a timeline that ensures it is done correctly.

- Enhance our internal ability to counter the insider threat, such as those by the radicalized jihadists like the Army psychiatrist, Nidal Hasan, who killed 13 at Fort Hood, Texas, or the Washington Navy Yard shooter. There is an Executive Order to this effect that has been largely ignored, or slowly implemented, by government agencies.

More on this in subsequent chapters. In the meantime, we should all embrace Muslims as they have been, for most of time, a peace-loving and moderate people. They represent about 1% of the U.S. population now, a figure that will grow significantly based on birth rates. Over 3000 now serve honorably in our Armed Forces. They must, however, leave behind their silent-majority status, and speak out against radical elements who terrorize in the name of Islam. We should also remember the words of Cardinal Theodore McCarrick, the Archbishop of Washington D.C., shortly after the 2001 attacks, *"We must seek the guilty and not strike out against the innocent or we become like them who are without moral guidance..."*

The Western Pacific region and China: Several years ago the Administration implemented a decision to re-focus our defense strategy through a "pivot to the Pacific." If you believe that all strategy is somehow rooted in economic concerns, then understanding the economic significance of the Pacific Rim is a good place to start. 44% of the world's population lives within 140 kilometers of the sea and 90% of the world's commerce travels by sea.

The Western Pacific is, foremost, a vast maritime domain. The economic interests of the dominant economies converge at the South China Sea. Of the several strategic straits, the Straits of Malacca links the Indian and Pacific oceans and the economies of China, India, Indonesia, South Korea, Japan and others. 50,000 ships a year, some of which this author has assiduously tried to avoid hitting while standing the deck watch at sea, transit this sea lane carrying a quarter of the world's trading goods, including oil.[65]

China, after centuries of transgressions, civil and land wars, is now relatively secure on its borders and focused on economic and military growth. The dynamics of an emerging regional power, strategic shipping routes driving multinational commerce, U.S. commitments, and treaties, and rising territorial disputes all combine to make the Western Pacific, in general, and the South China Sea specifically, a region of great national importance – hence the 'pivot to the Pacific.'

The Association of South East Asian Nations (ASEAN) holds an annual conference to discuss political, economic and security issues of common interest, one of the seemingly more strategically important conferences to the U.S., and which the President skipped in 2013, causing some to doubt the U.S.'s real commitment to the region. One of the ongoing and potentially combustive issues involves territorial claims, the most sensitive being the Spratly's (Vietnam, China, Taiwan, Brunei and the Philippines) and the Senkaku Islands (called the Diaoyu in China). Japan purchased the three Senkaku Islands from a private Japanese landowner in 2012 and, in response to that, a perceived more aggressive Japanese government under President Abe, and just possibly President Obama's skipping of the ASEAN conference, China in late 2013 established an expanded air defense identification zone (ADIZ) in the East China Sea, prompting immediate international response and increased tensions in the region. The U.S., Japan, and South Korea all then flew within this newly pronounced ADIZ, to reinforce international airspace.

These recent events mark China's first attempt to expand it's territory since 1949, and seems contradictory to the statements made by the President Xi Jinping of a "new type of great power relationship" with America, as well as China's decades-old policy of "strategic patience" first adopted by Deng Xiaoping 35 years ago.[66]

Although we can hope that an emerging powerful China can be our competitor and not our adversary, hope has never been a compelling strategy. The 12-mile limit of territorial seas has long been recognized and was formalized under the UN Convention on the Law of the Seas (UNCLOS) in 1982, which also recognizes a further 12-mile Contiguous Zone and exclusive economic zones (EEZs) extending to 200 miles. China is now claiming a poorly defined nine-dashed line (sometimes called the "U"), shown next, which includes the disputed areas and conflicts with UNCLOS which China ratified in 1996. China, as of April 2015, has yet to file any claim as to what this line actually represents.

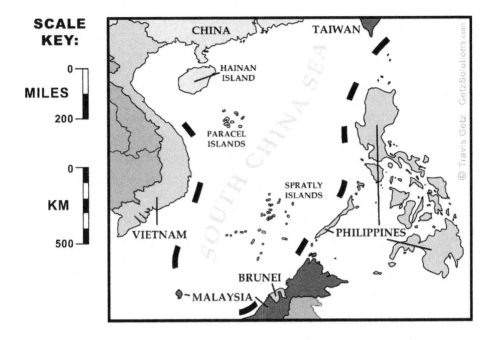

The pivot to the Pacific was a wise strategic move, with an announced buildup of naval power providing a centerpiece for long-term stability in the region. In the meantime, China, which holds over 1 trillion of our debt, continues to invest in our companies and, according to The Economist, one U.S. mayor lands in China every 10 days offering tax breaks and other incentives to Chinese firms to open shop in their respective hometowns. [67] It brings back memories of Texas Governor (and past presidential hopeful) Rick Perry's long courtship of the Chinese firm Huawei Technologies who he announced would open U.S. operations in Plano, Texas. Huawei was founded by a former PLA (People's Liberation Army) officer and is now the largest telecommunications equipment maker in the world with over 140,000 employees and several research and development plants in the U.S. This despite multiple warnings of the security risk associated with Huawei from the past two Administrations, accompanied by allegations of spying (from a former NSA director) and of its support for the Taliban, Iran, and corporate espionage. It is a long-running issue of U.S. or state economic interests facing off with national security concerns.

China's rogue behavior in response to the disputed island chains, announcement of this Nine-dash Line claimed territory that nearly encompasses the entire South China Sea, and economic outreach particularly to the Latin America's Pacific countries, have concerned its neighbors in the region who still look for American leadership as a stabilizing influence and to balance China's rise.

Good initiatives for the U.S. is to continue the buildup in Guam and complete the Trans-Pacific Partnership recently negotiated (discussed more in the foreign policy chapter). The next twenty years and beyond will see a remarkable focus on this region of the world with the emergence of China, whose economy is still growing and whose defense budget has seen a double-digit expansion for many years running.

> *"If ignorant of both your enemy and yourself, you are certain to be in peril."*
>
> --Sun Tzu

LEADERSHIP AND ACCOUNTABILITY

One of the ethos taught early and repeatedly heard in the military is that "with authority comes responsibility, and with them both comes accountability." Since the founding of our country the U.S. military has distinguished itself in battles won and lost; it is not surprising that the military continues to rank highest in polling among institutions that Americans most admire and trust. With the battlefield dynamics and pressures of war come occasional accidents and even atrocities, from the infamous My Lai massacre of hundreds of unarmed civilians in Vietnam in 1968 to the more recent abominations at Abu Ghraib prison to pictures of troops urinating on Taliban corpses. Yet as one historian has ably, and correctly, stated "the pre-Gates norms stubbornly persist. If fault is found, it invariably fixes responsibility and imposes penalties at echelons well below those occupied by the people said to be in charge. The fall guy ends up being the little guy."[68]

This is particularly troubling since the rigid test of accountability has been one of the most, if not the most, hallmark traits of the military services. Firings of Admirals and Generals has stepped up in recent years, ranging from issues of gambling, inappropriate conduct and inept leadership dealing with nuclear weapons, among others. That's a good trend, yet many still slip through; once such case being the former head of the Missile Defense Agency (MDA) who retired at grade, given an apparent free pass by the Service Secretary following a scathing IG report documenting an extremely abusive leadership style. A more recent headline involved a Navy Flag so drunk he locked himself outside his hotel room, naked. One of the enduring traditions is that, if found guilty of some misconduct at a high rank, you still get to retire with full benefits at the 'last rank at which you honorably served.' Worse yet, we read repeatedly about senior officers that have been found guilty of disgraceful offenses only to be given an administrative warning and then retained on active duty. Absolute nonsense! If you fail to perform and/or meet the ethical standards of a General or Flag Officer, then you should not retire at any rank equivalent to a senior officer. The same standard applies for all who serve, but the senior leadership must be judged by the strictest criteria.

Nothing quite compares to the revelations of sexual harassment and assault in the military that erupted several years ago. The lid blew off when Lieutenant General Craig Franklin, the Commander of the 3rd Air Force in Europe, overturned the court-martial conviction of Lieutenant Colonel James Wilkerson for assaulting a sleeping woman, stating that he could not believe that the "doting father and husband" could commit such a crime. The uproar infuriated members of Congress and millions of Americans as well. In the meantime, Wilkerson was accused by a second woman of adultery and fathering a child out of wedlock, an allegation that was substantiated and Wilkerson was retired. It is sad to continue to read how military commanders bungle sexual-assault cases by failing to take action; worse yet when the commanders themselves are the perpetrators and, when caught, receive a slap on the wrist and full retirement benefits.

Senator Kirsten Gillibrand (D–NY) and Senator Claire McCaskill (D–MO) led the hearings and legislative battle to remove commanders in the chain of command on decisions over prosecution, trial, punishment and review of sexual-assault cases. One of the most disappointing hearings I witnessed was the Joint Chiefs of Staff testifying in support of the status quo, in the face of mounting evidence of widespread problems and command inattention regarding sexual harassment and assault in the military. The 2014 Defense Authorization Bill made significant changes. Short of removing commanders from the chain of command and deferring cases to a military prosecutor, they include not allowing commanders to overturn sexual-assault jury convictions, requiring civilian review if a commander declines to prosecute, requiring a Dishonorable Discharge (DD) if a conviction results, affording legal counsel to victims, eliminating the statute of limitations and criminalizing retaliation. Unfortunately, the bill was silent on false accusations, which has to be addressed as well, and will be someday. Only time will tell if the military leadership has the conviction and ability to right the ship.

In two high visibility cases, retired 4-star Generals Cartwright and Petraeus stood accused of unauthorized disclosure of classified information, the latter famously to his paramour and biographer, Paula Broadwell. As a reminder, information that is classified as Top Secret, which General Petraeus admitted to leaking in a plea bargain, is defined as information that could cause "exceptionally grave damage" to national security if made public. Petraeus also lied to the FBI and retained classified information in his home after signing a document to the contrary, which was later discovered when the FBI raided his home.[69] The announcement in late 2015 that the Army planned no further action against Petraeus came as no surprise.

I've known some highly competent enlisted personnel and junior officers who sank their careers by the inadvertent mishandling of secret material, which is a much lesser offense. What signal does it send to them and the entire military establishment when very senior officers go unpunished, or receive light rebuke, for equal or greater offenses? I have a reasonably good idea what would happen to a junior officer who intentionally leaked Top Secret documents, and subsequently lied to law enforcement: it's called a Courts Martial, and a long stint at Fort Leavenworth prison. I have a very hard time arguing that a chronic double standard doesn't exist. The case of General Cartwright, suspected of leaking information about the Stuxnet worm, apparently remains under investigation by the DOJ, apparently over security concerns if he is prosecuted. Time will tell how this is resolved, but he is another Administration favorite. Both cases are influencing other cases, specifically referenced by the defense in the sentencing of Jeffrey Sterling, the former and allegedly disgruntled CIA agent who leaked highly classified documents to NY Times reporter James Risen, who printed them.[70]

Where is the accountability?

In a Veterans Affairs survey of 1500 women who deployed to Iraq or Afghanistan, one in four said they experienced sexual harassment—ranging from unwanted groping to rape.[71]

Every mother, father, guardian, family member, friend or neighbor should know with certainty that anyone who joins the military service may serve in harm's way, and may pay for that service with the ultimate sacrifice. They should have the same certainty, however, that whoever serves will be provided covenant leadership where they can grow personally and professionally, serve with honor, and never be harassed or assaulted by their fellow comrades in arms. Anything less is unacceptable. The standards of conduct have to be exacting and the consequences for transgressions severe.

The Border Defense Establishment. Over the past couple of years, there has been a lot of controversy regarding some of our elite agencies, namely the NSA and the CIA, that I have categorized here as part of our broader defense establishment.

In 2014, the CIA was back in the news with the release by Senator Diane Feinstein of the Senate investigation of harsh interrogation tactics, frequently called enhanced interrogation techniques (EITs). Although the report cost $40 million and took five years, it contained little new information and ostensible flaws that cast the U.S. in an extremely bad light and served as a shining recruitment tool for radical elements. I have a great deal of respect for Senator Feinstein, but it is still not clear to me why this report needed to be made public, which is not to minimize the abuses that occurred. While much has and will be written about these excesses, the most basic fault rests with a failure of congressional oversight by our intelligence committees and select staff. Senator John McCain was one of the authors of the Military Commissions Act that addressed EITs; his is the final word on this subject, as it should be.

After the Snowden leaks, the NSA's collection of bulk data under the Patriot Act Section 215 and other Executive Orders came under intense scrutiny. The Patriot Act authorized court orders to compel phone companies to turn over phone data. The President's Review Group made some recommendations to address this issue, and network providers and phone makers are taking steps to comply. While many changes have been made, the debate will continue as to the tradeoff between our privacy concerns under the 4th Amendment that protects us from unreasonable search and seizure, and the need to protect citizens from attacks, both from outside and within.

However, we manage this balance, I am certain that we need a fully functional NSA and CIA, with their staffs of highly-skilled and motivated employees, as we face an increasingly dangerous world from nations who are aggressively anti-U.S., to non-state actors to insurgents who would do us harm. Behind these headlines, there are superb Americans, often working in adverse and dangerous places, to protect us all. We should all be grateful.

Here are some final thoughts on Defense:

- Reduce military strength as planned, but no further. Reduce DOD civilian strength by 10-20% and contractor professional service support back to 2003 levels following recommendations of the Defense Business Board (DBB.) Modernize the civil service system to weed out under-performing members and grade creep (the unbalanced growth of senior levels.)
- Continue to add to the numbers and capabilities of the Special Operations Forces. Without other combat troops on the ground, these elite forces will be needed in far greater numbers.
- Stabilize acquisition budgets. Constantly changing funding contributes to cost and schedule overruns. Continue to invest aggressively in the development of new technologies,

such as those produced by the service research laboratories and the Defense Advanced Research Projects Agency (DARPA), which is critical to pace the threat, as the current SECDEF well understands.

- Keep the AVF, but pass legislation that promotes national service. Protect the post- 9/11 GI Bill to encourage recruiting and reward service.
- Pursue a dramatic reform of the organization of the Defense Department to reduce acquisiton redundancy, Defense Agencies and Geographic/Combatant commands. Take the next step to responsibly modernize the military retirement system.
- Finally, kill the sequestration law.

While some of these measures may seem stark, particularly given the fact that we are still fighting in multiple theaters. If correctly implemented, they will enable the enduring success of the defense mission and the readiness of our forces to our fight, equipped with the right hardware and technology to deter and prevail in combat when called upon.

Some would argue that the world will be better, maybe even safer if multiple countries shared power on the world stage. Thinking who these other countries might be, frankly, makes me very uneasy. And that is why we need to do what is necessary to have a strong military and the ability to project force where and when needed, based on a *sound economy.*

As Truman stated in the conclusion of his 1947 State of the Union Address: *"National Security does not consist of only an army, a navy, and air force. It rests on a much broader basis. It depends on a sound economy, on prices and wages, on prosperous agriculture, on satisfied and productive workers, or a competitive private enterprise free from monopolistic repression, on continued industrial harmony and production, on civil liberties and human freedom in all the forces which create in our men and women a strong moral fiber and spiritual stamina."*

CHAPTER 3

HOMELAND SECURITY

Homeland Security is a pretty broad topic, but I guess any discussion needs to start with a discussion of *The DHS,* its mission and organization, and how it functions. Understanding the Patriot Act is a second topic for discussion, followed by Cyber Security and the range of other issues involving privacy as protected by the 4th Amendment (protection from unreasonable search and seizure) and the needs of government agencies to keep us safe from terrorists and criminal elements. Much of what the Defense Department, DOJ, Treasury, and law enforcement agencies routinely do all contributes to our national and homeland security. To begin, let's trace the creation of the DHS.

Following the attacks of September 11, 2001, a 9/11 Commission was established to assess the "circumstances surrounding 9/11 and to identify ways to guard against future terrorist attacks."[72] The ten commissioners were chaired by Thomas H. Kean (former New Jersey governor) and Lee H. Hamilton (former Congressman from Indiana). The Commission Report, which was released in July of 2004, summarized significant events and shortcomings leading up to 9/11, and offered suggestions for preventing future attacks. Below are a few highlights of events preceding the attack:

- While the attack was a shock, it was not a surprise. The attempted attack on the World Trade Center in 1993, the shoot down of the U.S. helicopter in Somalia in 1993, the 1998 bombings of U.S. embassies in Kenya and Tanzania and the 2000 attack on the USS Cole, among others, were early indicators of the growing terrorist threat, some linked to al-Qaeda.

- In 1998, bin Laden issued a self-styled fatwa; publicly declaring that it was God's decree that every Muslim should try his utmost to kill any American, military or civilian, anywhere in the world, because of the American occupation of Islam's holy places and aggression against Muslims."[73]

- By late 1998 or early 1999 bin Laden and his chief of operations, Mohammed Atef, had agreed on a plan called the "planes operation" brought to them by Khalid Sheikh Mohammed (the mastermind who was waterboarded 183 times and is still held at Guantanamo Bay).

- From 1999 up to the 9/11 attacks, U.S. intelligence followed many leads surrounding suspected terrorists and al-Qaeda in particular. During 2000, President Clinton tried unsuccessfully to have the Taliban expel bin Laden from Afghanistan, where multiple terrorist training camps had found sanctuary.

- "During the Spring and Summer of 2001, U.S. Intelligence agencies received a string of warnings that al-Qaeda planned something very, very, very big."[74]

- As a Presidential Directive was complete and awaiting President Bush's signature, one that would authorize armed Predator attacks against al-Qaeda leadership, we were attacked on 9/11/2001.

Recognizing that clarity comes with hindsight, the Commission found, among other things, that leaders had not fully grasped the extent of the threat. The Defense Department was not sufficiently focused on al-Qaeda threat. (In fact, the Quadrennial Defense Review, or QDR, of defense threats, capabilities, and priorities was nearly complete without any mention of these asymmetrical threats. That's but one example. It was completely re-written post 9/11). Both the CIA and FBI were hampered in intelligence collection/analysis and prosecution options. (There was no National Intelligence Estimate (NIE) conducted between 1995 and 9/11/2001). Protecting borders and immigration control was not a priority before 9/11. Pakistan had been uncooperative in repeated efforts to evict al-Qaeda leadership. Since 9/11 the U.S. has given Pakistan over $21B in foreign aid, and relations are only now slowly improving.[75]

Congress, likewise, did not see the rising threat. Altogether, the nation was wholly unprepared for the attack. The recommended strategy from the Commission included an integrated 3-prong strategy: "(1) attack terrorists and their organizations (2) prevent the continued growth of Islamist terrorism and (3) protect against and prepare for (future) terrorist attacks."[76] We tried to do all three in the intervening years, with varying degrees of success. Among the specific recommendations for reorganizing government were five major ones:

1. Unifying strategic intelligence and operational planning against Islamist terrorists across the foreign-domestic divide with a National Counterterrorism Center (NCTC).
2. Unifying the intelligence community with a new National Intelligence Director (DNI).
3. Unifying the many participants in the counterterrorism effort and their knowledge in a network-based information sharing system that transcends traditional governmental boundaries.
4. Unifying and strengthening, congressional oversight of DHS to improve quality and accountability.

5. Strengthening the FBI and homeland defense.

Well prior to the Final Report of the 9/11 Commission in July 2004, Congress had passed the Homeland Security Act (HSA) in November 2002. HSA created the DHS and a new cabinet position. This was the most sweeping federal government reorganization since the creation of the Defense Department in 1947. It combined 22 separate agencies into one cabinet-level department, to include the Immigration and Naturalization Service (INS)—now part of the Customs and Border Protection Service, the U.S. Immigration and Customs Enforcement (ICE), the U.S. Coast Guard, the Transportation Security Agency (TSA), the Federal Aviation Administration (FAA), U.S. Customs and Border Protection Agency, FEMA, the Secret Service and many others. Some have suggested that the current problems that have surfaced with the Secret Service in recent years stemmed from this massive reorganization, and I would not totally disagree with that assertion.

HSA also laid the foundation for follow-on acts to include the Critical Infrastructure Information and the Cyber Security Enhancement Acts, both enacted in 2002 as well. As noted in a 2011 report card update, a lot has been accomplished. The Nationwide Suspicious Activity Reporting Initiative, using the FBI Guardian database, is a repository for suspicious activity from local police and is rapidly expanding to the Defense Department's National Crime Information Center. Airline travel is much safer as all checked and carry-on bags are screened (DHS prescreens 100% of the 14 million flyers coming to, from, or flying within the U.S. and 52,000 transportation security officers are deployed at over 450 airports across the country), and first responders are better trained, organized and resourced.[77]

Despite this progress, several serious problems have yet to be addressed, most notably what has been termed the "balkanized and dysfunctional oversight of the DHS."[78] When DHS was created by bringing together these 22 agencies into one large department, there were 88 congressional committees and subcommittees with oversight responsibilities. The 9/11 Commission Report, already discussed, recommended that Congress consolidate oversight to "a single, principal point of oversight and review."[79] Instead, the number of committees and subcommittees has now grown from 88 to 108, more than three times that of the Defense Department, though oversight is really concentrated in two Authorization and four Appropriation committees. Although attempts at reform have been initiated on many occasions, and there is a general consensus that DHS oversight is still broken, and politics and turf battles have prevented any meaningful progress.

Back in 2007 then DHS Secretary Chertoff wrote to Rep. Peter King (R—NY), the then Chair of the House Homeland Security Committee, regarding the burden of so much congressional oversight. According to one report, DHS officials spent "about 66 work-years responding to questions from Congress in 2009 alone." That same year, Homeland Security officials say they answered 11,680 letters, gave 2,058 briefings and sent 232 witnesses to 166 hearings. All this at a cost to taxpayers of about $10 million."[80] In 2010 former DHS Secretary Janet Napolitano wrote to King allowing that officials were spending more time responding to congressional requests and requirements than executing their mandated homeland security responsibilities.[81] As former chairman and former New Jersey Governor Tom Kean has stated, "That's confusion. It's not an oversight, it makes things dysfunctional. It means that the DHS spends so much time preparing and testifying that they're not spending their time protecting us."[82]

In May of 2015, we learned that TSA had failed, 95% of the time, to detect suspicious objects during screening, an incredibly high percentage which raises serious questions about the processes and standards implemented by the TSA. The Heritage Foundation[83] and others have proposed reasonable and workable ideas for consolidation of DHS oversight. Mike McConnell, a former DNI has suggested that only another attack would provide the impetus for the oversight change needed at DHS; hopefully that statement is an overreach.

Here are some fairly simple recommendations derived from the report card that still need to be implemented by our congressional leaders:

- Reduce HLS congressional oversight to six committees, 3 in each House, along the lines of the Heritage Foundation recommendations.
- Implement nationwide standards for secure identification documents and a secure biometric screening system. Legislation was passed to this effect in 2004 and still hasn't been implemented. As I state elsewhere, I've been in favor of a National ID card for many years, for many reasons.
- Review the intelligence enterprise for effectiveness, especially the Office of DNI (ODNI) which has grown disproportionally to the mission.
- With the DOJ, provide a clear legal framework for the detention of terrorists.

The Patriot Act (now replaced by the USA Freedom Act) has been a topic of much debate and legislation since first enacted in 2001 and extended seven times by Congress. I think all Americans should be conversant with the broader issues raised, as these will continue to be debated in future years and elections.

The Patriot Act was first passed in the weeks following the September 2001 attacks and signed into law by President Bush on

26 October 2001. The USA PATRIOT Act stands for "Uniting (and) Strengthening America (USA) by Providing Appropriate Tools Required to Intercept and Obstruct Terrorism." The Act, which initially passed the Senate by a vote of 98-1, made changes to some existing laws and incorporated a series of sunset clauses. *Senator Feingold (D--WI) was the only negative vote*; Senator Landrieu (D—LA.) did not vote. It contained ten main articles ranging from enhanced surveillance (Title II) to border security (Title IV) to Improved Intelligence (Title IX).

The law has been controversial, particularly regarding the protection of our 4th Amendment rights against unreasonable search and seizure. Over time, the law has been amended and reintroduced as courts have struck down some of the provisions, but most of the sunset provisions, which were to expire in 2005, have become a permanent part of the law. The Act was first reauthorized and expanded in 2005, enhancing seaport security, Secret Service authorities and means to combat terrorism financing. Controversy regarding many provisions of this Act has crossed party lines. During the re-authorization process in 2011 Senator Rand Paul (R—KY) held up the vote, believing the act to be an abuse of privacy rights, and was criticized by Sen. Harry Reid (D—NV) for placing the national security at risk by delaying a vote. Interesting politics to say the least.

Here are the key things you need to know about the important, and sometimes controversial, provisions of the original USA PATRIOT Act:

- Allows increased information (Title II- Section 218) sharing from criminal probes and intelligence agencies, designed to break down the wall between organizations that allowed potential terrorists to slip through the cracks.

- Allows federal agents access to business records for intelligence/national security probes, with permission of the federal court (Foreign Intelligence Surveillance Court). This provision is similar to what was already available in criminal probes. (See the Joe Biden quote a couple of pages forward.)
- Allows roving wiretaps against individuals for national security investigations to track terrorists who often switch mobile phones, with court order, to cover a range of devices; once again similar to authorities that law enforcement had for many years.
- Sneak and peek warrants which allow law enforcement to search businesses or homes and notify the suspect after the fact (delayed notification), similar to what already exists in criminal probes. (This provision was later struck down as a violation of the 4th amendment, as was another provision that expanded the administrative subpoena authority of FBI agents.)
- Expanded the use of National Security Letters (NSLs) that allows the FBI to search financial records, email, and telephone records without a warrant and prohibited anyone who received an NSL from disclosing it (a gag order). Eventually, this provision was also ruled unconstitutional and attempts to re-authorize it failed.
- Lone-wolf provision that, while not technically part of the Act (an amendment to the Foreign Intelligence Surveillance Act, FISA), it allows authorities to obtain foreign intelligence information about non-U.S., as well as U.S. persons, suspected of terrorist activities not affiliated with a group or foreign nation.
- Other provisions allowed expanded search warrants to wherever terrorist activity might have occurred; allowed law enforcement assistance for computer hacking; enhanced border patrol and INS agents; expanded the Secret Service

into computer fraud; prohibited the harboring of terrorists, enhanced maximum penalties and lengthened/eliminated statute of limitations on certain terrorist crimes; expanded the authority of the Secretary of State to offer rewards to fight terrorism and expanded the authority of the Secretary of the Treasury to regulate financial transactions between and among individuals and entities to prevent money laundering and improve reporting of suspicious activity.

While most provisions are now permanent law, roving wiretap, court-ordered searches of business records and surveillance of non-American lone-wolf suspects without terrorist ties, require renewal authority. Despite the delaying tactics of Senator Rand Paul, the 2011 re-authorization passed the Senate 72-23 and the House 250 to 153. In May of 2011, President Obama signed a four-year extension of these three key provisions of the Act: conduct of surveillance of 'lone wolves', searches of business records, and roving wiretaps.

One of the most controversial aspects of the Act stems from Article 215 by which the NSA, through the FISA court, collected telephone metadata from telephone providers. This was exposed by former Booz Allen Hamilton employee Eric Snowden, raising heightened concerns over both privacy and the adequacy of congressional oversight. In fact, the NSA can only access the content of any recorded calls based on reasonable suspicion that a particular phone number is being used by terrorists – there is no data mining of any content otherwise – and only a small fraction of collected data is ever analyzed. As one member of President Obama's Review Group on Intelligence and Communications Technology acknowledged, "9/11 would have been prevented had the metadata program been in effect in 2001."[84]

While privacy concerns are real, I am not sure the metadata collection program was the greatest threat to our privacy, given that it was only collected and still needed authorization to search, although that was almost always granted. Furthermore, China and others are exploiting the very same information we would deny the NSA. Anyone who attended the annual homeland security (GovSec) exposition in Washington D.C. or the Consumer Electronics Show (CES) in Las Vegas the last few years, both widely reported on in the media, are well aware of the rapidly expanding gadget industry that includes everything from hidden cameras and audio devices in alarm clocks to GPS tracking devices for less than $300 that can be hidden in a razor and tucked away in a car seat.[85] Miniature cameras are everywhere, and we are constantly photographed without our knowledge. News articles about the FBI's use of cellphone tracking devices that simulate a cellphone tower largely miss the point that our enemies have access to this same technology, which is expanding at lightning speed. New laws will be required to preserve some semblance of privacy in the future, but privacy as we all have known it is rapidly slipping away.

> *"The FBI could use wiretaps to investigate the mafia, but they could not get one to investigate terrorists. To put it bluntly, that was crazy! What's good for the mob should be good for terrorists."*
> --Then-Senator Joe Biden in the Senate floor debate.[86]

On 1 June 2015, the Senate by a vote of 67-32 passed the USA Freedom Act, amid much debate, including an 11-hour marathon filibuster again by Senator Rand Paul, and criticism again by his colleague Senator Harry Reid, among others. The bill was quickly signed by the President since the authorities had expired a day earlier. It short, it renewed the surveillance authorities on lone-wolf suspects and the roving wiretaps provisions, tightened other surveillance measures and increased transparency by requiring significant FISA court disclosures, and significantly curtailed the bulk collection of telephonic metadata by the NSA. Now, telephone companies retain that data and authorities can only access it by court order based on greatly restricted criteria.

Significantly, all three provisions are now permanent law, not subject to further sunset clauses. The debate is far from over, however, as some in Congress want to further modify the new law. Additionally, section 702 of the FISA Act, which allows NSA listening on foreigners outside the U.S., must be reauthorized in 2017.

Cyber Security: Richard Clarke, the former counterterrorism chief to Presidents Bill Clinton and George Bush, spent much of 2001 warning members of the Bush Administration about the possibility of an impending al-Qaeda attack. In a book he co-wrote and published with Robert Knake in early 2012, *Cyberwar: The Next Threat to National Security and What to Do About It,* he sketches a scenario in which hackers could hypothetically cripple the United States from behind a computer screen. "A cyber-attack could disable trains all over the country... it could blow up pipelines. It could cause blackouts and damage electrical power grids so that the blackouts would go on for a long time. It could wipe out and confuse financial records so that we would not know who owned what, and the financial system would be badly damaged. It could do things like disrupt traffic in urban areas by knocking out control computers. It could, in nefarious ways, do things like wipe out medical records."[87]

Particularly vulnerable to attack are the nations' power/electrical grids, nuclear facilities, and financial institutions. Few would argue the emergence of the cyber threat to our military, government, and private sector networks and infrastructure. There have been some highly visible attacks, a foreboding of what is still to come. A theft of F-35 Joint Strike Fighter plans in 2009 (now available worldwide). Attacks against Estonia and Georgia in 2008. A breach in 2009 of the U.S. electrical grid. Intrusions into the oil and gas sectors by a Chinese hacker in Shandong province. eBay, PayPal, CitiGroup hacks resulting in stolen credit-card information on 360,000 people. And more ID thefts involving Target (affecting 40 million customers credit and debit information), Home Depot and Neiman Marcus.

In late 2014, Chinese hackers used the Forbes website to hack into U.S. defense contractors and financial institutions. In that year we also we had the Sony hack and in 2015 we learned that the White House has been hacked, followed by the June 2015 announcement that the Office of Personnel Management (OPM) had been hacked and millions of files stolen (including this author's), files that list current and previous residences, financial data, names and addresses of family, and any derogatory information that could be used for blackmail.

Back in 2008 the NSA discovered that malware had infected classified military networks containing sensitive information, much of it dealing with the then ongoing war efforts. An NSA team was able to disable the malware, which was likely propagated by causal use of thumb drives, but the exact source of the virus was never conclusively determined (although Russian origin was suspected.) Significantly, this watershed event gave rise to the creation of the DOD Cyber Command, jointly commanded by the head of the NSA.

One of the problems dealing with Cyber Security has been defining its terms. I think the easiest definition is that "cyber" in anything that touches the Internet or secure networks. In the military, a distinction is made between Cyber Network Attack (CNA), Cyber Network Exploitation (CNE) and Cyber Network

Defense (CND). Although some will take issue, Cyber Command, which is a 4-star command working for DOD, is largely responsible for CNA and CNE, which are offensive operations, as well as defense of the military networks. There is a fairly well-accepted escalation terminology, ranging from exploitation to disruption to destruction. Stuxnet, the computer worm that infected Iran's nuclear plant, is a good example of an offensive cyber-attack, in this case, one whose origins still remain unknown, at least officially. *Cyber theft* is mostly against commercial entities, while *cyber espionage* is generally focused on military and security targets.

Most incidents, to include those referenced above, have been data mining for theft or espionage purposes, which falls short of cyber-attack. Figures vary, but recent estimates of intellectual property (IP) theft against U.S. companies ranges around $300B annually, with 50-80% attributed to the Chinese. Worldwide estimates are closer to $1Trillion. As one author summed it up, "we must recognize that most malicious actions in cyberspace directed against the United States come from hackers in two countries: China and Russia. These nations encourage their hackers to go after networks, data, money in the United States, and they protect them from prosecution. Russia allows criminal groups to steal from Western banks. The Chinese prefer to use military units to steal intellectual property."

In 2013, the White House informed over 3000 companies that they had been hacked. The FBI has over 1000 people working on cybersecurity investigations at its 56 field offices and the Secret Service investigates financially motivated cyber crime.[88] The CIA is reorganizing, to include a significant expansion of its cyber espionage capabilities. Both Russia and China together account for most, maybe 80%, of the intellectual property intrusions.

Military and other officials generally stay away from the terms cyberwarfare or cyber-attack, since those references carry with them far greater implications and response options. As former Deputy Secretary of Defense Bill Lynn has stated, "Although we cannot dismiss the threat of a rogue state lashing out, most nations have no more interest in conducting a destructive cyber-attack against us than they do a conventional attack."[89] It's a fair question. Why would China attack Wall Street when we owe them over $1 trillion dollars in borrowed debt?

In 2012, twelve countries admitted to having offensive cyber capabilities.[90] While only five nations (China, Russia, U.S., Britain, and Israel) currently have the ability to conduct high-end cyber-attacks like the Stuxnet virus that destroyed Iranian centrifuges in their nuclear program, many other nations are in hot pursuit; foremost among them Iran and North Korea. North Korea, you recall, was linked by the FBI to the 2014 hack of Sony in response to the humorous film "The Interview" which was then pulled from theaters quickly. It is, arguably, the most devastating attack on a U.S. firm to date. China's defense minister has announced the existence of an elite PLA unit called, Army Blue. In July of 2014 alleged Chinese hackers breached the networks of the U.S. Postal Service, potentially stealing information on up to 800,000 employees, and is thought to be behind other intrusions into the company USIS and the OPM breach mentioned above.

There is a big distinction between economic cyber theft and cyber espionage. In September 2015 Chinese President Xi Jinping pledged that China would no longer conduct economic spying in cyber, which was followed by broad agreement at the subsequent G-20 meeting in Ankara Turkey. And the Chinese have arrested the hackers presumed responsible for the OPM data theft. Whether Xi remains faithful to that pledge, or if he can even enforce it, remains to be seen. In the meantime, cyber espionage against military and government targets, continues on.

Underlying the military and strategic approach to cyber as a new warfare area is an interpretation of what is known as the Law of Armed Conflict (LOAC) and what constitutes an armed attack that justifies a proportional response. Under Presidential Policy Directive 20, only the President can currently authorize a cyber (counter) attack. It is estimated that over a hundred foreign national intelligence organizations routinely conduct operations against our computer networks and that our U.S. military networks are probed more than 6 million times a day from across the globe. A far greater threat is this capability in the hands of a terrorist group or the accidental release of a debilitating malware. With the rise of virtual private networks (VPNs) and proxy servers in accommodating countries, it is increasingly difficult to track hackers through IP addresses alone.

So why is cyber covered in the section on Homeland Security? The simple answer is that the DHS handles the Cyber Security policy of the U.S. (in other words outside the military circle, essentially to protect the.com and.gov versus the.mil domains), and it operates the DHS National Cyber Security Center. Most observers feel, with the establishment of Cyber Command and better resources, the DOD is far ahead of the DHS in protecting networks.

In 2010, the Obama Administration rolled out a new strategy that establishes a partnership between the Defense Department and the DHS, designed to export the active defense tools developed by the NSA to DHS (the Einstein 3 tool now being used as one example.) Although this partnership seems to be working better and cooperation increased, the line of responsibilities between the DOD (Cyber Command-NSA) and DHS remains a source of controversy. Another source of controversy, discussed before, is the dual-hatting of the NSA Commander as the Cyber Command leader, an alignment that President Obama retained subsequent to the NSA review following the Snowden leaks. A third controversy is why U.S. Strategic Command has oversight of Cyber Command, a legacy relationship beyond the understanding of this author.

In 2015, President Obama signed an Executive Order promoting government and private sector sharing of information. But more is needed, to include legislation that allows commercial entities access to the same advanced network tools used by the government. Senator McConnell attempted to introduce just such provisions to the military authorization act in 2015 but, without sufficient debate, it was defeated.

So here are a few simple things to consider:

- Require all Internet providers to have certifiable registration information for all users as a means to reduce espionage. I am generally against more government regulation, but in this instance we need to move swiftly beyond voluntary compliance toward regulation.
- Clarify the military (CyberCom's) role in protecting networks beyond only military infrastructure. An opportunity for enhanced security and less industrial espionage is being wasted by not allowing the sophistication of the NSA tools to be shared with the private sector. In fact, that opportunity may have been lost after the Snowden bust.
- Congress needs to streamline oversight of the DHA Department, a long acknowledged problem that fails to get resolved (and is going in the wrong direction with the increase from 88 to 108 committees as previously discussed). It would also go a long way to improving the

morale of the workforce. In 2013, DHS, for the second year in a row, was ranked last in an annual survey of "Best places to work in the Federal Government," with 53% of employees saying they were dissatisfied with their jobs and only 42% saying they had effective leadership.[91]

- Finally, require that all debit and credit cards replace magnetic strips to chip and PIN technology. In 2012, payment card losses were over $11B, much of that to credit-card issuers and merchants in the U.S. Industry has begun moving that way anyway since the costs of not doing so are mounting. Hacked credit-card and personal information are a thriving business on the dark web.

- Insider threat can be a particularly perilous threat, caused by a disgruntled or otherwise motivated employee. From physical security to access control and firewalls to utilizing new software that continuously monitors employees for anomalous behavior is part of a growing need for a vibrant insider threat program and training regime, both within government and commercial entities. Every government entity that handles classified information is now required to have a program and a new job code has recently been established for this profession, but implementation is very slow.

- In 1998, Presidential Decision Directive 63 (PDD-63) encouraged critical infrastructure centers to set up information sharing organizations, which has resulted in many Information Sharing and Analysis Centers (ISAC), both for economic sectors as well as municipal and commercial companies. Nike, Gap, and Target set up one such center after the Target attack. (The Economist, Cyber Security report, 7/12/2014). These centers quickly share threat information and alerts, assess vulnerabilities, etc. Many cities, such as Chicago, are considering such an arrangement for companies that operate within the city limits.

- Maybe most importantly, we need to sit down with both our allies and adversaries and come to an understanding of what constitutes a cyber-attack that requires a proportional response. A state-sanctioned theft of four million government records goes beyond aggressive intelligence gathering and cyber espionage, which all countries do, and borders on attack criteria that demands more than a weak presidential statement of lament and protestation.

DHS has a critical role to play in our nation's security, and all 22 organizations now subsumed under DHS play an essential part. Whether DHS is properly sized, and what is the best structure for oversight and management of the department, should be high on Congress' agenda. So too should be regulation to better protect our infrastructure (networks, power grids, financial institutions) from a nation state or malicious attack.

Privacy versus Security. For 2016 and beyond, the debate will continue over the government and law enforcement's need for access to metadata and communications, versus the privacy rights of citizens. In 2015, Congress was working on legislation that would protect companies who shared data with the government from privacy lawsuits. That's one step, but technology is moving very fast in a side direction where companies may no longer have access to that information. As Google and Apple and long-haul communication companies install greater encryption devices, in response to news reports and advocates for privacy, it becomes increasingly difficult for authorities to catch those who would do us harm. In fact, the Apple iPhone now defaults to encryption that can't be unlocked by Apple, only by the owner. Similarly, individuals are turning to devices like the Wickr app that encrypts all emails to another individual who also has that app, and

Protonmail that is securely encrypted. There are still vulnerabilities at the point of encryption and receipt, but the problem for law enforcement and intelligence agencies is getting more difficult, lacking the ability to retrieve data on encrypted phones. In July of 2015 the FBI director testified that ISIS is moving all recruits to encrypted devices, which the FBI can't access. Various proposals are being discussed, such as requiring multiple key holders to access data, or requiring providers to build in back-doors. This debate will be with us for a long time. Requiring phone providers to compromise on privacy will drive business elsewhere. After the Paris attacks in late 2015 that killed 129, there were renewed calls for tougher encryption laws as both law enforcement and terrorist concerns grow. Since I see no such encryption legislation on the horizon, our technology experts, it appears, are going to have to carry the burden to minimize the threat. In the meantime, NSA's bulk collection of megadata is now ended, but specific phone records can be accessed by court order.

CHAPTER 4

FOREIGN POLICY

"The World is a dangerous place, not because of those who do evil, but because of those who look and do nothing."

--Albert Einstein

When I ask the question: "What is our country's foreign policy?" I get some amazing looks and strange answers, which is fascinating since we have interests all around the globe, and the security of our nation rests to a great extent on our foreign policy and our nations' role in international affairs.

I read in a book review that it is tough to write about foreign policy because so much changes before the piece of work can ever get published. That's certainly true to some extent, but I also think we can still discern some obvious trends across the globe that won't change dramatically over the next 4 to 8 years. These include the continued rise of jihad extremism and expanding terrorist recruitment and threats; 'Putinism' and Russian aggression; ongoing Israel/Palestinian fighting and the growth of anti-Semitism; Iran's delayed (but eventual) path to a nuclear weapon and expanding state-sponsored terrorism; China's economic and military emergence and probing territorial ventures; North Korea's continued nuclear buildup and erratic behavior; persecution of

Christians and the gradual ebb of democratic governments across the globe; the continued unraveling of the Middle East (especially Syria, Afghanistan, and Iraq); growing pressures on Saudi Arabia, Pakistan, and Turkey, expanding income inequality and human rights violations, and general unrest and instability worldwide worsened by economic strife.

I am categorically an optimist, but those are the trends I see and why the world looks first to the United States to provide leadership to face these enormous challenges and act as a global stabilizing influence. It is the role expected of a nation whose primacy in the world order has long been established.

But more and more we read that America is viewed as being a nation in decline on the world stage. Rife partisanship between the White House and Congress gives no level of comfort. The President's disapproval ratings on foreign policy have far exceeded his approval ratings for years. Our allies are nervous and our adversaries emboldened by the lack of American leadership and a clearly articulated and understood foreign policy.

Maybe it was because we couldn't determine who we could trust, we nevertheless took no action in Syria where Basar al-Assad (supported by Russia and Iran) has gassed, tortured and murdered his own people... a humanitarian disaster exceeding 250,000 now dead with roughly half of the population displaced and children regularly dying from malnutrition and disease. All of which leads to the terrible European refugee crisis we've seen well reported in the media. Iraq has disintegrated into outright civil war. Radical jihad is spreading and the calls for a caliphate growing with the emergence of ISIS and other groups pledging allegiance.

After 9/11/2001, homes in every neighborhood and automobiles across the nation proudly displayed our nation's flag. Where are they now? Is the threat any less? More than ten years later most Muslims have an unfavorable opinion of the U.S., according to Pew Research figures and attitudes of disillusionment permeate many of our allies. The solidarity and compassion toward America that emerged from the events of 9/11 has long since dissipated.

> *"To brush aside America's responsibility as a leader and – more profoundly- our responsibilities to our fellow human beings would have been a betrayal of who we are."*
> --President Obama after Gaddafi's ouster in Libya

Those words obscure the sad truth of Libya today, post-Gaddafi, and leave unexplained our lack of leadership in international affairs; but more on that later.

In years past, we could usually discern the important aspects and the precise core of our foreign policy. The Truman Doctrine (communist containment) and Reagan Doctrines (diminish Soviet Union influence) being just two examples of such precisions. Far less so the current Administration, which seems to have embraced a foreign policy referred to as a doctrine of restraint, following the President's speech at West Point in May 2014. Others have labeled it overly cautious. Elements of that include disengagement, building large coalitions, using soft power (diplomacy, sanctions) and restraint from military action unless our national security interests are clearly and directly affected, however that might be defined. It is a risk-averse doctrine, once summarized by White House staff as 'don't do stupid stuff.' Secretary of State Clinton, as you may recall, referred to that phrase as not being a coherent foreign policy, causing some rift with the President.

So what is the scorecard? We now have civil wars in Libya, Syria, Iraq, and Yemen, the rise of ISIS, Iraq shattered after the pull-out of U.S. troops, Afghanistan on the brink as the U.S. draws down and the Taliban re-emerges, Iran continuing to spread terrorist activity, Putinism at full throttle, and a mischievous China in the South China Sea and elsewhere.

What might have been if we had never invaded Iraq in the first place? Or not disbanded the Iraqi army, or even canned Iraqi President Malaki when we should have? What if we had left stabilizing troops in Iraq and (presumably) Afghanistan as we did in Japan, Germany, and South Korea following WWII and the Korean War? We assisted in efforts to rid Libya of Gadhafi in 2011, and now we have chaos with two groups governing, and multiple new terrorist organizations cropping up.

The world expects the U.S. to lead from ahead, not from behind, to coin a phrase sometimes invoked to describe the current Administration's leadership approach. That means engagement (not necessarily kinetic or military force). It means a clear set of priorities and principals, reassurance to our allies, and red-lines that mean something. The world is a dangerous place and getting more so, especially with non-proliferation nearly bankrupt as an objective.

So what are the essential elements that constitute our foreign policy? Experts spend whole careers in this field, achieve advanced degrees and write voluminous articles and books, none of which applies to this author. But it seems clear, however, that we do need clearly articulated goals and vision to frame our foreign policy.

What follows is an issue-based discussion. So what might appear to be a slight to our allies in Europe, the Americas, or down under, that is not the intention. It is rather a focus on the close-in imperatives. *These are simply my views*, and they start by ensuring we remain strong economically and militarily, that we reassure our allies and stand tall for human rights and democratic principles and ideals.

GLOBAL LEADERSHIP – THE LONG VIEW

Frequently we hear the terms Interventionist or Isolationist to describe the overarching philosophy of a politician, elected official, or even the mood of the country regarding our approach to foreign policy. Are we the world's policeman? Or should our focus be more domestic and let the EU, and some of our regional allies, bear a greater global burden? When we look at our soaring debt, failing infrastructure, hungry children and struggling schools, should we not take the time to fix America first? What is America's role in the world? What is the threshold for military action? What are the global consequences of an inward focus, or isolationism policy, as generally captured by the libertarian non-intervention views of Sen Rand Paul (R—KY). Can we be effective engaging in the Middle East at all, particularly with fragile governments, as the Sunni-Shiite conflict broadens? Do the Muslim nations need to solve their conflicts without Western influence, or are we now morally committed having invaded Iraq and ousted Saddam Hussein?

Almost everywhere you look you see writings exclaiming the decline of American influence and leadership in world affairs. In late 2015 America is tired of war after 12+ years of conflict. As seen in Syria and later in the Ukrainian crisis, the perceptions that America will not intervene leaves us in a precarious position. Following the Potsdam conference with Truman, Churchill and Stalin in July of 1945 following World War II, Stalin reported back that 'Truman was weak.' What is the perception now?

I think allies and adversaries see the U.S. as a global superpower on the wane, and many Americans agree with that view. Our economy, the largest in the world, will be overtaken by China at some point, sooner rather than later. If we relinquish our role as the world superpower, then that void will certainly be filled by another country or alliance. Not only is America's security endangered by that acquiescence, but the stability of the world unsettled, just as it has been by our premature troop pull-out in Iraq and continued drawdown in Afghanistan. Complacency in world affairs will have disastrous consequences.

For America to retain its role (I would argue, its rightful position) as the world's leader, the most important underlying element is a stable market-based economy. Not one based on trillions of dollar of debt, annual deficits, and the world's highest corporate tax rate that drives business offshore. A thriving economy begets an affordable, strong and ready military that can influence, deter and, if necessary, prevail. Economic prosperity does not necessarily equate to geopolitical power, but I would argue that you can't have the latter without the former. Without the changes needed to revive and sustain the American economy we are, indeed, *on borrowed time.* We clearly need a new model for the future.

A renewed, and appropriate, foreign policy needs to begin with the notion that we won't fight other nation's wars but we will act in our own national interest, and that our resolve remains strong. If we look inward, allow complacency or indifference to seep into international affairs, we do so at our own long-term peril. That leadership void will be quickly filled by other nations. In his book, *On Watch*, Elmo Zumwalt quotes Henry Kissinger back in the 70s as believing "that the U.S. has passed its historical high point like so many other civilizations. He believes (the) U.S. is on (a) downhill and cannot be roused by the political challenge."[92] A lot of so-called experts agree with Kissinger's purported (and maybe misstated) view. I don't accept the premise, but I worry whether the country has the resolve to effect a different outcome.

If American power and world engagement wanes, the economic order would slowly unravel. Countries like Ukraine and Taiwan would be increasingly vulnerable, as would the shipping lanes so vital for international commerce. Our singular focus on radical jihad and the War on Terror has drained our resources and sapped our political will. Because of it, we mostly missed the emergence of China on the world scene and, to a lesser extent, Russia's increasing aggression. Only the U.S. can provide the security blanket that assures international order. That doesn't mean we do it all, but we must lead from out front, with a clear purpose, and from a strong economic base.

The use of military power is a tool of foreign policy and one that has been overused in the past decades. Intervention with military force, certainly with land forces in scale, should generally be a last resort, but always be available and credible if needed. In 1946, Ho Chi Minh told the French that "you will kill ten of our men and we will kill one of yours, and in the end, it will be you who tire of it."[93] He was correct, of course, a lesson we have re-learned since 9/11. Americans are war weary again, but we need to remain strong, determined, yet prescient about the employment of troops where other options remain. There may well be, and probably will be, near-term military deployments that are a necessity when our national security interests or treaty obligations can be clearly defined. We need to ensure that we have a strategy and outcome in mind, and fully understand the political and diplomatic consequences (and possible unintended consequences) in advance. Our moral compass and legitimacy need to be intact. As argued by two military officers assigned to then-Chairman of the Joint Chiefs, Admiral Mike Mullen: America needs to move to a new model of sustainment, focused on critically neglected infrastructure, education, water, food, and energy, and away from the old containment model."[94]

There is a massive rebalancing going on, from China, Russia, Brazil, Iran, Saudi Arabia and others who no longer march to either U.S. leadership or United Nations (UN) guidance. Our strategy must adapt and should encourage all countries to undertake a transformation, meaning economic conversion to a market-based free economy, an education transformation that produces the graduates who can compete in the new marketplace, social reform that promotes human rights and equal opportunity, and accept the rule of law as a baseline.[95]

I firmly believe that our future security and credibility on the world stage lies chiefly in our future economic prosperity, and we aren't doing nearly enough to ensure that future for the next generations. We need a 'whole of nation' approach that encompasses a strong economic underpinning, a rebuilding of our infrastructure and commitment to our youth, strong deterrence, and an inclusive and accepting perspective for the sovereign rights of other countries.

TREATIES AND ALLIANCES

The United States has a long history of Treaties and Alliances which inform and, in many instances, bound our actions. This involves mutual defense cooperation, governance forums, trade agreements, weapons limitation agreements and more, an exhaustive list. These agreements, some of them long-standing, form the starting point of our nation's foreign policy, and, therefore, should be generally understood by all Americans, at least those agreements of most significance. Here are just a few, and why they are important:

The UN

The League of Nations, which was established after World War I, did not include many world powers (like Germany, USSR, and Japan) and proved ineffective in responding to incidents that led to

World War II. The UN was championed by President Franklin Roosevelt after WWII to be a more inclusive and influential body than its predecessor, with a focus on peacekeeping missions.

It was formally established in October 1945 with 51 members, including the five permanent members of the Security Council, commonly referred to as the P-5: France, China, the Soviet Union, the United Kingdom and the United States. In 1971, the People's Republic of China was given the Chinese seat formerly held by the Republic of China (Taiwan). The UN has five primary structures, but those most often referred to are the General Assembly with over 190 members represented and a 2/3 vote requirement; The International Court of Justice (The Hague) in the Netherlands; and the Security Council, which is made up of fifteen members, ten non-permanent with 2-year terms, and the five permanent Security Council members mentioned above, each of the five with veto power over any resolution.

Since inception, UN forces have been involved in many peacekeeping missions from Sierra Leone to Sudan to the more recent UN observers sent to Syria to supervise the removal of chemical weapons. Along the way have come criticisms, such as the failures to prevent ethnic cleansing in Bosnia or genocide in Rwanda. The UN is also active in Human Rights issues and arms limitation treaties. Despite criticism, the UN is a vital institution for addressing key issues around the globe and a critical component of our foreign policy and leadership engagement.

NATO: The North American Treaty Organization:

Signed in April of 1949, it is one of several major mutual defense treaties to which the U.S. is a signatory, where the Parties agree that an armed attack against one of them is considered an attack against them all (Article 5) although the means of response are not specified, but implied. Article 5 is important to understand. It states that all Parties agree "to assist the Party or Parties so attacked by taking forthwith, individually and in concert with the other Parties, such action as it deems necessary, including the use of armed force." Initially, there were twelve NATO member countries, now expanded to 28, which has been one of the controversial issues.

The French left NATO under Charles de Gaulle in 1966, but returned to full membership in 1999 under President Sarkozy; likewise, Greece withdrew in 1974 when Turkey invaded Cyprus, but rejoined in 1980. The most topical issue has been Russia's outsized concern with NATO expansion eastward.

Following the Soviet Union's rejection for NATO membership in 1954, the Warsaw Pact was formed (Soviet Union, Hungary, Albania, E. Germany, Poland, Romania and Bulgaria) in 1955, as a prelude to the Cold War. Since the dissolution of both the Soviet Union and the Warsaw Pact in December 1991, many new nations have joined NATO to include former Soviet Block and Warsaw Pact nations: Poland, the Czech Republic, Hungary, re-unified Germany, Bulgaria, Romania and other Northern and Eastern European countries. Bosnia-Herzegovina, Macedonia, and Montenegro are being considered for membership. Ukraine and Georgia have also been told they would eventually be allowed NATO membership, which has drawn sharp rebuke from Russia (Putin), as did NATO plans for putting a missile defense system in Poland (subsequently moved to a naval ship-based system by President Obama with evolving early warning components).

Some of this concern is ostensibly now playing out since the March 2014 Crimea annexation and follow-on Ukraine crisis. Although Russia is advancing the concept that NATO non-expansion was expressly promised to Gorbachev, most scholars (not all, however) dispute that assertion. Militarily, NATO has intervened in Bosnia (1992), Yugoslavia & Kosovo (1999), and

Afghanistan (since the 9/11 attack on the U.S. was an attack on a member).

In addition to the 28 members of NATO, another 22 nations participate in a program called the Partnership for Peace. While the structure, membership, and troop employment of NATO has evolved over time, *our membership in NATO drives a significant element of our foreign policy.*

The challenge for NATO now is how to deal with Russian belligerence and to assure members, who feel threatened, of NATO's absolute commitment to Article 5. This applies particularly to the Baltic nations of Lithuania, Estonia, and Latvia, which were once a part of the Soviet Union, and two of which border on Russia, who feel especially threatened and are repeatedly provoked.

Just as important, NATO needs to get on with expansion to those countries who are ready and qualified to join. Starting with Montenegro, Macedonia, and Georgia. Failure to do so, out of fear of alienating Putin, plays right into his strategy. Under a different Article 4, any country can ask for consultations when they feel their security or territorial integrity is at risk and Turkey did so in July 2015. Afterwards, the Ambassadors of the 28 countries convened as required.

The U.S. now carries about 75% of the financial burden for NATO, and only a few countries besides the U.S. spend the agreed upon percentage of GDP (2%) on defense. NATO will need to be strong to cope with a resurgent and unpredictable Russian head of state. It remains to be seen if Putin, by his actions, has given NATO a cattle-prod to step up the alliance, or whether it will be a signal missed altogether. If Putin starts unrest in Estonia or Latvia, following Crimea and Ukraine, NATO is bound by treaty to respond. Some believe that Putin will arrange just such a challenge in due time, maybe post-Syria, in an attempt to render NATO moot. Based on recent Pew polling, many if not most EU citizens would not support military action as required by Article 5, with the German's lowest at 38%.[96] This polling, I suspect, is not lost on Putin.

Strategic Arms Reduction:

These discussions started back in 1969. Sometimes called SALT (Strategic Arms Limitation Talks), the talks concluded when then Soviet President Brezhnev and then U.S. President Nixon signed the two treaties designed to limit the number of intercontinental ballistic missiles (ICBMs), submarine-launched ballistic missiles (SLBM), multiple independently targetable re-entry vehicles (MIRVs, missiles with multiple warheads) and, finally, anti-ballistic missile (ABM) systems. SALT II was negotiated and signed by Brezhnev and President Carter, but never ratified by the Senate following the Soviet invasion of Afghanistan in December 1979.

These were next followed by START treaties in 1991 and 1993. In parallel, in 1991 the Nunn-Lugar Cooperative Threat Reduction (CTR) act was passed, as the Soviet Union was disintegrating and the safety of the vast inventory of nuclear weapons was cause for concern. CTR has been hugely successful in eliminating thousands of tons of Russian chemical weapons, nuclear delivery vehicles and over 7600 warheads.[97]

The latest version of these arms control efforts is the New START Treaty, signed 5 February 2011 which requires these limits: 700 deployed missiles or heavy bombers with nuclear bomb capability, 1550 total warheads, and 800 deployed launchers and bombers. [The number 1550 can be exceeded by several hundred based on counting protocols.] Both Russia and the U.S. are permitted eighteen site inspections per year. One of the first threats from Russia and Putin during the Crimean crisis in 2014 was to threaten withdrawal from this inspection protocol.

Another significant and related agreement is known as the Non-proliferation Treaty (NPT) which became active in 1970, with 190 countries now signators to the treaty. It recognizes the five permanent members of the UN Security Council as Nuclear Weapons States: The U.S., Russia, China, United Kingdom and France. The five nuclear weapon capable countries agreed *not* to transfer weapon technology and the non-nuclear weapons states agreed *not* to acquire nuclear weapons. N. Korea signed but left the accord in 2003. Iran also signed but has argued that its uranium enrichment is for peaceful purposes, but more on Iran and the nuclear deal later. Pakistan, India, and Israel never joined the NPT countries, and all are widely known to have nuclear weapons capability (estimated at 200 warheads for Israel, and 100 each for Pakistan and India). Additionally, only eighteen of 193 member states of the UN have signed the Arms Trade Treaty which is aimed to stop the illegal sale and transfer of weapons, estimated to be between $60B to $85B annually!

Non-proliferation of nuclear weapons is, sadly, not working as hoped, and a serious challenge for future Administrations and all peace-loving peoples. Regardless of the specifics of the recent Iran deal, it is probable that Iran will become a Nuclear State fifteen or so years down the road, and what impact that has on Israel and other Mideast nations remains to be seen.

Biological and Chemical WMD are generally governed by what is referred to as the Biological Weapons Convention (BWC), which became effective in 1975. It bans the development and stockpiling of biological agents and toxins, delivery vehicles and transfer of or assistance to anyone trying to develop a program. Although there are 170 signators to the BWC, this Convention lacks enforcement and there are *no inspection or verification mechanisms*, this despite seven review conferences held over the years. Not surprisingly, there have been gross violations of the BWC by signators to include the Soviet Union (now Russia), Iran, Iraq (Saddam Hussein's chemical attack against the Kurdish people that killed thousands), Libya and, most recently, Syria (where Assad has gassed his own people, including civilians and children.) New strains of Anthrax, as one example, made possible by genetic engineering, are potentially devastating as WMD. The BWC needs teeth and more signators as Chem-Bio threats continue to mount and will, with all probability, increasingly become a weapon of choice for terrorists. This Chem-Bio threat scares me as much any element of the potential terrorist arsenal.

Finally, there are any number of other bilateral and multilateral treaties that bound our nation's foreign policy. The Security Treaty with Japan signed in 1960 (which replaced the 1951 agreement) recognizes that an armed attack against either Party would result in action in the common defense. This applies to the ongoing dispute between Japan and China regarding the sovereignty of the Senkaku Islands, which only partially explains the U.S. concern with this confrontation. This Security Treaty also forbids Japan from maintaining more than a Self-Defense Force, which was codified in the Japanese constitution, but which has become a politically hot issue in Japan in recent years as some, led by Prime Minister Shinzo Abe, are pushing for a stronger and more capable military. The Treaty provides for the continued presence of U.S. forces in Japan.

In 1955, the Sino-American Mutual Defense Treaty was enacted and provided that both Taiwan and the U.S. would come to the other's defense if attacked. After the U.S. recognized mainland China in 1979, President Carter terminated that treaty with the one-year notice that was required. The U.S. Congress subsequently passed the Taiwan Relations Act, which carries over some of the content of the previous agreement, but no longer guarantees military assistance in the event of an attack on Taiwan. It says merely that a forced attempt at reunification would be deemed a "threat to peace and security of the Western Pacific and of grave concern to the United States."

Some of the other major treaties include those with Australia. New Zealand, the Philippines, and South Korea where we continue to have troops stationed and the threat of conflict is high given the succession of unpredictable leadership in North Korea.

Most nations recognize the 12-mile Territorial Limit to their contiguous coast as well as the EEZ stretching up to 200 nautical miles offshore. One variable is that of an Extended Continental Shelf for resource development, if you can prove the extension and if you are a signatory to UNCLOS, mentioned in the earlier Defense chapter. UNCLOS was adopted over 30 years ago and deals with the international conduct of deep-seabed mining, the exploration and exploitation of rare minerals from the ocean floor beyond the Extended Continental Shelf and the EEZ, territorial disputes, and military activities. Based on initial objections by President Reagan in 1982., some provisions were changed favorable to the U.S. There are still many opponents who feel that the authority of the International Seabed Authority to determine royalty payments relinquishes jurisdiction over much of the ocean, despite the agreement that the U.S. will assume a leadership role. Although signed by the U.S. in 1994, the Senate has yet to accede to the Convention (requiring 67 votes), although we do generally accept and abide by the provisions. Among many issues are Rare Earth elements, such as nickel and copper, a market once controlled by the US, but now mostly controlled by China. New technology has now made deep-sea mining more feasible and economical and the U.S. needs to accede to the Convention to drill. Concerns over loss of sovereignty are valid, but on balance we need this agreement. Once ratified and signed into law, as it should be some day, it will be an important treaty for our country's future in the increasingly volatile maritime domain.

GLOBALIZATION AND TRADE

> *"Globalization depends upon secure sea lines of communication for trade and energy transfers: without the U.S. Navy, there'd be no globalization"*
>
> --Robert Kaplan[98]

Globalization and trade are both important drivers of our foreign policy. The U.S. Trade Representative is a cabinet-level position in the President's Executive Office who develops and recommends trade policies. It is not a small job. The current U.S. trade representative, Michael Froman, was the chief negotiator for the recently completed Trans-Pacific Partnership (TPP) agreement.

The term economic globalization has been around for a long time, as have been the trends toward a more unrestricted global economy. Although many different definitions can be found, at a macro level globalization means the more open flow of commerce and integration of markets for technology, capital (financial) investment, and goods and services across international borders. There are proponents and opponents of the increasing role of globalization in the U.S. economy, arguing the industrial base impacts and, in particular, the flight of jobs overseas, especially in the manufacturing sector. We talked about globalization in the Economy chapter, but expand the discussion here; exporting of jobs and impending treaties will be a hot topic leading to the 2016 presidential elections, and beyond.

Proponents argue that wider access to the global marketplace has resulted in greater competition, lower trade tariffs, lower consumer prices, better jobs, improved health, overall better standards of living and a direct correlation between the fact that the

percentage of the developing world living in extreme poverty –
defined as living on less than $1 per day – has been cut in half.[99] As
a former President of Mexico stated, "In every case where a poor
nation has significantly overcome its poverty, this has been
achieved while engaging in production for export markets and
opening itself to the influx of foreign goods, investment, and
technology." [100] Further, some emphasize that globalization has
actually reduced income inequality in nations that have embraced
it, although opponents argue otherwise.

Our foreign policy is guided or impacted by some crucial
trade alliances. Following WWII, the General Agreement on Tariffs
and Trade (GATT) was formed with the purpose of encouraging
trade without bias, opening markets and lowering tariffs, with 23
countries initially members. The World Trade Organization (WTO)
was founded on 1 January 1995 to update and replace GATT and
currently has 159 member countries, including 75 of the GATT
members. The nations of the EU, which was formed in 1993 (the
Euro was introduced in 2002 and is the currency of nineteen of the
28 EU states) are also members of the WTO. The significance of the
WTO is that "all members are required to grant each other most
favored nations status, such that trade concessions granted by a
WTO member to another country must be given to all members." In
2001, China was admitted to the WTO, and Russia joined in August
of 2012.

One goal of the WTO is to monitor isolationist trends,
something many fear may increase in the coming years. Not directly
related, but of similar importance, the World Bank-International
Monetary Fund (IMF), which began operations in 1945, now has
over 180 countries as members and makes loans to countries in
need, among other financial objectives. The IMF has loaned $17.5
billion to Ukraine, a badly needed financial infusion to that country.
Nations contribute to the IMF based on a quota system that also

determines their respective power within the IMF. There is general consensus that the WTO, World Bank and IMF are all in need of serious reform. In the 2016 Omnibus Spending Bill, Congress finally approved a long overdue commitment to increase U.S. backing for the IMF. It's a good, if belated, start.

The G-8 is another structure, an informal one, that included the U.S., France, U.K., Italy, Japan, Canada, Germany and Russia, the last to join in 1998. The G-8 summit agendas encompass a range of issues to include trade, terrorism, health, environment, and others. Based on the March 2014 Russian annexation of Crimea and subsequent adventures into Ukraine, many advocated that the G8 be dissolved altogether, or reduced to a G-7, sans Russia. Russia was subsequently expelled in late March of 2014 and was not present at the 2015 meeting held in Brussels. The G-8 is now the G-7. A similar forum is the G-20, established in 1999 and which consists of around nineteen individual nations plus the EU. It meets annually to discuss high-level economic policy decisions, and recently concluded the 2015 conference in Turkey, shortly after the deadly Paris attacks.

NAFTA - The trade alliance most frequently talked about and debated, until recently, is the North American Free Trade Agreement (NAFTA) which was championed by President Bill Clinton, although opposed by most of his fellow Democrats, and signed into law in 1993. NAFTA signatories are the U.S., Canada, and Mexico. According to one report, on the 20-Year Anniversary of NAFTA, instead of the gain of 200,000 annual jobs promised by Clinton, the country had lost a million jobs. Nearly 850,000 relatively well-paying jobs in the manufacturing sector alone have been lost, and the annual trade deficit with our close neighbors now stands around $180B (up from $27B in 1993, the last pre-NAFTA year.) Of the displaced workers, only about 2/3 have found new work, most at wage reductions of 20% or more.[101] Conceding that prices of goods for the consumer have dropped, opponents argue that this has not been enough to compensate for the job and wage losses.

Defenders of NAFTA point to numerous other considerations beyond lower prices that benefit all consumers, to include the impact of exports on GDP. The effects of globalization on income equality are hard to measure – certainly there has been a loss of jobs and wage reductions, but they have also lowered the cost of goods in the marketplace, helping those at the lower end of the income scale. One expert suggests that 10-20% of the increase in income equality is attributable to trade as U.S. workers resort to lower paying and less skilled jobs, although there are offsetting opinions as well.[102]

All these arguments have re-emerged as the next rounds of trade treaties, the TPP and farther out Transatlantic Trade and Investment Partnership (TTIP), are being discussed. TPP, recently negotiated, has resurrected NAFTA controversies and was a hot topic for the 2016 elections until recently; more discussion on TPP shortly.

A trade surplus exists when exports of goods and services exceed imports; a deficit is just the opposite (imports exceed exports.) The highest recorded trade deficit, sometimes called the trade imbalance, was a staggering $753 billion in 2006. In 2011, the trade deficit was $560B, which dropped to $ 535B in 2012 and to $471B in 2013, primarily based on expanded fuel exports, then back to $504B in 2014. A few of years ago almost 60% of our trade deficit ($332B out of $560B) was sent overseas to buy crude oil, a figure that is now closer to 10%. The biggest contributors now to our trade deficit include automobiles and consumer products such as electronics, clothing, drugs, furniture, etc. Absent a resurgence in

America's manufacturing base, it is hard to imagine how we can someday again balance our trade.

Our primary trading partners are Canada (16.1%), China (14%), Mexico (12.9%) and Japan ($5.7%).[103] The reason that trade deficits matter is that they are financed by debt. So each year that the U.S. has a trade deficit (the last year we had a surplus was 1975) it contributes to the $19 trillion national debt in a circuitous, but real manner. For example, in 2013 the trade deficit with China alone was over $300B (as it was in 2012 and 2014) so as those dollars went overseas, China could then notionally finance another $300B of our debt.

Some would argue that bilateral trade imbalances don't matter, that it is only the overall trade imbalance that matters. However, bilateral imbalances do matter as they directly impact (or are impacted by) our foreign policy, and overall imbalances also matter because they indirectly affect the national debt, the economy, and U.S. jobs. There are two very significant trade initiatives now in various stages of negotiation or implementation: the TTIP with the EU, and the more imminent TPP with eleven key Pacific Rim nations.

These impending treaties have renewed arguments about the impact of NAFTA and spurred new globalization and trade protection concerns worldwide. Realizing that getting any new trade agreements through Congress would be difficult, President Obama asked for what is called Fast Track authority, which is formally called the Trade Protection Authority (TPA). This authority, which last expired in 2007, allows the President to negotiate a trade alliance and then present it to Congress for an up or down vote, without amendment. Democrats, led by Harry Reid, along with 151 Democrats in the House who signed letters of opposition, have embraced the union position that NAFTA has shipped our good paying manufacturing jobs overseas, which has then translated into increased income inequality as those displaced workers either take lower paying jobs or find no work at all. Some Republicans also opposed Fast Track because it gives the President more authority, but they are generally more trade friendly. Estimates are that TPP and TTIP could boost world output by $600B, of which $200B could accrue to the U.S.[104]

In mid-2015, much focus was on TPP and the Trade Pact Authority (TPA.) As with any international agreement, the details matter. Senator Elizabeth Warren argued that TPP would primarily benefit large foreign investors and concurrently compromise U.S. sovereignty through the establishment of an international panel of arbitrators.[105]

Presidential candidate Bernie Sanders, an admitted socialist, has campaigned from the same perspective. President Obama said Senator Warren is "absolutely wrong." Once again, as with NAFTA, we have a Democratic president leading the charge, widely opposed by his own Party. National Security Advisor Susan Rice says that TPP is one of Secretary Hillary Clinton' key achievements while Secretary of State, and it is true that Clinton pushed passage for years with our Pacific partners; she was all for it before she was against it as a Presidential candidate. Those who oppose the TPP legislation also argue that it was negotiated in too much secrecy, fails to adequately address climate change, human rights, sanctions for currency manipulation, or comprehensive re-training for displaced workers, and generally benefits big business and investors and not U.S. workers.

Proponents argue that without TPP the U.S. will be left on the sidelines and that our Pacific regional allies, who are already nervous about China, will see this as another step away from our pivot to Asia. They cite the Asian Investment Bank and a competitive trade agreement being negotiated by China. Proponents stress the economic benefits of trade as well, that it has boosted average consumer purchasing power by thousands of dollars annually, and that the movement from a labor-intensive to capital and technology-intensive market was well underway regardless.

Most economists that I have read have assessed little overall direct impact on the labor market from these agreements. I'm not totally convinced. Despite impressive new job creation in the U.S. in the last quarter of 2015, and 292,00 new jobs in December, wages remain flat and the manufacturing sector lost 17,000 jobs last year, continuing a long trend.

The TPP is one of those difficult issues, like Keystone pipeline and health care that you have to work through pre-conceived beliefs, misinformation, and emotions and try to focus on the facts. No one quite agrees on what those facts are, however. Trade alliances are never ideal, but strong trade relationships remain good ways to strengthen long-term nation alliances, and help avoid future conflicts.

Clearly there is an intersection between economic and foreign policy. The trick for the U.S. is to structure these agreements in ways to best protect U.S. workers and manufacturing jobs, avoid further flattening of wages and incomes that exacerbates income inequality, incorporate measures on climate, currency manipulation, trade barriers on our exports and human rights and, in doing so, not so clutter any treaty that it self-defeats. The current alignment has President Obama and most Republicans supporting TPA and TPP (and TTIP next), and most Democrats and unions opposing both. The President has pledged that any agreement will accommodate both environmental and labor concerns that are enforceable.

Although Congress initially defeated TPA in mid-June 2015, twelve days later it passed the Congress and gave the President Fast Track authority for six years. Entering Fall 2015 some issues remained unresolved to include import of dairy products into Canada, Japanese concerns over rice imports, intellectual property rights protection for pharmaceuticals among others. On 5 October 2015 12 nations announced that TPP negotiations had been completed. Immediately, to no one's surprise, alarm signals were sounded by some congressional members on both sides, as well as unions, impacted industries and human rights organizations.

The prescribed timeline was that Congress get the documents shortly after negotiations were completed, which happened in early November 2015, and had 30 days to review them before they are made public. Next followed a 60-day public review, so the earliest that the President could sign any legislation was 90 days from the date that Congress receives the documents, which he indicated he intends to do. The U.S. International Trade Commission is required to do an assessment, then, Congress has 90 days to vote the implementing bill up or down, requiring only a simple majority based on TPA. However, Senate Majority Leader McConnell, realizing that passage was unlikely in the heat of the 2016 election, took TPP off the table until after the election is over. TPP discussions will be back, but not until 2017, probably after President Obama leaves office.

It seems widely accepted that years after NAFTA and China's acceptance into the WTO, poverty worldwide has been reduced. Since the economic calamity of 2008, however, globalization appears to have entered a new period where nations seem more cautious about boundless free trade and opening markets to international companies, more selective of trading partners, and more protective of national industries. The emergence of national interests over broader free market initiatives, if a definite trend continues, will unquestionably make these international trade alliances more difficult in the future. Overarching issues of nationalism (seen in the 2014 French elections), intellectual property rights, and multinational corporations will further complicate the landscape.

How America balances these challenges will have strategic implications as well as economic. America already lost some ground with the Chinese Infrastructure Investment Bank. If the U.S. walks away from TPP, China will fill the void and in my view, to the detriment of both our economy and national security. Vietnam and the other 11 Pacific Rim nations want the deal. Better that China and South Korea join the TPP after it is approved by all twelve nations and implemented, agreeing to abide by the rules that have been negotiated. Besides, the U.S. and China are closing in on a separate Bilateral Investment Treaty (BIT) that has been in negotiations for years. A future TTIP between America and the EU will spur growth and makes sense strategically for all parties, but will be an even harder lift given populist sentiments. I also think these trade agreements are essential to the long-term preservation of the dollar as the world's reserve currency, but that is another long discussion altogether.

HUMAN RIGHTS

> *"Moral values and commitment to human dignity have not been an appendage to our foreign policy but an essential part of it, and a powerful impulse driving it."*
> --Former Secretary of State George Shultz

One of the most important areas for the U.S. to remain as the world leader and principal advocate is in the pursuit of Human Rights. It is our heritage and our obligation to call-out abuses, even in the face of criticism and international pushback. Consider some of the disturbing facts on this list, which is far from inclusive:

- The Armenian Genocide, Ottoman Turkey: in 2015 we recognized the 100-year anniversary of the slaughter of 1.5 million Armenians and dislocation of millions more in April 1915, an event that Turkey to this day does not recognize as genocide (the word genocide requires intent, and Turkey objects to this term to describe the events).

- Cambodia: Between 1975 and 1979 the Khmer Rouge in Cambodia systematically killed an estimated 2 million babies, intellectuals and Vietnamese; roughly 25% of the country's population.

- The Rwanda Genocide 1994: The majority Hutu slaughtered at least 800,000 Tutsi minority (and some moderate Hutu) and raped more than 250,000 women, dismembering victims and killing children in front of their families. President Clinton later apologized for American inaction in this tragedy.

- Bosnia: estimates of 50, 000 girls and women raped and/or killed by Bosnian Serbs during the 1990s war, partially for ethnic cleansing. In 1995, before the 1995 Dayton Peace Accord late that year, 8000 Muslim men were killed in Srebrenica by Serbs under Ratko Mladic, as ethnic cleansing continued. Although international courts have determined Srebrenica to be genocide, Russia vetoed a UN resolution calling it just that, on the 20th anniversary of the massacre in 2015.

- North Korea: On February 17, 2014, the UN Human Rights Council issued its 400-page report, concluding a year-long investigation of human rights abuses in North Korea. The panel, headed by Australian Michael Kirby, chronicled horrendous human rights abuses.

- Bangladesh Genocide 1971: Around 500,000 killed (accounts vary) and hundreds of thousands of women raped (as the Nixon Administration stood silently by, ceding humaniarian concerns to the political propsective of an opening to China).
- Civil wars and internal armed conflicts: Lebanon - 100,000 killed, Iraq - 100,000+ killed, Algeria - 200,000 killed, Sudan - 300,000 killed, Syria - 250,000+ killed. In August 2013 alone, Assad launched a chemical attack on opposition forces outside Damascus, killing over 1400, including many children. Sri Lanka, upwards of 100,000 killed in a 25-year civil war that ended in 2009.[106]
- Stalin's created famine in Ukraine in 1932-1933 that killed 2.5 to 7.5 million Ukrainians (7 million is believed to be an accurate, approximate, total).
- Mao Tse-tung, from his victory in 1949, through the Cultural Revolution and Great Leap Forward, is believed to have killed 70 million Chinese; 30 million from starvation alone, including hundreds of thousands of Christians.

Those are incredible numbers of human lives tragically lost, and I didn't even mention the Holocaust.

In 2012, the U.S. provided $48.4B in economic and military assistance: $17.2B in military aid and $31.2B in economic assistance of which $11.75 was under the U.S. Agency for International Development (USAID), created in 1961 to focus on long-term social and economic development, and administer financial assistance programs. Maybe the most positive accomplishment of the George Bush presidency was his leadership to combat HIV/AIDS in Africa, with $5 billion a year invested, and untold thousands of lives saved.

As George Shultz stated in the quote at the beginning of this section, the U.S. needs to continue to be the vocal advocate for human rights and fundamental individual freedoms across the globe, even as it often puts us at odds with other, sometimes strategically powerful, nations. It is embedded in our foreign policy.

GEOGRAPHIC PERSPECTIVES

Israel and Palestine

All Americans should have a basic understanding of the history of Israel and the Israeli-Palestinian conflict, and how that ties into the entire Middle East landscape and the ongoing conflicts. It drives a lot of our foreign policy, especially with the tensions between the current Administration and Israel, made worse by the nuclear agreement with Iran.

Referring to the following map, the land commonly known as Israel and Palestine is at the Eastern end of the Mediterranean Sea bounded by Lebanon to the north, Jordan to the east, and Egypt in the south and west, although some of this area is in great contention. The Land of Canaan dates back two thousand years, with biblical references to Moses, King David, and his son, Solomon. The land was conquered and re-conquered over the centuries and was, at various times, part of the Roman or Ottoman Empires.

The modern day map starts with a significant event in 1917, during WWI, when the British issued the Balfour Declaration. This established a Jewish national home in Palestine, despite Arab opposition and arguing among the British, French and U.S. The next 20 years saw Arab riots, massive Jewish immigration as the result of religious persecution in Eastern Europe, and various efforts at partition (which the Arabs rejected) or immigration limitation.

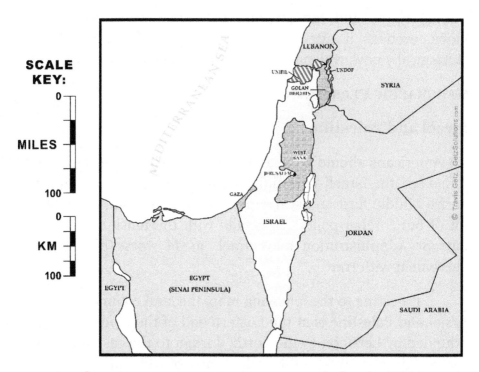

Another attempt at separation was made by the UN in 1947, following WWII and the Holocaust during which 6 million Jews were annihilated. Again the Jews accepted the partition, but the Arabs rejected it.

1948 began the Israeli War of Independence, which was fought against Egypt, Syria and (to a lesser extent) Lebanon for the Palestinians. In the Armistice of 1949, signed by Israel and the Arab states, Gaza fell to Egyptian control, Jordan controlled the West Bank (refer back to the map), and between 720,000 and 780,000 Palestinian refugees fled from Israeli land, the borders of which were never officially recognized by the Arab states.

In June 1967, following Egyptian President Nasser's closing of the straits of the Suez to Israeli shipping, Israel defeated the Egyptians and conquered the Sinai and Gaza, captured the West Bank from Jordan and the Golan Heights from Syria, in what is known as the 6-Day War.[107] As a result, Israel now had control over an area several times larger than the 1948 boundaries and about a million Palestinian Arabs under its rule. It also contributed to the rise of Islamic fundamentalism; Fatah (The Movement for the Liberation of Palestine) and the Palestine Liberation Organization (PLO) (which had in its charter the goal of destroying the Israeli state) were founded in 1957 and 1964 respectively by Yasser Arafat and Egyptian President Abdul Nassar.

In 1969, Arafat took over the PLO. In the Yom Kipper War of 1973, Egypt, and Syria launched a surprise attack on a largely unprepared Israel where thousands of Israelis were killed, but which eventually led to a peace treaty between Israel and Egypt in 1979 (for which Egyptian President Sadat was later assassinated).

In 1982, Israel invaded Lebanon to fight the PLO. Later that year Israel withdrew from the Sinai.

In 1987, at the time of the Palestinian uprising in Gaza and the West Bank, Hamas was formed and is one of the 28 groups officially labeled a foreign terrorist organization by the State Department, and financially backed by Iran.

In 1993, after years of Israel and the PLO fighting, each agreed to a peace treaty (in 1994) and to mutual recognition in a series of agreements generally referred to as the Oslo Accords signed in 1995. Israel withdrew from the Gaza Strip and most of the West Bank. However, some key provisions of the accord were not implemented. Israel continued to build (now over 300,000 settlers) in the West Bank. And the PLO, far from renouncing violence, did not revise its charter to destroy Israel. Jordan signed a peace treaty with Israel in 1994.

In late 2015, on the 20th anniversary of the Oslo Accords and amid renewed violence, Palestinian Authority President Abbas announced that Palestinians would no longer be bound by the Oslo Accords, blaming Israel for continued violence and settlement violations.

The preceding is a very simple introduction to a complicated issue and brings us to current day discussions. Numerous attempts at negotiating a permanent peace, mutual recognition, and a Palestinian state have been tried, without success, over the past twenty plus years.

In 2008 & 2009, Israel fought against the militant group Hamas in Gaza, with about 1400 Palestinians killed.

In 2010, Israel intercepted a humanitarian flotilla of six ships from Turkey headed for Gaza; nine people were killed. Israel's Prime Minister later apologized.

Many surrounding countries with whom Israel once had cordial relations, to include Egypt and Turkey, are now mostly coalesced against Israel, although dynamics on the ground are changing all the time. This partially explains why Israel and the Palestinians agreed back in 2011 to re-start peace talks. This was a focus of Secretary of State John Kerry for much of 2013 and 2014. The major stumbling blocks of those negotiations were, and remain:

- Palestinian demand for withdrawal to the 1967 borders before the 6-Day War, and a freeze on West Bank settlements. Israel continues to expand into land that would ostensibly be part of a future Palestinian state.
- Palestinian 'Right of Return' for the 1948-49 refugees and their millions of descendants.
- Israel's demand that the Palestinians recognize the Jewish state (the 1947 partition resolution was never accepted by the Arabs; and Mr. Abbas's Fatah, which controls the Palestinian Authority (PLO), has affirmed that position repeatedly).

- Gaza, which is now governed by a unity government, but which was ruled by Hamas from 2007 to 2014, was never a part of the recent peace attempts. It refuses to recognize Israel's right to exist. Hence, any peace agreement that might have occurred would apply only to the West Bank, and not Gaza.

In 2014, a breakdown of the peace process amid revelation of a vast array of Hamas tunnels leading to Israel and continued rocket attacks resulted in another outbreak of hostilities. Just before fighting, Fatah (West Bank) and Hamas (Gaza) had an apparent rapprochement, leaving uncertainty as to who actually represented the Palestinians, but ostensibly it was Abbas and the Fatah. (Abbas is now 80, not held in high regard by his people, and reported to be near retirement.) By the fall of 2014, and the third cease-fire, over 1500 Palestinians had been killed, of which about 200 were Hamas and over 1000 civilians, and hundreds of thousands more displaced.

Succinctly stated, Fatah, Hamas, and Iran all advocate the annihilation of Israel.

The apparent reconciliation between Fatah (the dominant party in the PLO and led by Abbas) and Hamas (which refuses to recognize Israeli legitimacy), certainly complicates any future talks of peace, as does the continued financial support provided to Hamas by our trustworthy friends in Iran.

The proposal for a one-state (all Israelis and Palestinians under a single Nation State) or a three-state solution (with Jordan again absorbing some portions of the West Bank, and Egypt the Gaza Strip), which has some historical significance, don't appear to be realistic options. Only a two-state final solution could work in my opinion, one based on the full recognition of Israel with the return of some occupied territories.

Although Israel destroyed the Hamas tunnels and inflicted severe damage to Hamas in 2014, it lost some sympathy with the West over the repeated press coverage of civilian casualties in the attacks.

In March 2014, President Obama warned Prime Minister Netanyahu, on the approaching peace talks, of the U.S.'s limited ability to control international fallout if they failed, which they did.[108]

More recent clashes have centered on the Temple Mount in the Old City, where Jews pray at the foot by the Western (Wailing) Wall and Palestinians pray at the Haram-al-Sharif, one of the holiest sites for Islam containing two important Muslim shrines, administered by King Abdullah II of Jordan. The Temple Mount is the holiest site in Judaism, last destroyed by the Romans, and the place where Jews hope that a 'final temple' will be built someday. Some Israeli agitators are pushing for Israeli access to the Haram, beyond tourist rights, a movement that should be shut down by Netanyahu.

It is clear that relations between Prime Minister Netanyahu and President Obama are frayed, to put it mildly. The invitation by then House Speaker John Boehner to Netanyahu to address Congress in early 2015, without approval or courtesy notification to the White House, was wrong. The Prime Minister's acceptance was equally wrong. Israel is our strongest ally in this part of the world; hopefully the current Administration and the Israel can patch that up in 2016, as we both have common adversaries who would do us great harm. Despite the uproar over his visit and address to Congress, Prime Minister Netanyahu was re-elected and will continue to be the leader we must deal with. He says he still favors a two-state solution. The U.S.–Israel relationship will be a top priority for the next president.

In the meantime, Gaza has hardly recovered from the war of 2014. The accord between Fatah and Hamas hasn't amounted to much. West Bank settlements continue. The bad blood between Obama and Netanyahu is further aggravated by the Iranian nuclear deal, although Israel's Atomic Energy Commission endorsed it. Egypt's al-Sisi abhors Hamas, and the Iranian-backed Hezbollah in Lebanon, currently distracted by fighting in Syria, poses a grave threat to Israel's north.

There is a growing movement, fairly or unfairly, to boycott Israel for their treatment of Palestinians, the latter still pushing for the International Criminal Court in The Hague to investigate war crimes.

In the fall of 2015 clashes and retaliation between Israelis and Palestinians are again becoming commonplace. Any talks of a long-term solution have apparently dissipated, at least for the immediate future, and likely well into a future president's tenure.

Russia

For most of my adult life I believed, and hoped, that Russia and the United States would become allies and partners at some point, following the break-up of the Soviet Union. I have been immensely impressed by the hospitality and warmth of the Russian people during my short visits. Friends of mine who attended some of the Olympic events in Sochi came away with the same experiences.

Sadly, Russia is governed by a despotic leader who could have built strong nationalism through a more diverse economy and raising the standard of living of the Russian people, and risen to be a global leader for good. Unfortunately for the international community, and especially the Russian people, Vladimir Putin continues to support his greedy oligarchs and despots. One example is Syrian leader Assad, who has now butchered over 250,000 of his countrymen-women and children, and many more foreign fighters, nevermind the displacement of large populations and the scores of wounded. After Crimea and Ukraine, there should be little doubt as to Putin's intention to rebuild a grander Russia. He continues to limit the freedoms of citizens, arrests protesters, controls the media and prosecutes territorial expansion.

The Cold War actually ended at the December 1989 Malta summit when President George H. W. Bush and Mikhail Gorbachev agreed that the premise for the Cold War, that the U.S. and the Soviet Union were enemies, was no longer valid. Putin was in the KGB office in Dresden Germany and witnessed the events in East Germany in 1989. The break-up of the Soviet Union into fifteen separate countries happened later, beginning in tumultuous 1991, an event that Putin has repeatedly stated ended tragically, and which appears to form the centerpiece of his grander vision.

From the Russian perspective, subsequent events have eroded the goodwill that initially followed that summit. Among them are the NATO expansion to include former Warsaw Pact countries, beyond the Russian understanding of the break-up according to some (including Gorbachev), the threat of missile defense systems deployed to Europe,[109] to the more recent stand-up of a NATO Command Center in Bulgaria. Although NATO expansion east was never codified, Gorbachev considers it a violation of the spirit of the agreements and assurances that were given, although most experts discount this premise.

In 2008, Putin invaded Georgia, and Russia still occupies Abkhazia and South Ossetia. President Obama unsuccessfully tried a reset with Russia, but the current Administration is seen as weak on foreign policy and the meager Western response to events in Crimea and Ukraine serve to reinforce that view.

Putin has already annexed Crimea and continues to provide military support to the rebels in eastern Ukraine. He has broken multiple treaties and agreements, including the 1994 Budapest Memorandum that guaranteed Ukraine's sovereignty and independence (in exchange for giving up its nuclear weapons to Russia, and the subsequent deterioration of the Ukrainian army). Russia has also violated the 1949 Geneva Convention by having thousands of military troops, in combat, without uniform or military insignia. The downing of MH17 with the tragic loss of 295 lives and the absurd Russian spin following the shoot down tragically underscores the ongoing bloodshed. These crimes, by the way, should be investigated by the International Criminal Court (ICC) at The Hague.

The history of Ukraine suffering at the hands of despots is appalling. In the 1930s, Stalin sealed Ukraine's border and, by spring of 1933, *10,000 Ukrainians were dying each day.*[110] The horrific details are almost beyond description. Sadly, Russia is again at the doorstep of this beleaguered nation. For the U.S. and the EU, there is an urgent need to provide more immediate assistance to Ukraine.

Ukraine itself has started meaningful reforms but needs to do more to control the oligarchs and reduce corruption and graft, which President Poroshenko knows. The West, in turn, must help with serious debt restructuring and write-offs, and loan guarantees, such as the 2015 IMF loan. The EU and it's 28 members must, as they have signaled, keep sanctions in place until the conditions of the Minsk II agreement signed in February 2015, have been met. These provisions include cease-fires, removal of heavy weapons from the front lines and monitoring, among others. Unfortunately, as of this writing, there is mounting evidence that Russia in not abiding by the agreement, has a fully functioning military base in eastern Ukraine with almost 10,000 troops, is violating the cease-fire and seems poised to advance further. This sad situation has all the makings of another foreign policy disaster as the West has not responded adequately, either economically or with defensive weapons, to the needs of the Ukrainian government and their brave people.

Aside from Crimea and Ukraine, Putin has pursued his international outreach with some apparent success. In February 2014, the Russian Defense Minister announced plans to establish military bases in eight nations: three in Latin American countries (Cuba, Nicaragua, and Venezuela) and five in Asia. This was before the U.S. and Cuba re-established diplomatic relations. In May of 2014 Russian President Putin and Chinese President XI Jinping signed a huge deal to send $400B of natural gas to China over the next 30 years, which includes a $70B pipeline, although a combination of sanctions and falling gas prices have delayed any projects from starting. Vietnam has granted Russian ships port visit privileges at the old U.S. Naval Base at Cam Rahn Bay and India recently signed a trilateral agreement with Russia and China to "strengthen coordination on global issues."[111] As further evidence of the evolving relationship between Russia and China, Russia is selling its S-400 air defense system to China, which will provide China significant capability over the disputed South China Sea territories. On 9 May 2015 China's President, Xi Jinping, was Putin's guest of honor celebrating the 70th anniversary of the defeat of the Nazis.

In watching Putin's international push, the U.S. and Europe should pay attention to the "Stans" as well; Kyrgyzstan, Kazakhstan, Tajikistan, Uzbekistan, and Turkmenistan, all of which will suffer economically as NATO withdraws from Afghanistan. Both the

Russians and Chinese have been quick to offer aid and fill the void of Western influence. Except for Kyrgyzstan, U.S. aid to all five countries is declining, and we should all ask why?[112]

On 1 January 2015, the Eurasian Economic Union came into being. It is Putin's answer to the EU, with Russia, Kazakhstan, Armenia and Belarus members, and Kyrgyzstan in talks. Turkey's Erdogan has threated to join it, instead of joining the EU. Putin has all but walked away from nuclear talks regarding the expansion of the 2010 New START Treaty as well as other arms limiting agreements. Moving in the opposite direction, he is rather increasing nuclear delivery capability and rhetoric and was selling S-300 air defense missiles to Iran while sensitive nuclear capability talks with that country and the P5+1 were still ongoing.

Most recently U.S. intelligence was again surprised by Russia's move into Syria. At the UN in September 2015, his first visit to the UN in ten years, Putin was critical of the U.S. policy of backing rebels rather than legitimate governments and the U.S. insistence that Assad be ousted. A couple of days later air strikes began, not on ISIS targets as claimed, but against the anti-Assad rebels. With the U.S. flying airstrikes in some of the same airspace, and Russia bombing anti-Assad forces, the engagements created a real possibility of unintentional misqueues. When a Russian bomber subsequently flew over Turkish airspace it was shot down, resulting in Russian sanctions and escalated tensions between those two countries.

Putin's motives in Syria are not too difficult to see because we've seen them before. Protect the Russian military seaport at Tartus Syria and extend Russian influence in the Mediterranean. Prop up Assad, who is possibly his only supporter in the region. Enhance his stature at home to further solidify his power. And re-direct attention away from the military offensive and humanitarian crisis he has precipitated in Ukraine. The Ukrainian people no longer associate with Russia yet Putin has put their country on ice and calls the shots. Once Putin has accomplished what he has set out to do in Syria, he may well come to the negotiating table. Our options in Syria and the President's reaction are discussed below when we venture into the quagmire called the Middle East.

Putin, it seems, doesn't care much about public opinion (although his popularity is well over 80%). The only things that threaten his power and stolen wealth (by one estimate over $40 billion) is the corrupt and inefficient government, suppression of protests, media control, the increasing rollback of individual rights and basic freedoms, and the downward spiral of the Russian economy. Hundreds of tons of foreign food have been destroyed while Russian families go hungry. Putin has yet to see any real consequences from the Western sanctions, although the drop in oil prices has hurt the economy substantially. The IMF has estimated that the Russian economy will contract by 3% in 2015, and the S&P has downgraded Russia's credit rating to Junk status. One estimate is that Putin's cash reserves may only last a couple of more years.[113]

Within Russia Putin continues to oppress the media and any signs of protest. The Magnitsky Act, named after a Russian lawyer who uncovered a $230M embezzlement scheme by Russian officials and who was later imprisoned, severely beaten, and subsequently died in 2009, was passed in 2012. In early 2015 activist Boris Nemtsov, who uncovered widespread fraud at the Sochi Olympics, was shot in the back by unknown assailants. Putin said he would personally take over the investigation, a heartwarming reassurance to be sure. Who killed Nemstov and who ordered the killing may never be known, although most signs point to Chechen strongman and Kremlin puppet Ramzan Kadyrov. There were some initial arrests, but as of fall 2015 nothing further on the investigation. *And I am shocked, truly shocked.*

There no longer seems much doubt regarding Putin's intentions, and it is unlikely that he will stop until Ukraine is back under Russian control, like Crimea. Some believe that Putin wants to reestablish the historic Novorossiya boundary which would push Russia hundreds of miles to the west of current territory.

At the start of 2015, Russia, with a budget that is highly reliant on oil and gas, was on the verge of a currency crisis, with high inflation and impending recession. The combination of sanctions and dropping oil prices are accelerating the downturn. However, Putin continues to inflame nationalism to offset the economic strife and enjoys very high approval ratings as a result. He has fully embraced the old Lenin axiom that "a lie told frequently eventually becomes a truth." With the national fervor, he can withstand sanctions for some time, and the Russian people are pretty resilient. The EU will need to exhibit strength in dealing with this challenge, backed by U.S., which will not be easy given poll results that show a lack of popular will, and the economic ties that currently exist. Russia has already been dis-invited from the G-8 (now the G-7) forum, following the Crimea annexation, which the Russian leader brushed off. For the U.S. and our allies, here are some other options, as things sit in late 2015:

- Strengthen our own economy. Lacking a position of domestic economic strength, no foreign policy will be successful. This is a recurrent theme of this book.
- Consider stiffer sanctions and publish the results; "banks instead of tanks" as Russian dissident Kasparov has stated.[114] Follow the money and freeze assets of all the oligarchs and their family members who have stashed billions in Western banks. Sanction Sberbank, Russia's largest bank, and financial centerpiece. Our EU friends will need to match these sanctions, which is a riskier proposition, since Russia is

Europe's third biggest trading partner with more than $400B exchanged between the two annually.[115]

- Encourage the EU to build more interconnectors, increased storage and more import and export (U.S.) terminals. Europe gets about 1/3 of its natural gas from Russia and Ukraine about 2/3. All this will take time. The Department of Energy has many projects under review that can be accelerated, in addition to those already approved and under construction. Delisting one of Russia's largest oil company, Rosneft, from the stock exchanges, although not without consequence, should also be seriously considered if Russian aggression continues. The EU is now taking on another Russian oil company, Gazprom, for charging unfair prices, so the timing is right to accelerate crude oil and gas exports, even as oil prices are depressed and will remain so for some time. Recent Congressional action to repeal the 40-year-old ban on crude exports is a welcome move in the right direction.

- Continue to comply with the 2012 Magnitsky Act. That Bill, sponsored by Senator Benjamin Cardin (D—MD) and Representative Jim McGovern (D—MA), freezes assets and strips visas from any Russian officials involved in Magnitsky's torture and death, as well as other officials involved in gross human rights violations. Sergei Magnitsky was the accountant who exposed large scale theft by the Russian government, as previously mentioned. (In response to this act Russia halted all U.S. adoptions of Russian children.)

- Continue to expose the crackdown on human rights and complete disregard for ordinary citizens that has increased dramatically since Putin was re-elected in 2012.

- Publicly name, and call-out for accountability, Russian military officials who are caught in violation of the Geneva

Convention by instigating violence without wearing a military uniform, as required by Geneva Convention.

- Complete the TTIP treaty discussed earlier.
- Finally, maybe most importantly, help the Ukrainian people and support President Petro Poroshenko to establish a government that is inclusive, free of corruption, and capable of developing a growing economy. The Western response has been tepid. Ukraine's economy is a disaster and needs reforms and significant loan restructuring, and possibly defensive weapons, for which we should not be timid and fearful of the consequence.
- Accept only a full withdrawal of Russian forces from Ukraine as a condition for the lifting of sanctions.

Hopefully, over time, the Minsk protocols will be allowed and would see Russia leave eastern Ukraine and agree to elections in Crimea. In exchange, NATO might decide to withhold membership of Ukraine for some short period of time, maybe until 2025. Maybe the Russia-U.S. nuclear talks could then resume. Both sides would need to be interested in a solution, but Putin has shown no such interest to date. A more likely scenario is that Putin, post-Syria, will test NATO resolve by provoking unrest in Estonia, Lithuania, or Latvia, all NATO alliance countries that we are bound to protect under Article 5. Our intelligence should not again, *be surprised*.

In the final analysis Russia, except for its nuclear arsenal, though it fails under Putin's leadership to conform to any decent set of norms governing responsible international behavior, poses little direct long-term threat to the U.S. It is a country in rapid decline with a defunct economic model heavily dependent on the government, that will eventually collapse. In the shorter term, however, Russia's behavior is a threat to Ukraine, NATO, and its neighbors. As long as Putin's survival depends on fostering the idea of the West as the great enemy, not much will likely change.

"In my view, our primary enemy is the U.S. and the North Atlantic bloc."
--Senior Russian Defense Ministry Official, Sept. 2014

China and the Pacific

China is an emerging power that will drive much of our foreign policy, as well as defense posture, well into the future. It is re-visited in this chapter in a broader context as the Asia Pacific region's importance continues to grow. While America is a relatively new country and short on memory, China's history is rich and should inform us as to how they view their place in the world order.

The Tang Dynasty from 618-907 A.D. was considered the golden age, with economic and cultural advances, a strong army with successful military campaigns and robust trade along the ancient Silk Road trade route that linked the Mediterranean with Asia. China enjoyed primacy in Asia and was highly respected by neighbors such as Japan, Korea, and Vietnam. Sometime after that, China's decline began. The British defeated China in the Opium Wars that covered the period 1839-1860, which opened up ports to trade and Hong Kong was ceded to Britain, ushering in the modern era. (Hong Kong was reverted to Chinese sovereignty on 1 July 1997, ending a 99-year lease.)

During World War II, China was occupied and its people brutalized by the Japanese. There still remain some survivors of the famous Nanjing massacre where Japanese soldiers slaughtered 300,000 and raped an estimated 20,000 women and girls in the *first month of occupation alone,* usually killing their victims to cover the crime. Although expressing 'remorse', not fully acknowledging these war crimes continues to cause friction between the countries.

In 1949, after the war, Mao Tse-tung defeated the army of Chiang Kai-shek and his Kuomintang (KMT) Party, which fled to Formosa (now Taiwan.) Chairman Mao founded the Peoples Republic of China (PRC) and China became communist where religion, both Buddhism and Confucianism, which had flourished, gave way to a Karl Marx doctrine and allegiance to the state; and where *hundreds of thousands of Christians* were put to death.

As pointed out in the Human Rights discussion, Chairman Mao, who is still revered, killed an estimated 70 million during his reign. In March of 2013, Xi Jinping became General Secretary of the Communist Party, President of the PRC and head of the military. Considered the 5th generation of leadership, he holds all three posts and is also an ex-officio member of the governing body, the Politburo. The son of a communist, he rose through the ranks and is steeped in China's history as a dominant nation in Asia.

China's more recent adventurism in the area goes back decades. When China took the Paracel Islands from the Vietnamese in 1974, it killed dozens of Vietnamese Navy sailors, and began a series of occupations of Philippine reef shoals since. China claims a vague Nine-dash Line (shown in the Defense chapter) to claim sovereignty in the South China Sea. This, in what is generally acknowledged as international waters, is not recognized by either Vietnam or the Philippines, (or any other country).

Anti-Chinese protests in Vietnam in May 2014 were in opposition to the new $1B Chinese oil rig located in what Vietnam claims is in the Vietnamese EEZ, apparently tolerated by the sympathetic pro-China Vietnamese communist leadership. The announcement by China of an ADIZ in the East China Sea, and the escalating Diaoyu/Senkaku island disputes are keeping Japan-China tensions elevated in the region, and causing worry among other neighbors, especially Vietnam and the Philippines.

In early 2015, China completed building a series of small military bases along disputed shoals and reefs, and by September 2015, when Xi Jinping arrived for an official visit, construction of airfields on three man-made islands was well in progress. Despite Chinese claims to the contrary, their clear intent is to militarize these reefs, which lie within the Spratly Islands, with naval ships, anti-aircraft weapons, and planes.

China has warned that a future ADIZ might someday encompass the South China Sea as well as the East China Sea, and when complete these facilities will enable just that. *We should not be surprised!* The vital importance of the region and the growing influence of China largely explains the U.S. policy decision to 'pivot to the Pacific,' although what that means is entirely vague regarding our foreign policy for the region. Asian nations are increasingly skeptical of what looks like a U.S. policy in rhetoric only.

Continuing to build our relations with the Philippines and Vietnam makes strategic sense, encouraging Japan to assume a greater military and regional role to the fullest extent allowed by its constitution, and re-setting of Japan/South Korea relationships should all be U.S. priories. China is courting South Korea to further its agenda of a playing a key role in the region. Taiwan is another issue altogether. China views a (peaceful) unification as only a matter of time, and the current Taiwanese President Ma Ying-jeou (Chinese Nationalist Party, or KMT)), who was elected in 2008 and re-elected in 2012, has continued rapprochement efforts. He and Chinese President Xi met in Singapore on Nov. 7th 2015, ahead of elections in January. Opposing him is the Democratic Progressive Party (DPP), with ties to the former Kuomintang that fled to (then) Formosa after the civil war in the 1940s, and who favor declaring independence. In the late 2014 local elections, the DPP won a resounding victory which sent a strong signal to President Ma and his KMT Party, and a warning shot for what might be the outcome of the January 2016 presidential elections. In October 2015 the KMT, sensing defeat, replaced their candidate with the party chairman, Erik Chu. The DPP looks to be in a good position to win, with important ramifications for both countries. The 16 January election will take place just as this book goes into final edit.

China's economy and widespread unrest are other two issues to be watched closely. The past three decades have witnessed enormous growth and the predictions are that China's economy, now the world's second-largest, will eclipse America's before long. Yet there are many signs that the 9% GDP growth cannot be sustained and is predicted to fall to around 7% in 2015, still robust by world standards.

China's workforce population will decrease by nearly 10% by 2040 (due in large part to the one-child policy, only recently relaxed), and it is now the second-largest net importer of oil in the world. It was self-sufficient in 1990.[116]

Many economists are warning of the overinflated Chinese stock and housing markets, and we saw a dramatic stock market swing in July and August 2015 that impacted the world markets. The same events in January 2016 sparked stock market losses worldwide. The general consensus is that China's new President, Xi Jinping, will need to implement significant economic and political reforms to continue growth and stimulate greater consumer spending to achieve what he calls the Chinese Dream, the details of which are just now beginning to come into focus, and discussed more in a few pages.

Despite crackdowns and many high-profile arrests, corruption remains widespread, corporate espionage commonplace, the currency still undervalued (estimates as high as 40% at one point), inequality profoundly manifest (about 1 billion of the 1.3

billion population are poor), air quality horrendous, and the mostly state-owned economic model grossly inefficient.

About 60 million Chinese children are left to the care of a single parent or other relatives while parents leave for urban areas to find jobs, what The Economist calls 'the left behind children.'[117] Add to that the popular unrest, mainly from the disenfranchised Tibetans and Uighur minorities, human rights violations, crackdowns on lawyers and the media, and you have the seeds of discontent.

China's debt has increased to over 200% of GDP. Almost 750 million people live in the cities (projected to be 1 billion by 2030), with demands that will strain infrastructure for services and products.

In June of 2014, we somberly remembered the 25th anniversary of the Tiananmen Square massacre that killed two to three thousand Chinese civilians, an event that Chinese officials remember very well and what drives much of their internal policies.

China holds about $1.3 Trillion in U.S. debt, but any attempt to unload that debt would cause a global recession and be counter-productive to all.

China is suspected of being behind most of the Defense Department hacking and industrial espionage of the past few years, including the theft of over five million records from the OPM. When President Xi Jinping visited the U.S. in September 2015, he and President Obama reached an apparent accord on cyber hacking, as discussed in chapter 3. The G-20 later affirmed the intent to stop corporate intellectual property theft. Most experts don't believe anything will change, either because Xi cannot deliver on the promise, or because he won't. As discussed in the Homeland Security chapter, it is past time for establishing international agreement on what constitutes a cyber-attack that would initiate a proportional response.

As I mentioned before, the TPP appears more beneficial than not and will probably be approved in 2017 post-Obama, without China initially, although that should be open for future discussion, whereby China will need to abide by the standards already set. China has already surpassed the U.S. and become the largest trading country in the world. This treaty will help restore some balance to the increasing share of Chinese markets and goods. Both countries should complete the Bilateral Investment Treaty (BIT) mentioned earlier in this chapter on terms that benefit both. The pivot to Asia needs to continue, but without provocation. As Robert Kaplan points out in his recent book, "nearly 7 billion of the world's 9 billion people will generally live in East Asia, Southeast Asia, South Asia, the Middle East and South Africa."[118]

The South China Sea will be of staggering future importance for commerce and the free flow of trade worldwide, which is why we worry about the aggressive build-out. As China continues to rise on the international scene, with an expected corresponding rise in nationalism, it will be important to maintain a balancing coalition of Asian countries that should be led by the United States. This will require long-term diplomatic skill and a foreign policy that promotes Chinese immigration and studies, that ensures Japan remains faithful to its constitution, and a larger U.S. Navy fleet with an increased presence in the Pacific to ensure the future stability of the region and the all-important South China Sea. This will also help offset the threat posed by North Korean President Kim Jong-un as he continues his quest for nuclear weapons. Kim may have all the necessary components to be operational in a few years, by some estimates. China, the only country capable of stopping this buildup, has not done so, more concerned apparently that any intervention would destabilize the leader and country even further. So a nuclear-capable North Korea may only be a few years away, and the hopes of South Korea for a peaceful reunification ever beyond reach. As with China, the increasing availability of news and the Internet will certainly lead to increased unrest within the oppressed of both countries.

There seems to be little debate that China is set on establishing what it considers to be its historical and rightful leadership position in Asia. What President Xi calls the Chinese Dream may have visibly kicked off with the establishment of the ADIZ in the East China Sea in November of 2013. Next we saw rapid reclamation in the disputed Spratly Islands by pumping sand into coral reefs and the construction of airfields soon to be capable of landing combat aircraft. Should China eventually declare an ADIZ over the entire South China Sea, most of which falls under the Nine-dash Line, it would represent a new level of provocation and an even clearer signal of intent to the West, requiring a response. There are already signs of rising military tension as other countries, including the U.S., exercise their right to free navigation of international waters, which all must do without hesitation.

The second leg of the dream seems to be China's focus on manufacturing and managing the supply chain, which remains strong despite rising wages.

Third is the establishment of the AIIB with 50 original members including many U.S. allies who rushed to join (Britain, Germany, South Korea, and India among others), which will help finance new infrastructure for Chinese manufactured exports and oil and gas imports.

This Chinese Dream now appears to also entail a Maritime Silk Road, which ties to the expansion activities in the South China Sea and Spratly reclamation projects, as well as an Economic Belt

Silk Road that links the Ungur region in China's northwest with the Gwadar Port on the Arabian Sea in Pakistan.

China, which has for so long been land-centric, is now building a powerful navy and fully embraced sea power as critical to global commerce and influence in the region.

In addition to the stalled oil deal with Russia which appears to heavily favor the Chinese, China has now signed with Pakistan for $46 billion in supporting projects. President Xi is also reaching out to other countries in the region to include Malaysia, Cambodia, Laos, Myanmar, and Laos.

There remains considerable debate as the whether China can or will pursue this dream peacefully. There is also debate as to whether China's goals remain Asia-centric or across a wider sphere, and whether the reach into Africa, India, and other regions is driven by economics or politics.

I disagree with those who explain away recent aggressive behavior largely in a historical context, dismiss the outreach (maybe overreach) to Africa as purely market driven or justify the military buildup it terms of some rationale security concerns – from whom, North Korea, Japan?

The Chinese actions in the region skirt the international law and are carefully orchestrated to avoid direct confrontation. Still, America will need to concede that China is an established world power with far-reaching influence and work to maintain normalized relations. It is, after all, through America's victory in WWII that China survived and reached this critical point in its history, a fact that America should frequently take the time to remind. Americans are quick to forgive and forget; many of our staunchest allies were enemies in WWII. China, on the other hand, plays the long game;

hostilities toward Japan and others still drive their foreign policy, even long after they remain any threat.

How China handles critically needed economic reform, unrest in Hong Kong and large Muslim and Tibetan areas, political dissent and the media, religious freedom (to include Christianity) and behaves with neighbors in the South China Sea will reveal much to us about Chinese leadership's intentions, sooner rather than later. Xi has established himself as the most decisive leader since Mao. His anti-corruption campaign seems to be taking hold. Yet it is entirely unclear if Xi will make the political and economic reforms so desperately needed. Will he pursue continued censorship of dissent and the media? It's equally unclear if the one billion poor will become increasingly restive as wealth accrues to the upper middle-class and corrupt leaders, leaving so many more behind, mostly those concentrated in the large urban areas and prone to unrest.

The PLA remains paranoid about the West and America in particular, and Xi's ultimate motives and those of the Politburo remain aloof from any real foreign understanding. Former President Deng Xiaoping stated in his now famous foreign policy quote: *"Hide your strength, bide your time."* President Xi appears to be taking a much different and very activist approach to foreign policy. The West, with leadership from America, must remain fully engaged in and committed to this region of the world.

It would be far better if China rose peacefully and assumed a non-threatening role in the Pacific. It would be better yet if American-Chinese relations could advance, business expand in both directions, cyber hacking end, and free commerce prevail in the South China Sea. Improved relations benefit the peoples of both countries and will help the economies of both to grow. That should be our objective. In time, we shall see.

Africa

Fifteen of the twenty most fragile nations in the world – those on the brink of collapse in 2014 – are in Africa, as are more than half of the U.S. embassies that the State Department calls high risk.[119]

It is a vast continent with challenges ranging from bloody conflicts, famine and hunger, corruption, sexual violence against women and a growing radical terrorist movement. Here are a few facts to consider:

- Congo: when civil war broke out in 1998, more than four million died in the conflict that lasted from 1998-2003 and another million in the aftermath of starvation, conflict or preventable disease. Tens of thousands of children were forced to become soldiers and as many as 2/3 of all women were victimized by rape or similar sexual violence.[120]
- Niger: has become an increasingly brutal target for jihadists where a weak army and government, poor economy, and widespread poverty provide opportunity. UNICEF has estimated that half of Niger's populations face severe malnutrition. Refugees by the thousands have come in from neighbors Mali and Nigeria, an estimated 50,000 from Mali alone.
- Sudan: particularly the ongoing Darfur genocide in western Sudan, has displaced hundreds of thousands and seen up to half a million deaths as well, by most estimates. Human Rights Watch documented the mass rape of 220 women by Khartoum's army in Tibet in 2014, findings which the Russians dismissed at the UN.
- Nigeria: now with a new President (Muhammadu Buhari, who succeeded Goodluck Jonathan in May 2015 in a peaceful transition) is fighting against the Islamist terrorists of the al-Qaeda-affiliated group known as Boko Haram in the Muslim

north, and fighting poverty where most of the population lives on $2/day or less. In mid-April 2014 over 200 school children were abducted by Boko Haram, which translated means, Western education is forbidden. This terrorist group is every bit as deadly as the more renowned ISIS, having displaced over 2 million citizens and killed over 20,000 since the uprising began in July of 2009 according to Amnesty International, including an estimated 2000 dead from the January 2015 Baga massacre alone.

Affliction and poverty throughout Africa remain widespread, and a perfect source for al-Qaeda recruitment. Bloody conflicts continue in South Sudan, the Central African Republic, and the Congo. Liberia was devastated by the Ebola outbreak. Islamist attacks in Kenya, such as the American Embassy bombing in 1998 that killed 213 and the Nairobi Westgate Mall killings of 67 in September 2013, have increased since Kenya deployed troops into Somalia to fight al-Shabab.

Yet, there are some signs for optimism. Elections held in Mali, with the help of French forces and UN supervisors, is promising. Chad, which has resources and a tested army, is fighting Boko Haram. Nigeria has restated its annual GDP at over $500B, making it Africa's largest economy (ahead of South Africa). The country is rich in resources, oil in particular, which is drawing foreign investors and companies. Nigeria's new President Buhari has raised expectations that he can tackle widespread poverty and corruption, spark economic growth, and deal with the expanding threat of Boko Haram, whose total brutalization of women threatens Nigeria's future.

Even though oil and other commodity prices have fallen, these economies have generally remained afloat due to increased diversification. As Secretary of State John Kerry wrote in The

Washington Post, "The best-untold story of the decade may be the story of Africa. Real income has increased more than 30%, reversing two decades of decline. Seven of the world's 10 fastest-growing economies are in Africa, and GDP is expected to rise 6% per year in the next decade. HIV infections are down 40% in sub-Saharan Africa and malaria deaths among children have declined 50%." The U.S. is re-engaging in Somalia, site of the Blackhawk down in Mogadishu in 1993, now that the country has a new President and constitution and is actively fighting the terrorist group al-Shabab.

Some of these trends are encouraging, but much of Africa still suffers from civil strife, corruption, abuse of women, poverty, the constrained but still real Ebola threat, and general instability. There are other worrisome signs, with democracy slow to take hold and the population on the continent projected to double by 2050.

In 2014, President Obama hosted leaders from 50 African countries, hopefully sending the message of the importance of the continent and a genuine commitment to continued aid and investment. In his July 2015 trip to Africa, the President pledged greater support to the Somalia and Kenya governments to fight terrorism. There is much for the U.S., the UN, and other countries to do on this continent to help overcome widespread malnutrition, promote human rights, and defeat radical Islamic groups such as Boko Haram in Nigeria and al-Shabaab in Eastern Africa. Without concerted and sustained action, these jihadist groups will leverage poverty and disaffection, continue to recruit militants, and spread terror like cancer across the continent.

The record of the Obama Administration toward Africa falls short in comparison to that of his predecessor, and much more needs to be done, both to offset the Chinese who are moving in, but more importantly to help all of Africa fight terrorism, poverty, and hunger.

Pakistan and India

The history of Pakistan is intimately intertwined with India and British colonial rule. Most Americans don't remember that Pakistan was once part of India. Although Hindus and Muslims were for years unified in their quest for independence from Britain, the idea of states took hold sometime in the late 1930s and was endorsed by the Muslim League in 1940.

During the buildup to the partition of India, an estimated eight million people gave up jobs and homes and migrated across borders, fearful of being dominated by a different ethnic majority; an estimated 1 million Muslims, Hindu, and Sikh became victims in the ensuing violence.

Pakistan was formally established on 14 August 1947. Almost from inception, Pakistan and India have since considered the other a rival, fought several wars, and now both possess nuclear weapons, estimated at around 100 warheads each. While India had existing infrastructure following the 1947 partition, Pakistan did not, and has suffered extended periods of military rule, widespread corruption and instability. Twenty-three years following partition, in 1971, the Pakistani army dominated by Punjabis, killed an estimated 500,000 Bengalis (and raped hundreds of thousands more), and forced about 10 million to flee to India. American indifference, led by Kissinger and Nixon and portrayed in the book "The Blood Telegram" by Gary Bass, was politically motivated to pursue the grander opportunity of relations with China.

Both India and Pakistan continue to grow military budgets, with the former keeping a wary eye on China, and the Sunni-dominated Pakistan a wary eye on Iran. In March 2015, Pakistan fired their new missile, the Shaheen-III, which reportedly has a range of 1700 miles and would be capable of reaching across all of India, and delivering a nuclear warhead as well.

Although much of the history of both countries is intermingled, India and Pakistan are also part of the complicated mosaic that makes up the larger Middle East and southern Asia regions. Recently, both countries have relatively new leaders on whom much hope rests.

Narendra Modi is India's new Prime Minister, promising to reinvigorate India's declining GDP and generate jobs, something he was successful at as chief minister of Gujarat, a state of about 60 million people, notwithstanding the sad events of 2002 where thousands of Muslims in Gujarat were killed. It remains to be seen if he will be a leader for all Indians and institute reforms needed to create jobs and improve the economy. His initiative to invest $7.5 billion in smart cities may be too ambitious when many slums and lack of basic clean water still exist throughout the country, but it is a step in the right direction. Lack of Inoculations and malnutrition, especially among the children, is widespread. Prime Minister Modi has also reached out to China. He and China's President Xi Jinping have exchanged state visits, despite the fact that both share an uneasy 2500-mile border and fought a short war in the early 1960s. India remains wary of China's expansion into the South China Sea and is fully aware and suspicious of Pakistan's long- standing relationship with China. Modi has also reached out to Japan, establishing a close relationship with Mr. Abe; both leaders share a mutual distrust of China's motives.

Since June of 2013, Muhammad Nawaz Sharif has been Prime Minister of Pakistan. On May 26 of 2014 he attended Mr. Modi's inauguration, a real signal of more cooperation for the future, although Modi had been less receptive to increased accords over time, until he made a surprise stop-over to visit Sharif in December 2015, following a trip to Russia. This marked the first time an Indian Prime Minister had visited Pakistan since 2008, and raises hope.

In December 2014, the Pakistan Taliban killed 145 school children is what may be a turning point for that country. Pakistan's military had begun a crackdown on the groups in the country that had long enjoyed a safe haven and terrorist training ground, specifically the Pakistan Taliban, the Afghanistan Taliban and al-Qaeda. In September 2015, the Taliban killed 29 at a Pakistani military base, mostly those at a mosque preparing for morning prayers. The Pakistan Taliban immediately took credit and claimed it was in retaliation for the crackdown.

We can all hope that Pakistan's military will continue to put increasing pressure on these terrorist groups that have long had safe sanctuary. There is evidence in late 2015, that Pakistan is stabilizing with less frequent terrorist attacks and some improved infrastructure, although much of the population lives in poverty and without jobs.

With the leadership of Prime Minister Sharif in Pakistan and Prime Minister Modi in India, there is reason for encouragement toward easing of long-standing frictions, and for an eventual accommodation in Afghanistan. Sharif remains close to China and is an essential part of the Chinese vision of an economic Silk Road running to the Pakistani deep-water seaport town of Gwadar, which would also benefit Pakistani manufacturing. Sharif (Pakistan is over 80% Sunni) recently angered his Sunni neighbor in Saudi Arabia, to whom he is personally indebted and from whom the country receives financial support, by not supporting the call to assist with the war in Yemen.

For the U.S., the stakes are high for continued improving relations with both countries, not only for peace prospects in the Middle East, but for stable relations in southern Asia.

The Greater Middle East

The Arab Spring was primarily a movement toward democracy, free markets and increased rights for women. With the widespread availability of Internet access and social media, it would have happened eventually in my opinion, whether or not we invaded Iraq.

Except Tunisia, where the Arab Spring began, the end results have been the opposite of the hopes, with wider suppression of human rights and media freedom. From the ongoing civil wars in Libya, Yemen, and Syria, to the rise of ISIS, nations appear to be morphing into religious states. Sometimes the U.S. has had to back leaders or groups who were the lesser of two bad choices, often labeled as making common cause with our enemies.

Egypt, with army general and now President Abdel Fattah al-Sisi, having ousted the Muslim Brotherhood, now seems to have settled into an uneasy calm and embarked on economic reforms, but with increased internal repression; more on Egypt later.

As Henry Kissinger has stated, our policy in the Middle East and surrounding areas has been guided by three core objectives for more than half a century:

> *"Preventing any power in the region from emerging as a hegemon; ensuring the free flow of energy resources, still vital to the operation of the world economy; and attempting to broker a durable peace between Israel and its neighbors, including a settlement with the Palestinian Arabs. In the past*

decade, Iran has emerged as the principal challenge to all three."

--Henry Kissinger, The Washington Post,
3/3/2012

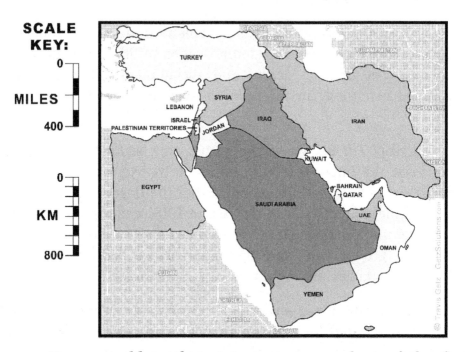

You can add to that statement, as a subset of the first objective, a goal to prevent a nuclear arms race in the Middle East, something that many feel more likely, post-Iran deal. Time will tell.

While the history of the region would take us back centuries, let's start with recent events that begin with the Islamic Revolution (or Iranian Revolution) in 1979 that overthrew the Pahlavi dynasty and ousted the Shah of Iran, who left in exile. On 1 April 1979 Iran voted to become an Islamic Republic and the Ayatollah Khomeini became the Supreme Leader of the country by the end of that year. Fifty-two American hostages were taken prisoner (The Canadian Ambassador saved six Americans, made famous by the movie, ARGO). After a couple of failed rescue missions, they were released following 444 days in captivity, immediately following President Reagan's acceptance speech. Following years of legal battles, the 2016 Omnibus funding bill authorizes up to $4.4 million per hostage ($10,000 per day of captivity) in compensation, 36 years later, as well as some compensation for those in the Beirut bombing attack, discussed below.

President Reagan went on to rebuild our nations' military capability and create the Special Operations Command. On October 19, 1983, terrorists bombed the Marine Barracks in Beirut, Lebanon, killing 241 service members and injuring hundreds more. No senior official was ever held accountable for the Beirut attack (much like Benghazi Libya in 2012.) Thirty years later, a U.S. District Judge ruled that Iran (are you surprised?), its President, and Hezbollah (Iran's proxy in Lebanon) were responsible for that bombing.[121]

The U.S. and allied forces quickly withdrew, a fact noted by Osama Bid Laden, which leaves us to wonder if the events of 9/11/2001 could have been avoided by a different Western response to the Beirut bombing. Clearly the attacks on the U.S. on 9/11/2001 provided significant momentum to the radical Islamic movement.

In 2010, a series of protest movements began in Tunisia in what is now called the Arab Spring, mentioned above, that moved on to Egypt, Libya and Syria and other countries. Much of the conflict can be traced to the ages-old conflict between Shiite and Sunni Muslims, as well as hardline Islamists who would impose strict Shi'a law, versus those Muslims who are more secular and tolerant. One sad result of the failed Arab Spring has been the targeting of Christians. Christians in Iraq, who once numbered around a million in 2003, have mostly fled persecution or been killed

Tracking the many ethnic groups, growing militias and terrorist affiliates that make up the region, and that so influence our national interests and resultant (if opaque) foreign policy, is challenging even for those who follow the Middle East closely. Surprisingly to me as I researched and wrote this, Shia Muslims make up only about 12% of the world's Muslim population, and are a majority in only a few countries that includes Iran, Iraq and Bahrain. Sunni Muslims constitute the other 88% of Muslims. Being in the ethnic majority does not necessarily equate to authoritative rule, as Saddam Hussein in Iraq was Sunni and Assad in Syria is Shia, but understanding the ethnic balance does enlighten us on how relationships and support are aligned.

Here is a short list of some of the larger groups across the region, but the list frequently changes as new splinter groups or affiliates arise, so this list is far from inclusive:

- Hezbollah: The Iran-backed terrorist group in Lebanon; Hezbollah is an Iranian IRGC (Iranian Revolutionary Guard Corps) proxy. Although its stated claim is to defeat Israel, it has re-focused on fighting alongside Assad, losing some respect in the Sunni Muslim world as a result.
- Houthi: The Iranian-backed Shia rebels who seized the capital in Yemen and toppled the pro-American government.
- Hamas: The Palestinian organization that essentially controls the Gaza Strip and is labeled a terrorist organization by the State Department. Although backed by Iran, it has allegedly cooled on Iran somewhat based on continued Syrian atrocities.
- Kurdistan Workers Party (PKK): A Kurdish group within Turkey that has been fighting for independent rule for several decades. It follows a Marxist-Leninist doctrine and is labeled by the U.S. a terrorist organization (the PYD, a Syrian- Kurdish organization, is loosely affiliated with PKK).

Recep Erdogan, Turkey's President, has been urging both the PKK and PYD to enter the fight against Assad. Then there is also the YPG (Kurdish People's Protection Units) fighting in Syria and doing well, although it is tough to tell whom the group is supporting.

- Syrian Kurdish People's Protection Units (YPG): Another Kurdish group that had co-existed with Assad in Syria until early 2015, when it began fighting against the Syrian Army. The YPG's affiliation with the PKK is disputed.
- Muslim Brotherhood: a strict Sunni Party that rode to prominence following the Arab Spring, but has now been displaced and discredited in both Egypt and Tunisia.
- Al-Qaeda: the original terrorist group headed by Osama bin Laden that now vies for influence with the more radical ISIS. Al-Qaeda has generally disavowed ISIS for another terrorist group, the Jabhat al-Nusra Front, its Syrian affiliate.
- Jabhat al-Nusra: A Sunni rebel group aligned with al-Qaeda and fighting Assad in Syria. Some see al-Nusra as a terrorist threat almost equal to ISIS, and well positioned in post-Assad Syria.
- Taliban: A Sunni fundamentalist group that follows strict Sharia law and was dominant in Afghanistan for years and still threatens the country's rule. It is renowned for its brutal treatment of women. As discussed later in the Afghanistan section, with the reported death in 2015 of leader Mohammad Omar two years after he actually died, the future direction that the Taliban leadership will take is uncertain.
- ISIS: ISIS or ISIL (The Islamic State of Iraq and the Levant), who have captured large areas of Iraq and claimed a new caliphate under Abu Bakr al-Baghdadi. Not recognized as a legitimate caliphate, they have been most visible for the ongoing beheadings of foreigners and atrocities against other Muslims in territories it captures. Recently, world leaders

have been using the term DAESH, which is the proper Arabic name for the Islamic State, but one now forbidden to be used.

- Boko Haram: The Nigerian radical Islamist group responsible for the kidnapping of 200 school children and other terrorist activities as discussed in the Africa discussion previously.
- Al-Shabaab: the jihadist terror group operating in Somalia and expanding into Kenya and Ethiopia.

There are many more, too numerous to cover, with new affiliates all the time, but those are some of the more notorious, and recognizable, non-state actors in the region.

Iraq, Afghanistan, and Syria

Syria and Iraq to the west of Iran, and Afghanistan to the east; I've grouped these countries together since these has been the areas where most of the fighting is ongoing and has taken place in recent years (not to exclude the civil wars in Yemen and Libya).

Each country and the challenges are unique. Syria is 70-75% Sunni (but Assad is Shia, which explains Iran's support to Assad). Iraq is also 70- 75% Sunni and Afghanistan 80-90% Sunni. Simple ethnic majority facts, however, oversimplify the many complexities that make up the many ethnicities and tribal structures.

Former Secretary of State Hillary Clinton says she voted to invade Iraq and admits she got it wrong. The current Secretary of State, John Kerry, stated twice in 2013 that he opposed the invasion, but the record shows he voted for it and spoke publicly of his support on many occasions. Then-Secretary of State Colin Powell made the case at the UN that Iraq possessed and was hiding WMD, which about everyone now knows was based on flawed intelligence. And Powell himself remained highly skeptical of the evidence that the CIA was providing, including reassurances from then-CIA Director George Tenet. The Commission on the Intelligence Capabilities of the United States Regarding WMD, referred to as the Robb-Silberman Report, found that the U.S. Intelligence Community was wrong in almost all of its pre-war judgments about Iraq's WMD, constituting a major intelligence failure.

That's the quick background, but what we now face traces directly back to our invasion of Iraq in 2003. This was possibly the worst foreign policy decision in a century, right up there with our appeasement of Hitler and our misadventure into the Vietnam conflict.

The last U.S. forces left Iraq on 18 December 2011 as agreed in the negotiated Status of Forces Agreement (SOFA). We spent over $1 Trillion, suffered 4,487 casualties and another 32,223 seriously wounded. By not leaving a stabilizing force as we could have, and with the Shiite government of Prime Minister Nouri al-Malaki leaning toward Iran and failing to be inclusive of the Sunni majority, some predicted the unraveling that followed.

The campaign against the Sunni majority was orchestrated by none other than Qassem Suleimani, head of the IRGC, who is now leading the Iranian-forces fight against ISIS and who clearly played an unofficial role in the recently negotiated nuclear talks. (Suleimani by the way, who is responsible for the deaths and wounding of thousands of Americans in Iraq, and who violated sanctions by visiting Russia while talks were ongoing, will have sanctions against him lifted as part of the final nuclear deal negotiated by the U.S. and others in the P5+1.)

Malaki refused even to pay the Sunni tribal militias that were created to battle the more radical Sunni al-Qaeda in Anbar province. IRGC-aligned Shia militias trained in Iraq and crossed borders to support Bashar al-Assad in Syria. Predictably, or it probably should have been, disenfranchised Sunni radicals eventually formed ISIS and are far more hardline than the core Sunni al-Qaeda operatives, as we have all witnessed graphically on multiple videos.

Two of our other biggest mistakes in Iraq (besides the invasion) were the 2003 dissolution of the Iraqi army, and by continuing to support Malaki (Vice President Biden, among others, was key in this) after 2010. When many senior officials were warning that his retribution against Sunnis would have consequences. Malaki may have initially been the only good choice with the authority to lead the country, but he should have been pushed aside far earlier.

Basically, we had achieved a major milestone after the 2007 Iraqi surge success, but the current Administration was more interested in withdrawal than stability–an epic opportunity squandered. It is both ironic and a tragedy that the U.S., with senior level Administration and CIA involvement, propped up both Maliki in Iraq, when in 2010 the Iraqis voted to elect pro-American Ayad Allawi, nd Karzai in Afghanistan, when in 2002, 75% of the delegates to the Afgan Loya Jirga (Grand Assembly) signed a petition for King Zahir Shah.

The prospects for Iraq look dim right now with ISIS, well known the world over for their brutality, beheadings and destruction of priceless artifacts, now controlling large parts of the country. (In the summer of 2015, ISIS beheaded the Syrian archeologist who for years preserved the antiquities in Palmyra Syria.) Despite the neutralization of Malaki for a more moderate Prime Minister Haider el-Abadi in 2014, Sunnis, Kurds, Shiites, Iranian influence, and various sectarian lines make it problematic in my view that any central government can now govern effectively, at least not for some time.

In late 2015, having pulled all troops out of Iraq, the current Administration now has over 3500 stationed back in Iraq, in a reported advisory or training role supporting the fight against ISIS. Iran's IRGC and militias, Iranian-backed Hezbollah fighters from Lebanon, the Kurdish Peshmerga forces, and airstrikes from Egypt are also contributing to the fight behind the fragile Iraqi army. Abadi says he not getting enough U.S. support.

U.S. intelligence was once again surprised by the stand-up of a joint Iraq-Iran-Russia-and Syrian joint intelligence center in Baghdad in September 2015 representing a clear and foreboding picture of the new alignment of countries in the region.

Once ISIS is neutralized, which will take some time, there may yet be hope for an inclusive Iraq with shared leadership, free from dominant Iranian oversight, and an independent Kurdistan in northern Iraq. Prime Minister Abadi has proposed some reforms, with the apparent approval of Iran's leadership, but discrimination and sectarianism against Sunnis are well entrenched. The issue of an independent Kurdistan will come, but only with a nod from Bagdad and Turkey, and with agreement on exactly where the border will be drawn.

Getting Iraq free from the grip of ISIS, and free from Iranian influence, will be a long struggle and last well into the next president's term, and beyond. The more likely long-term outcome for Iraq will see the Iranian militias filling the void in Iraq post-ISIS, heavily influenced by the government in Iran, representing anything but an inclusive government.

Now on to Afghanistan, where we have spent over $2 Trillion; these costs, like those associated with Iraq, do not include the funding that will be needed to reconstitute our force structure, nor the long-term health care required for our veterans, all of which would drive the numbers infinitely higher. We have seen about 3,500 allied troops killed of which almost 2,400 were Americans, and close to 20,000 wounded, a loss beyond any cost.

Combat operations officially ended in Afghanistan on 31 December 2014, when the International Security Assistance Force turned over in Kabul, but roughly 13,000 troops remained at the end of 2014, mostly Americans, with a focus on training, advising and assisting the 300,000+ AFGHAN National Security Force (ANSF). The Administration plans were to have all American troops out by the end of 2016, a timeline and goal that was controversial, and just happened to coincide with the end of the second presidential term. Afghanistan, with over a dozen languages spoken and thousands of clans and villages and rampant opium cultivation and addiction, is difficult for any central governance model to be effective.

Despite threats of Taliban violence, voting for Karzai's successor in 2014 went relatively well and the two contenders, Ashraf Ghani, and Abdullah Abdullah ultimately agreed to share power. Amid all the challenges, much has been accomplished since the Taliban ruled. Especially worth noting: child mortality has been cut in half and maternal mortality by 80%, access to health care has expanded by 60%, and three million girls and five million boys are enrolled in school, a figure that was less than one million under Taliban rule.[122]

Yet, significant challenges remain, starting with Taliban advances back into the country in the north, the beginnings of ISIS emergence, corruption, poverty, addiction, and a fragile economic system heavily reliant on billions annually in U.S. aid. How Afghanistan progresses will depend on many variables to include the continued cooperative power-sharing agreement between Ghani and Abdullah, how the ANSF progresses, and Pakistan's continued crackdown on the Pakistan Taliban (TPP) terrorists that began in late 2014 following the school bombing. Ashraf Ghani has invested significant political good will in improved relations with Pakistan and its Prime Minister, Nawaz Sharif, in hopes that the Pakistani army will also continue its crackdown on the Afghan Taliban and Haqqani networks that focus their attacks inside Afghanistan.

The goal is continued pressure on the Afghan Taliban to enter peace talks with the government in Kabul, something talked about but not yet begun. With Taliban leaders divided on negotiations, and the acknowledgment in July 2015 that long time Taliban leader Mohammad Omar had died back in 2013, these talks have a long and uncertain road ahead. The 10 August 2015 attack on Kabul International Airport by Taliban forces sparked President Ghani to rebuke Pakistan for harboring the terrorist group, straining relations. The ANSF and Taliban have been fighting in and around the large northern city of Kunduz for over a year, with control going back and forth.

Since mid-2013, the Taliban has reclaimed much of the territory it formerly held. Although the current Administration had previously announced a hard timeline for combat troops to be out by the end of 2016, there remains a strong argument to maintain a continued presence at several key bases, such as Kandahar and Bagram, to avoid the vacuum and resultant chaos that we created in our hasty departure from Iraq.

In March 2015, the Administration announced that the U.S. would slow withdrawals at the request of President Ghani, and retain 9,800 troops in Afghanistan through the end of 2015. In October 2015, the President announced that 5,500 troops would remain through 2016, reversing previous policy on a complete withdrawal by the end of 2016. Although we don't know the specifics, this was probably again based on a request by the Afghan leader and comes after renewed advances by the Taliban.

In my view the troop strength should have stayed at a minimum of 9,800; the 5,500 figure generally attributed to the retiring Joint Chiefs of Staff (JCS) Chairman, is insufficient and sends a mixed signal. As many have said before, diplomacy usually follows events on the ground. Continued U.S. presence and aid will hopefully allow the ANSF to mature into a real fighting force, the Ghani-Abdullah government to take firm hold, and allow for the continued possibility of some political accommodation with the Afghan Taliban.

The Taliban is closely watching the U.S. commitment, and it would be a shame to make the same mistake again in Afghanistan, as we clearly made in Iraq and lose the gains this country has made over the past decade.

Former Secretary of State Colin Powell said to President Bush before the Iraq invasion, words to the effect that "If you break it you are going to own it." We did, and we now have an obligation as a nation to see Afghanistan through to a successful transition. Pakistan's involvement and sustained pressure on the Afghan Taliban will be critical to any ultimate success as well. In the long-term, it is Pakistan's best interests to have a secure and stable Afghanistan on their mutual long border. America also has an obligation to re-settle many Iraqi and Afghan citizens (and families) who supported us throughout these conflicts, and whose lives may now be in danger, just as did following Vietnam.

Now to Syria, which as everyone knows is simply a mess, period. Much as he did with Putin, President Obama offered the olive branch to Syria after being elected, and the results are self-evident. One of the risks of being in a leadership position is that everything you say is on record, and can be played back. And so it is with Secretary of State Clinton who in 2011 argued against intervention stating of President Bashar al-Assad: *"Many.... Believe he's a reformer,"* and later predicted that Russia would back a transition plan, which may actually now be in play once the ground conditions are favorable to Putin. None of our early foreign policy approaches in Syria worked and our political miscalculations have proven costly in terms of lost lives as well as America's standing in the world.

Recall the President's famous Red Line to al-Assad in 2012, which was quickly discredited when Assad subsequently used chemical weapons, killing an estimated 1,400 of his citizens. The Syrian fatality count is now over 250,000 and growing, with escalating desperation, hunger and massive dislocation occurring; an estimated 11 million people have been displaced and millions have fled to other countries.

Russia is supporting Assad and the Iranian-backed Hezbollah leader in Lebanon, Hasan Nasrallah, has sent thousands to enter the fighting. The rebels are supported by Saudi Arabia and various Sunni Gulf states. ISIS, with headquarters in Syria, is now fully engaged as the border between Syria and Iraq becomes more porous each day; it controls about a third of Syria's territory.

The Syrian war is impacting all its neighbors; over one million refugees have pushed Lebanon to a breaking point and exacerbated Sunni – Shiite relationships. [123] Lebanese limited support for the war effort against Assad has heightened violence by militants against Lebanon's police forces. Many believe that the U.S. should have supported moderate rebels, such as the Free Syrian Army (FSA), long ago, a move that would have been applauded by our Sunni friends in the region and probably led to the early ouster of Assad.

In September 2014, the U.S. began bombing missions against ISIS in Syria, indirectly helping Assad by inflicting damage on ISIS jihadists fighting the Syrian dictator. Another example of making common cause with the enemy is Iran's IRGC now fighting against our common enemy, ISIS, in Iraq.

By August of 2015, a coalition of Turkey, Saudi Arabia, and Qatar was also heavily engaged in defeating Assad. Then, in late September 2015 the Russians entered the conflict in support of Assad, but bombing the moderate rebels and not ISIS, and further complicating the landscape. We already discussed Putin's motives, so the important question is what the U.S. should do now, having missed the chance to remove Assad long ago. (By the way, does anyone think that Reagan, having put down a red line, would have walked away?) Now we have a raging civil war and a European refugee crisis of epic proportions, as witnessed on news highlights all around the world.

So it is a mess, and probably changed further by the time this book goes to print. Nevertheless, in late 2015, here's a short list of what I think we should consider, drawn from many sources: Institute with our allies no-fly zones and safe havens with the will to enforce them for humanitarian and security reasons; continue to arm the Syrian Kurds (known as the YPG) despite their ties to the radical KPP (which angers Turkey but is necessary to fight ISIS); arm moderate rebels and the FSA (we know what they need and it should not require congressional authorization); continue to bring the fight to ISIS as we have been doing with a broad coalition and by going after their sophisticated financing and recruiting apparatus. Much of this is in progress. If Russia sends in ground combat troops, we have another serious escalation.

It is hard to see a clear end-game in these countries, with the possible acknowledgment that a post-al-Assad Syria is inevitable at some point in the not too distant future; what that looks like is entirely unclear. Any accommodation to Assad's continued leadership would drive more disenfranchised Sunnis toward radical groups. The border between Syria and Iraq, opaque now, will become virtually indistinguishable once the regime changes. What takes its place remains to be seen, possibly the emergence of the al-Qaeda affiliate al-Nusra, who some see as a lesser of bad choices, but clearly not the moderate solution we want. For now, the best course for the U.S. is to continue coalition building to fight ISIS, freeze the troop drawdown in Afghanistan at 9,800, support Iraqi PM Abadi and his reforms, and arm the Kurds and who are desperate for weapons and have the proven ability to fight ISIS.

We may yet achieve a negotiated settlement in Syria, and there was momentum for negotiations to begin in early 2016, followed by a monitored cease-fire. On his way out Assad may yet escape what he should get, which is a date with the ICC at The Hague in the Netherlands. We have a long way to go in Syria, before that.

The next President will not inherit a safe and secure Middle East, free of U.S. involvement – far from it.

Saudi Arabia and the Gulf Cooperative Council (GCC), Egypt, Jordan, and Turkey

All of these countries are, to one degree or another, our allies in the region and maintaining close relations is critical as the dynamics of the Middle East change over ISIS and Iran's support for terrorists.

Saudi Arabia and five other countries (Bahrain, Oman, Qatar, UAE and Kuwait) formed the GCC in 1981. All except Bahrain are Sunni majorities, Muslim, enforce Sharia law to various extents, have authoritative monarchs and prescribed dress codes, with Kuwait being the most open and moderate of the nations.

Saudi Arabia, our longtime ally in the Middle East, was largely unaffected by the Arab Spring that saw governments toppled in Libya and Egypt and started the unrest that led to the ongoing violent civil war in Syria.

The U.S. decision not to support the moderate rebels in Syria caused a serious strain in U.S.-Saudi relations, as did the Administration's decision to negotiate with Iran on the latter's nuclear weapons program, which the Saudi government ultimately expressed support for, however grudgingly.

There are rules within the House of Saud that govern succession to the crown. Following the death in January 2015 of King Abdullah, Crown Prince Salman became King and the first grandson of Ibn Saud, Prince Muqrin, became the Crown Prince and next in line to the throne. Then in late August 2015 King Salman, now 79, replaced Prince Muqrin with Interior Minister Prince Mohammed bin Nayef, making Nayef next in line to the throne, and made his son (Prince Mohammed bin Salman, age 30), Nayef's deputy. There have been many reports of discord between Prince Nayef and his deputy ever since.

Differences among GCC members on Iran, Egypt and especially Syria, have divided the countries. Saudi Arabia has branded the Muslim Brotherhood a terrorist organization and is active in curtailing the influence of al-Qaeda and jihadists in the region. Qatar, which caused a rift by supporting the Muslim Brotherhood following the Arab Spring, has now joined Egypt, UAE and Saudi Arabia's decision to label the Brotherhood a terrorist organization, although Qatar continues to support radical Islamists in Libya, but in turn is fighting ISIS. Kuwait, while denying any official support to terrorist groups, has many private groups and wealthy Kuwaitis that provide funding to al-Qaeda elements fighting in Syria.

Jordan, not a GCC member but which shares a border with Syria, is cracking down on terrorists and hardline Islamists fighting in Syria. It began bombing ISIS following the 5-day starvation and then barbaric murder by fire of a captured Jordanian pilot in a cage, which was broadcast worldwide in early February 2015. Jordan is a constitutional monarchy, and King Abdullah II one of the most influential and respected leaders in the Arab world.

Our relationship with Saudi Arabia is long-standing and of strategic importance. Many complain of their human rights violations and limited rights for women. All legitimate issues that the House of Saud must deal with to address potential unrest, particularly with almost half of the population under 30. The issues now are less about oil and more about stability in the region.

Some Arab states are even beginning to reach out to Israel as they see a common enemy in Iran. Iran's aggressive backing of the Houthis in Yemen has caused the Saudis to take an increased leadership role in the region, which began with air strikes against the Houthis in late March 2015. Egypt, Turkey, and Pakistan, all large Sunni countries, are working through past and current differences as the landscape continuously changes.

One unanswered question is, with the recent Iranian accord over that country's nuclear weapons program, can we expect that other Gulf countries, led by Saudi Arabia, will pursue equal capability over time. Missile tests conducted by Iran in October 2015, which violated an existing UN Security Council resolution, suggest a greater arms race in the region. Another danger is that the fighting in Yemen between the Saudi coalition and the Iran-backed Houthi rebels will eventually become a Sunni-Shia battleground for a protracted civil war that could expand the conflict even further.

Saudi Arabia, Egypt, and Qatar all expanded their troops on the ground in Yemen in September 2015. Although the Saudi-backed fighters have made some gains, this might all change once Iran is released from sanctions and has billions more to spend on terrorist activities. A decade ago, King Abdullah II of Jordan warned us that by ousting Saddam Hussein the U.S. would create a "Shia Crescent" led by Iran. Warnings that were largely dismissed then, but now look prophetic.[124]

The U.S.–Egyptian relationship has seen many ups and downs over the years, but this relationship is also a critical one for our foreign policy in the region. Anwar Sadat, who ruled from 1970 to 1981, was pivotal to the Egyptian-Israeli peace accord at Camp David in 1979. After his assassination, certainly as a result of that accord, Hosni Mubarak was President until the 2011 revolution when Muslim Brotherhood candidate Mohamed Morsi was elected. In 2013, Morsi was ousted by General Abdel Fattah al-Sisi, in what many called a military coup, but which language the U.S. avoided since it would impact arms sales and aid. Although the relationship is strained, the U.S. continues to send aid to Egypt, $1.3 billion in 2015, and in March of 2015 released the sale of missiles, tanks and aircraft that had been previously frozen. While we continue to emphasize Human Rights concerns with President al-Sisi, the resumption of military aid to Egypt is a good decision for this critically important ally. Egypt has entered the fight against ISIS, which is July 2015 launched a missile attack on an Egyptian naval ship.

Besides fighting ISIS, Egypt can assume a key role in rebuilding Gaza and weakening Hamas (the Muslim Brotherhood affiliate). Such efforts might bring some stability to the Israeli-Hamas conflict, which will only get worse without an approach that includes reconstruction from the war, disarming the Hamas militants, and neutralizing Iranian militias in the Gaza Strip. As with most of the Arab countries, Egypt's economy is fragile, with unemployment running well over 10%.

Turkey, with the election of President Recep Erdogan to a third term, once seemed on the road to one-party rule with a focus much like Putin's, to reestablish the vision of a powerful Ottoman empire with primacy over the Sunni nations. That perspective helps explain Erdogan's anger that the U.S. was only attacking ISIS in Syria and not Assad, and resulted in his initial denial of usage of the air base at Incirlik to facilitate attacking ISIS, and his not engaging his own forces in the ISIS fight. Erdogan has long-standing internal problems with the Kurdistan Worker's Party (PKK), which the U.S. also labels a terrorist group. In July 2015, prompted by Assad forces defeats and ISIS western expansion, the U.S. and Turkey finally reached an agreement whereby NATO (of which Turkey is a member) could use the airbase at Incirlik for continued airstrikes against ISIS. This was part of a larger arrangement to establish a safe zone along the 60-mile Syrian-Turkish border that used to be an unimpeded ISIS supply line, and is to be turned over to moderate Syrian rebels. On 4 August 2015, the Pentagon announced that the U.S. had begun flying missions over Syria from Turkey. Shortly after entering the fight against ISIS, however, Erdogan also began bombing the PKK Kurds, an unfortunate political move designed to marginalize the Kurds, and effectively ended the ongoing peace negotiations. Kurdish retaliation was swift.

On the political front, Turkey held parliamentary elections on 7 June 2015 with very high voter turnout, and Erdogan's AKP party was denied the 50% majority that would have allowed him to rewrite the constitution and consolidate his powers as president. This vote was an amazing tilt toward democratic rule and against the authoritarian aspirations of President Erdogan. Before elections, Erdogan had reached out to the Kurdish population, which may have generated the Kurdish turnout for the pro-Kurdish HDP Party, with direct ties to the PKK, which achieved 13% of the vote. Erdogan had 45 days to form a coalition government or call for new elections, choosing the latter. Then on October 10th a couple of bombs detonated at an HDP rally in Ankara, killing about 100 and wounding close to 250 others. The bombings were thought to be ISIS related, possibly to inflame the Turkish government and KPP conflict. The ensuring elections took place a few weeks later on 1 November and, to the surprise of many, Erdogan's AKP party achieved the 50% majority vote, sending a signal that the voters were more interested in the economy and security, than Erdogan's ambitious and authoritarian agenda.

So Erdogan and Turkey has now entered the fight against ISIS, is battling Kurdish factions everywhere which weakens the ISIS battle, has threatened not to join the EU, supports Hamas and the Muslim Brotherhood, and is sometimes aligned with the al-Qaeda affiliate that is fighting Assad (Jabhat al-Nursa). The Turkish economy, like so many others dependent on oil revenues, is expanding but shaky. Erdogan's ongoing struggle with the PKK complicates any future resolution of the Kurdish situation. With the downing of the Russia Su-24 bomber over Turkish airspace in November 2015, Russia has imposed economic sanctions between the two countries. Although it remains a complex situation right now, Turkey is an important NATO ally, hopefully, a future member of the EU, and critically important to eventual peace in the Middle East.

Iran

As Kissinger was quoted previously, Iran is *the obstacle* to lasting peace and flowing commerce in the Middle East, which is why I have left this discussion toward the chapter end. Along with Sudan and Syria, it is one of only three countries in the world that the Department of State currently lists as sponsors of state terrorism. And, yes, we did just negotiate with them. There are many dynamics at work.

Iran's new president as of 3 August 2013, Hassan Rouhani, appeared a breath of fresh air after eight years of troublesome leadership from his predecessor, Mahmoud Ahmadinejad. Although he negotiated Iran's 2004 voluntary suspension of its nuclear program (since re-started) and is less conservative than his election challengers, his true colors remain in question, and he faces many internal obstacles. Foremost among them is that the Ayatollah Khatami, successor to the Grand Ayatollah Ruhollah Khomeini following his death in 1989, must approve all decisions. The far more conservative Iranian elements, led by Gen. Qassem Suleimani and the IRGC must also be dealt with.

There are other challenges that Iran faces: growing inequality with 40% of Iranians living below the poverty line; inflation once running at 30% is down closer to 17%, but still high, and a rapidly declining birth rate even though the median age is a youthful 28. [125] The economy, which is highly dependent on oil proceeds, shrank by 6.6% in 2012 and another 5.8% in 2013. Finally, although the U.S. helped Iran's goals by favorably disposing of a hostile regime in Iraq, Iran's subsequent and subversive overreaching in Iraq and Syria helped drive disenfranchised radical Sunnis to form ISIS, posing the possible creation of a hostile Sunni state along Iraq's 900-mile border with Iran. [126] In fact, many Sunnis have stated that they joined ISIS only because they believed it posed a lesser threat than Iran. Iran is clearly *the leading state sponsor of terrorism worldwide* and remains hugely repressive of its own people.

In early 2015, when the Iranian-backed Houthi rebels took control of the Yemen government the placards read "Death to Americans, Death to Israel, curses to Jews and victory to Islam." Are we to believe that a dedicated state sponsor of worldwide terrorism that so suppresses its own population would agree to, much less faithfully abide by, any agreement to limit nuclear weapons development? The probable answer is to buy time and to get sanctions lifted to re-start the economic engine, and re-focus on pursuing state-sponsored terrorist activities outside Iran. The world will find out in short order.

Which brings us to the nuclear negotiations themselves, which took place for over a decade in various forms, including a comprehensive proposal from Russia. In November 2013, a Joint Plan of Action (JPOA) was signed at Geneva with the group called P5 +1 (the five permanent members of the UN Security Council plus Germany.) Without being too detailed, the key components of that deal were the following: limited installation and use of centrifuges to halt production of 20% enriched uranium that can be quickly converted to usage in nuclear bombs; stop work on the heavy-water reactor near Arak and convert it to permanent domestic use; frequent inspections, and specific break-out capability. Iran would still be able to pursue nuclear power for domestic use as allowed in the Nuclear NPT, but it baffles me why an oil-rich nation that has the world's 4th largest oil reserves, would need nuclear reactors for domestic purposes. Really? In exchange for continued dialogue, Iran gained access to $4.2B in frozen overseas assets and easing of some trade restrictions; another $2.8B was unfrozen based on the 4-month extension of talks, which ran from July–November 2014.

In April 2015 in Lausanne, Switzerland both sides agreed to the parameters defining how a deal could be reached and a deadline for a resolution of June 30, 2015. In the week before this deadline Iran's Ayatollah Khamenei threw two new roadblocks into the negotiations by insisting on no inspections of military sites and accelerated lifting of sanctions. Inspections of facilities by the International Atomic Energy Agency (IAEA) remained the toughest issue throughout the negotiations. Another obstacle was a proposed Senate Bill, with significant democratic support, that would have increased sanctions if progress were not made on negotiations; it was vigorously opposed at the time by the Administration as being counter-productive to the ongoing talks. Then there was the much-reported address to Congress by Israeli Prime Minister Netanyahu in March of 2015, during which he warned of the dangers of the impending accord. Specifically, if rumors were correct, would involve a sunset clause on Iran's prohibition to build nuclear weapons, and create a window of time (notionally a one-year break-out time) when resumed efforts could be detected and known to the world community. To Netanyahu and many others, this simply codified the inevitable that once the timeline expired, if not before, Iran would have a nuclear weapon with delivery capability.

However, none of the details of the actual negotiations were officially announced while in the process. As I heard Senator Kelly Ayotte (R–NH) and others espouse prospectively, a good deal would have been one where Iran ended its nuclear and ballistic programs, ceased state-sponsored terrorism, and recognized Israel's right to exist, all before the lifting of sanctions. Of course, that's not what we got.

In July 2015, the deal with Iran and the P5+1 was concluded, and it followed closely along the lines of the JPOA that was agreed to in Geneva. Again, without too many specifics, it reduces the stockpile of low-enriched enriched uranium from 10,000 to 300 kilograms and reduces the number of centrifuges that produce enriched uranium for 15 years. The enrichment site and heavy-water reactor plant will be re-purposed and the IAEA will be permitted inspections with 24 days of advance notice. A UN embargo on arms sales will be lifted within five years and on ballistic missile sales within eight years (Iran's Hahab-series nuclear-capable missiles, which already range to 1200 miles, could one day be capable of reaching the U.S.). And finally, there are automatic provisions for sanctions to snap back in the place for violations which need not be voted on by the P5+1. The break-out time, meaning the time that Iran could reconstitute the program that it has denied having, and build a bomb, is one year. In exchange, sanctions are gradually lifted based on compliance protocols, but initially Iran will get around $140 billion in frozen assets.

Critics of the deal were quick to point out that the inspection regime was insufficient (not anytime, anywhere). That the deal did not include the release of American citizens held in Iran. That the deal was not tied to Iran's increased terrorist activities in any way. That snap back sanctions would never work, and that the $140B to be released would likely be used to bolster the terrorist activities of the IPRG. Critics included both Republicans and some skeptical Democrats, who felt the deal would quickly precipitate a nuclear arms race in the Middle East. The Administration argued, not altogether incorrectly, that sanctions were already fractured, that Iran was already perilously close to the nuclear bomb it denied pursuing, with enhanced centrifuges and a heavy-water reactor being built, had the long-range delivery capability, and that negotiations presented the best hope of opening up a better dialogue with the West. Additionally, although there are sunset clauses on some parts of the agreement, the express intent of Iran's nuclear program is to remain peaceful. Issues such as hostages and IPRG sponsored terrorist activities supporting the Houthi rebels in Yemen, Assad in Syria, and Hezbollah in Lebanon apparently had to wait in order to focus on the nuclear aspects of the deal.

Once negotiated, the U.S. Congress had little option, and there was no real alternative at that point. Either we walked away from the P5+1 or accepted the deal as presented. Presumably, we should have negotiated a better result. The lifting of the sanctions on Qassem Suleimani, head of the IRGC, is especially shameful, given the great loss of American lives he has caused. The Administration has been strangely silent on the captured journalist

Jason Rezaian, so we can only hope that back-channel negotiations are ongoing.

In May of 2015, Congress overwhelmingly passed the Iran Nuclear Review Act that gave the President the authority to negotiate the terms of the deal and submit them for congressional review, rather than the normal treaty route that requires 2/3 Senate approval. (Sounds a lot like the Fast Track Authority for TPP!) One reason that President Obama created all the fanfare after the announcement was because he knew he had the votes to override a veto, enabling him to declare a foreign policy victory in the end.

The President's linking of those in Congress who opposed the deal, including democratic Senator Chuck Schumer, to the Iranian hardliners was in exceptionally poor taste. In August 2015, the six GCC countries all acquiesced and endorsed the accord in exchange for accelerated arms sales, more intelligence-sharing and increased humanitarian aid. Game over. If Iran adheres to the deal, and that's a big IF, it will be 15 years and possibly longer before it fields a nuclear weapon.

In December 2015, the International Atomic Energy Agency completed its investigation of Iran's nuclear weapons program, concluding that the program substantially ended in 2009, and clearing the way for the deal to move forward. Not to be outdone, in October 2015 Iran conducted multiple ballistic missile tests that were not authorized, generating a call for increased sanctions from both democrats and republicans, even as sanctions were being relaxed as part of the deal negotiated. Next Saudi executed 47, including four Shiite Muslims and a cleric, actions that resulted in the Saudi Embassy in Tehran being burned, and a break in diplomatic ties between the two countries in January 2016.

Iran is in an interesting country. For years the economy has been sagging, radical Sunnis are a growing threat, funding to support Hezbollah in Lebanon and Assad in Syria have been a drain on resources, and the impact of sanctions and declining oil prices all converged to pressure Iran to come to the negotiating table. The nuclear deal that was reached allowed Iran to preserve its dignity although, as former Secretaries of State Kissinger and Schultz argued during the negotiations, the agreement appears to 'concede to Iran the very capability that we are trying to prevent'. In fact, Iran's President Hassan Rouhani stated bluntly afterward that the deal met "all of our objectives," so it remains to be seen how much reform Rouhani will, or can, accomplish.

Now that the deal is complete, how this ultimately plays out is up to Iran. It is more probable than not that Iran, rather than assuming a responsible role in the Middle East as a strong Shia state, will pursue grander ventures of reestablishing the old Persian Empire, to include the ancient capital of Babylon which now resides in Iraq.[127] As we know, the IPRG is heavily engaged in Iraq now, fighting ISIS, as well as supporting Assad in Syria, Hezbollah in Lebanon, and the Houthi rebels in Yemen. Relations with Hamas are strained as (the Sunni) Hamas supported the rebels fighting Assad, and ties with Saudi Arabia now severed

This deal will be a centerpiece of the Obama Foreign Policy legacy. The Economist magazine has stated that the success of this deal will depend on the next U.S. president and Iran. I agree only in part, because whoever the next president is will certainly honor the agreement. I rather think it will depend mostly on Iran, who most believe will cheat on the nuclear program and continue to spread terrorism. It might also depend on how other Gulf nations behave. If any pursue nuclear capability, Iran will likely see this as a constructive change to the agreement and re-start the program. At a minimum I think we will see an escalated arms race in the Gulf area; equally likely - Iran will test the agreement, requiring swift response from the P5+1. As a strong America remains engaged in the Middle East, let's hope that Iran's behavior surprises us all.

Canada, South and Central America

Our neighbors that we haven't necessarily always treated as neighbors. Canada is irked on several fronts, notably dragging our feet on the Keystone XL Pipeline and mixed signals on any renegotiation of the 1961 Treaty on the Columbia River, among others. Although the current president has vetoed the pipeline, it will likely survive this Administration and may eventually see passage someday, if the TransCanada Corporation and Canada remain interested.

Several governments (Venezuela, and Ecuador) openly oppose the U.S., Brazil has been problematic ever since the Snowden leaks and Mexico feels slighted, even before the insults hurled by Donald Trump.

Just as we were slow to see the rise of China while bogged down in the Middle East, we are neglecting our neighbors' north and south. China on the other hand, and Russia to a lesser extent, have been engaged globally while the U.S. has been pivoting in apparent circles.

Venezuela should remain a focus for the U.S. for any number of reasons, Among them is that the country is a conduit for illegal narcotics globally, has the largest oil reserves in the world (larger than Saudi Arabia; CITCO is 100% owned by the Venezuelan government and the U.S., when oil prices were higher, pumped $70M a day to the Venezuelan dictator via CITCO). And it is a clear human rights violator. Venezuela, with recent encouraging elections, may be turning a corner – let's hope.

Mexico, although making slow progress, remains arguably a drug state with manifest government corruption and infrastructure neglect, and needs our continued support.

In all, the Americas need to be a discernible focus of our foreign policy, far beyond the effort we now exhibit while consumed with the Middle East, Russia, and China.

THE TERRORIST THREAT

While not confined to one geographic region, it is a major factor in U.S. Foreign Policy decisions. In fact, nothing has guided our foreign policy for the past 15 years more than the terrorist threat to our homeland. Yet very few understand the nature or magnitude of the terrorist network.

When our President tells us on the campaign trail that al-Qaeda is "decimated" and "on the run," (or the previous president stating, "mission accomplished") how do we explain the increasing threat and spread of terrorism worldwide? Does anyone remember the Paris attacks in January 2015? A recurrence just happened on 14 November 2015. The terminology is confusing. How do you define al-Qaeda or its affiliates? The original al-Qaeda organization founded by Osama bin Laden is now largely dysfunctional. Al-Qaeda in the Arabian Gulf (AQAP), al-Shabib in Somalia, and al-Qaeda in the Islamic Maghreb in Algeria, in Nigeria, and the Taliban in Pakistan are all basically affiliated. (Refer back to the Introduction to The Greater Middle East sections for some definitions.)

The picture became even more confusing in 2014 when al-Qaeda cut ties with the ultra-radical ISIS in Iraq, and the al-Qaeda affiliate in Lebanon (the Abdallah Azzam Brigades) launched attacks against the Iran-backed Shi'a Islamic terror group Hezbollah after the latter sent troops to fight alongside Syrian

President Assad against the primarily Sunni rebels. In early 2014 the President modified his previous statements saying that "Islamists were undermining the global, national security," and by inference, the national security of the U.S., one of his criteria for limited engagement.[128]

Even if you believe that we are midway through a 50-60-year movement as some, including former CIA director Michael Hayden, have opined, there is more we should be doing now, short of combat troops on the ground.

We covered the jihadist and ISIS movements in the Defense chapter and again throughout this chapter. Just look at the report card: Syria is decimated by civil war and facing regime change and Iraq is in civil war and fighting ISIS. Neither country will be the same, and the borders are almost gone now. Afghanistan is trying to stabilize under new leadership and an imminent U.S. drawdown of troops, and a problematic Taliban resurgence that is resisting peace talks. Libya is now close to a failed state with hardline and more moderate factions controlling different areas of the country (the more radical Islamists in Tripoli backed by Qatar and Turkey and the more secular government in the East backed by UAE and Egypt) making assistance very difficult. In Yemen the pro -U.S. government has been ousted by the Houthi rebels, with sponsorship from Iran.

All in all, a terribly complex landscape. Our first priority is seeing that ISIS is defeated, and the coalition is growing with Jordan, Turkey, Egypt, Iraq and even Pakistan joining in the fight against these violent jihadists. But some of our friends in the rich Gulf States continue to funnel large sums of money to the jihadist movement, something we have known for many years, yet never adequately addressed. There are some glimmers of good news, despite the downward spirals in Yemen, Libya and elsewhere. ISIS appears to be losing strength and is experiencing internal dissension. Tunisia has emerged from the Arab Spring as a democracy with an elected President, Beji Caid Essebsi, whose party ousted the Islamist leadership. The election of Joko Widodo (Jokowi) in Indonesia and Maithripala Sirisena in Sri Lanka are also positive signs for these largely Muslim countries.

One controversial issue for Americans, and many will feel uncomforatble with this conversation, is the need to energize the silent-majority of Muslims, particularly those that reside in the U.S. We need them to challenge groups like the controversial Council on American-Islamic Relations (CAIR), which promotes (some would say incites) activism among Muslims, refuses to denounce Hamas or Hezbollah, and which has been labeled a terrorist organization by the UAE. Various studies have concluded that between 15-25% of the world's 1.2 billion Muslims are radicalized, and 80% peaceful. Yet we hear far too little from the 80% silent-majority, who should be condemning Islamic jihad and terrorism. Estimates are that there are 3-7 million Muslims living in the U.S. and, using that same twenty percentages, would suggest that at least 600,000 are sympathetic to the more radical elements. It is probably inappropriate and inaccurate to suggest that these percentages extrapolate even approximately, but it still raises the question, emphatically, as to why the large majority of peaceful Muslim Americans do not stand up and be more vocal? Some few do, but not enough, maybe out of fear of the attention it would draw.

The Russian, Chinese, German and Japanese people were largely peaceful, while their governments slaughtered millions. History has taught us over again what a lack of moral clarity, that silent-majority, and appeasement will engender. Ultimately, this is an internal conflict for the soul of Islam, and thus can only be solved by Muslims, who largely and vocally reject the terrorist atrocities carried out in the name of Islam, and overtly challenge the legitimacy of jihad. The silent Muslim majority, especially in the U.S., needs to be more proactive and outspoken in condemning the radical elements of jihad and ensuring that what is taught in the schools and mosques is appropriate. I don't think that this is asking too much. I am a fan of M. Zuhdi Jasser, M.D., founder of the American Islamic Forum for Democracy (AIFD), who is seeking to counter the radical jihad ideology and instill American values. He is a vocal advocate and devout Muslim; we need more like him.

FOREIGN POLICY SUMMARY

For the better part of eight years, we've had a foreign policy of restraint with an Administration that had vowed to close Guantanamo Bay prison (with which I agree), and end our involvement in Iraq and Afghanistan, which is in progress and poorly executed. In our hasty retreat, we managed to basically double the national debt from $9 to over 19 Trillion dollars. The U.S. is no longer seen as an effective global leader for good; primacy and the ability to influence world events is in decline.

Because of our preoccupation with the Middle East we largely missed the rapid rise of China, lost opportunities to make a deal with Mexico on immigration, and lost sight of Putin and his expansionist aims. Into the void has come 'Putinism,' Chinese overreach, a worldwide decline of democracy, persecution of Christians, and the rise of the Islamic State (ISIS) and radical jihad with its powerful recruiting machine.

As one writer described this policy of restraint, "the world senses it, our friends from Israel to Poland to Taiwan – fear it; our enemies are counting on it."[129] The Economist has called it "The decline of deterrence."[130]

Just as Churchill and Roosevelt abandoned Poland to the Soviet Union following WWII, we failed to support the moderate secular rebels fighting Assad when asked for help, and missed the opportunity to oust the dictator. Just as we also did when initially asked to support drone strikes against ISIS, and as we are doing now by our tepid support to the Ukrainian President and the Syrian Kurds.[131]

Basically, however, the American people got what they asked for in a retreat from the global stage and Middle East conflicts. Complacency, however, is the enemy. I think that most would argue that, as a nation, our security is more at risk today than in 2008, and our rising debt an impending storm that threatens the future generations of Americans. Add to this assessment a dysfunctional Congress and we have a grim outlook unless an enlightened new leader emerges on the scene.

What I hope to see in the next president in a policy of active engagement, military restraint, and advocacy. I reject the 'so-called' Kissinger notion that America has peaked and is in decline. (I am not sure that Kissinger would approve of that broad paintbrush portrayal, but he might agree that we'd better quickly figure out how we're going to co-exist with China and resolve our own internal problems foremost.) I think rather that our nation is still rising and the shining light of opportunity for millions around the world who want to come here, and millions who are waiting patiently to immigrate legally. Active engagement and advocacy mean taking the lead on world issues, assuring our allies, calling out bad behavior and being a vocal advocate for human rights across the globe, underscored by military restraint.

I agree with the current Administration's goal to reduce our footprint in the Arab world; unfortunately, we did it very badly in Iraq and may yet repeat the mistake in Afghanistan. The U.S. is not going to solve the long-standing Muslim civil war, and nation building among weak governments is likely to be similarly unsuccessful, as we clearly and, unfortunately, saw in Yemen and Libya.

Russia, though nuclear-capable and poorly led, is a short-term but not a long-term threat, in my view. China's emergence as a world power in inevitable and should be respected, with hopes that with this emergence comes responsible behavior, something we are not yet seeing. Both Russia and China face huge growing internal and economic challenges.

As President Reagan taught us, there is peace through strength. We need both military and economic strength to restore our role of primacy in the world. We need to defeat ISIS and stay in Afghanistan with limited, but sufficient presence (read 9,800 troops), to ensure the stability of the Ghani government that may yet lead to eventual peace talks with the Taliban. Truman, a Democratic president, left stabilizing troops in Japan, Germany, and South Korea, all now important U.S. allies.

We need to reassure our longtime allies in the Middle East, Saudi Arabia and the GCC who fear a stronger, more assertive Iran now that sanctions are being lifted, and who see U.S. power and influence in decline. We need to send weapons to back both the (Syrian) Kurds and to Ukraine. Simply stated, we need to stay engaged, even if not with large scale combat forces on the ground.

We need a coherent foreign policy that supports and assures our allies and neighbors, reinforces our treaties obligations, enables strong coalitions in Asia, Europe, and the Middle East, and sets clear expectations for international norms of acceptable behavior. It would help if we appointed Ambassadors of stature who understand the culture and speak the language, something the current Administration has a terrible track record doing. Caroline Kennedy, the U.S. Ambassador to our important ally Japan, is a shining example of how we can do this right.

As a nation, we need the willpower to impose sanctions when necessary and adapt quickly to changing political and geographic challenges. There is always risk in taking action; there is sometimes greater risk in doing nothing.

Importantly, we need a strong Commander-in-Chief who commands respect, at home and abroad, with the leverage that only a strong and growing economy and enlightened diplomacy can assure. We hope to see all that in the next president. We have all witnessed vividly what results from a foreign policy vacuum.

As stated so well by Richard Williamson, the late, highly distinguished, public servant and former Ambassador to the UN Commission on Human Rights: *"America's foreign policy must be pragmatic, practical and proportional; grounded in reality and calibrated to constantly changing facts on the ground. But principles matter. They remind us who we are. They help us see a better world to which we should aspire. And a world of advancing freedom, the rule of law and in which human rights are respected, is a safer and more secure world for America."*

CHAPTER 5

IMMIGRATION

"By the end of my first term in office I will pass comprehensive immigration reform."

--Barack Obama 2008

He didn't even try!

Immigration reform is one of those issues that demonstrates the absolute hypocrisy that embodies Washington and seems to perpetuate the absolute worst of partisanship. President George Bush pushed immigration reform back in 2006 and delivered a national address on the issue. In 2005, Senators McCain (a long-standing leader in this effort) and Kennedy (another great statesman and advocate) pushed legislation. In 2007 it was Senators Kyl and Kennedy with the same results. Enough Republicans rejected reform on the grounds of amnesty and border security, and enough Democrats on grounds of protecting American workers, to defeat any legislation.

Which still leaves unanswered why President Obama failed to initiate reforms until six years into his presidency when he no longer controlled either House of Congress; he could have done it in 2008 as he promised he would. The official answer would likely be that there were other urgent matters of state; the cynic in me thinks it was, and remains, nothing but maneuvering for pure political advantage.

This issue is increasingly polarizing the country, and should have been addressed a long time ago. Most Americans (but not all) agree in concept on what needs to be done, as do most lawmakers. The precepts of a new immigration law should be relatively simple in my view: secure the borders first and foremost, and enforce visa overstays . Require English as the national language. Issue tamper-resistant National ID cards. Provide the American-Dreamers (children of illegal immigrants who came to the U.S. and have grown up here) and the other 10+ million here illegally a path to either a guest-worker permit or permanent residency (e.g. Green Card), and a normal path to citizenship (five years afterward an immigrant can begin the process of becoming a citizen). Give first priority to those who are waiting legally to enter. Ensure our immigration policies reflect more ethnically diverse representation. Expand guest-worker permits for skilled high-tech workers and highly educated college graduates and, finally, strengthen employer penalties for violations. Forget back taxes as some have suggested. Immigration reform should also revisit the family reunification and Central American child relocations provisions.

This formula won't please everyone, but it is fair and just. It will go a long way toward enhancing the security of our homeland, which is increasingly at risk, and welcome our new citizens to the greatest country in the world. We should stop using the pejorative term alien in favor of illegal immigrants. We should also accept the premise that we, as Americans, by our inattention and lax enforcement, particularly of the employer enforcement provisions of existing legislation, allowed the current situation—the 11+ million now in the U.S. illegally—to occur. So it is now time, well past time to address the issue as a matter of national priority and security.

Here is a bit of history on immigration to our great country that will help put the discussion in context:

We are, of course, mostly a country of immigrants. Beginning with settlers from England at Jamestown in 1607 and Plymouth in 1620, followed by the Spanish in Florida and Texas and French on the Gulf Coast. The first Dutch ship carrying slaves arrived in 1619 at Jamestown. The various influx of other European and Asian nationalities arrived and settled over the years. The Statute of Liberty, dedicated by France in 1886, is inscribed on the pedestal with the words, "Give me your tired, your poor, your huddled masses yearning to breathe free." A few years later, in 1892, the Ellis Island Immigration Station opened, through which millions of immigrants passed. The first real immigration bill called the 'Quota Law' and that included annual quotas on immigration, was passed in 1921. Another dozen laws dealing with various issues to include ceilings, refugees, family reunification, and preferences were enacted up until 1986, including the Immigration and Nationality Act of 1952 which became the basic immigration law for many years. The Immigration and Naturalization Act of 1965 was significant in that it dropped national quotas and instituted a family reunification provision. Since enacted in 1965, one naturalized or American born citizen can sponsor many relatives and the percent of the U.S. population born outside the U.S. has tripled in the intervening 50 years.[132] So when you hear so many saying that we need comprehensive immigration reform, be reminded that we've had over a dozen immigration reform acts in the past century.

The comprehensive, and bipartisan, Immigration Reform and Control Act (IRCA), sometimes referred to as the Simpson-Mazzoli Act, was passed in 1986 and signed by President Reagan, whose major features were to legalize immigrants (amnesty for about three million) who had lived in the U.S. since 1982 (including an estimated 125,000 Cubans who entered following the 1980 Refugee Act). It established employer sanctions against hiring illegal immigrants, created a 7-year agricultural worker program, but failed to address a workable non-immigrant visa program for unskilled workers. The final version of the bill watered down employer sanctions, at the request of businesses, requiring only a reasonable paper check on workers. The result is that we now have closer to 12 million illegal immigrants as opposed to the five million when Simpson-Mazzoli was passed. In 1990 and 1996 additional Acts passed Congress addressing various issues of both legal and illegal immigration. As the Chair of the U.S. Commission on Immigration Reform, former Rep. Barbara Jordan stated to Congress in her testimony on 24 Feb. 1995, "Credibility in immigration can be summed up in one sentence: Those who should get in, get in; those who should be kept out, are kept out; and those who should not be here will be required to leave... For the system to be credible, people actually have to be deported at the end of the process."[133]

The 1996 Illegal Immigration Reform and Immigrant Responsibility Act (IIRAIRA) added 5000 border patrol, authorized the 14-mile San Diego fence, expedited judicial review, increased some criminal penalties and required that states phase in, over six years, driver's licenses that were tamperproof, among other provisions. As the then President Clinton said, "We should honor every legal immigrant here, working hard to become a new citizen. But we are also a nation of laws."[134] When Clinton left office in 2000, there were about seven million illegal immigrants in the U.S.

The next major attempt at Immigration Reform was the Comprehensive Immigration Reform Act of 2007, which would have further expanded the border patrol, provided funding for 370 miles of fencing, an expanded guest-worker program and revised visa system for more highly-skilled workers. Several earlier, bipartisan versions of this bill were alternatively sponsored by Senators McCain, Kennedy, Cornyn, Kyl, Specter, and strongly supported by President Bush. Unfortunately, opposition from both the right wing and left wing of *both political parties* finally ended all hopes of passage of these efforts in 2007.

Since 2008, there have been several incremental changes, such as efforts to improve immigrant due process representation and deportation proceedings. One law in 2008, aimed at deterring sex trafficking, requires that Central American children receive temporary relocation and assistance while awaiting deportation proceedings. This law had unintended consequences in 2014 when tens of thousands of unaccompanied children crossed the border illegally, creating a humanitarian crisis and massive relocation throughout the U.S.

GAO estimates that completing the border construction, a part of border security would have cost about $7 billion in 2009, much less than enforcement is costing now. But as elections neared and partisan politics emerged, it became increasingly clear that an all-or-nothing approach would not pass, with some Republicans pressing for a border security first legislation.

Most recent legislative activity occurred in April of 2013 when eight senators referred to as, the Gang of Eight led by Senators Schumer and Rubio, introduced a bipartisan Senate Bill for immigration reform. It passed the Senate by a margin of 68-32 in June of 2013 and included many of the features previously attempted: national employment verification through the Social Security's e-Verify system, increased visas for skilled workers, an expanded temporary work program for lower-skilled workers, and a 13 year path to citizenship for the over 10 million illegal immigrants, and legal status for 1.7 million American-Dreamers.

The largest objection of the House of Representatives majority was the special path to citizenship in the Senate Bill that many Republicans felt was unfair to those who have followed the rules and were waiting in line, and rewarded those who broke the rules. Still, there was apparent room for compromise with Republicans signaling that a possible path for the 10 million (other than the Dreamers whom Republicans also supported for citizenship) to remain legally (if not with citizenship, but without the threat of deportation) if the borders were secured first.

The arguments for comprehensive immigration reform are compelling. The first is the issue of fairness to those who have followed the rules and are waiting for legal immigrant visas, now over 4 million. Next in line are the dreamers who came as children and have grown up here. Third are the other roughly 10 million who came illegally as a means (largely) to find work to support their families, something we would all do in similar economic conditions.

We have failed to enforce our own laws, so we need to now fix the situation we created and implement a path to guest-worker permit or residency and eventual citizenship. When tens of thousands of Central American children flooded the border in 2014 and were relocated, as happened again in late 2015, it was largely through a loophole in our own immigration law that permitted the entry. Expectant mothers from Mexico and China come to America to have their children, who by law are U.S. citizens and can one day sponsor relatives. "Birth tourism" is a thriving U.S. industry.

The second issue is the National Security imperative to secure our borders due to growing threats from terrorists, who could easily penetrate porous borders, and already have to some extent. There is the issue of transnational gang violence and horrendous gang rapes throughout our nation, such as the MS-13 gang, thought to be operating in over 33 states and involved in rapes, drugs, etc. The Custom and Border Patrol (CBP) and Immigration and Customs Enforcement (ICE) have their hands full, and we need more of both. There are several ways for foreigners to enter the country, the most prevalent being on a tourist, student or business visa, or Border Crossing Cards (BCC) that allow entry for short periods of time from Mexico and Canada.

In 2012, a Moroccan, Amine El Khalifi was arrested for plotting to bomb the U.S. Capitol. Like four of the 9/11 hijackers, he is one of the 40% of illegals who have overstayed their visas and the *DHS has no way to track them.* The 9/11 hijackers had more than 300 aliases, passports, and visas, which illustrates the requirement for a fraud proof verification system. Since 2004 Congress has required DHS to implement a biometric entry-exit system, yet in 2014 there is still no system in place, another example of non-enforcement of our own laws.

In 2011, GAO began tracking the DHS's management of foreign visitors and found a backlog of over a million records of arrivals without matching exits. [135] Approximately 1 in 5 illegal immigrants has a criminal record. There are about 1.4 million gang members in the U.S. and in 2014 a Texas state senator stated that 100,000 of them were in that state. From 2008 -2012 those 100,000 gang members committed half a million crimes that included 5000 rapes and 2000 murders according to that source. The year prior U.S. ICE released over 36,000 illegals who were awaiting final disposition or deportation and who had been charged with 88,000 crimes ranging from homicide to aggravated assault to sexual-assault. Prior to that ICE had released 68,000 illegal immigrants who they let go from jail rather than prosecute. [136] That is absolutely nuts.

The Boston Globe has done revealing research on illegal immigrants convicted of sex offenses and who were not deported and instead were released back into society, often without registration as a sex offender. I'd encourage everyone to read "ICE's sex offender policies under scrutiny" by Maria Sacchetti on 14 June

2015. There are multiple problems identified in this report. Based on a Supreme Court decision, ICE must release all offenders within six months if the home countries won't take them back (and most don't for obvious reasons). In many cases the individuals disappear, fail to register as sex offenders, and commit repeat crimes. Read the Boston Globe article.

In November 2014, President Obama issued an Executive Order that granted a legal reprieve from fear of deportation to about four million undocumented immigrants, many who are parents of legal residents of greater than five years, through expansion of the Deferred Action for Childhood Arrivals Act (DACA) of 2012. The executive action still left about eight million immigrants unaddressed. Twenty-six states have challenged the Executive Order as illegal and that challenge is working its way through the judicial system; in the meantime, the Executive Order is on hold.

Sanctuary city is a name given to a city in the United States that follows certain procedures that shelters illegal immigrants. These procedures can be by law (de jure) or they can be by action (de facto). Illegal immigration and the whole issue of sanctuary cities was front page news in July 2015 with the tragic murder of Kathryn Steinle in San Francisco. She died in her father's arms, apparently killed by Juan Lopez-Sanchez, who had been deported on *five* previous occasions. San Francisco had failed to comply with a statutory request from Homeland Security that Lopez-Sanchez be held for deportation before his prison release. He wasn't detained and Kathryn Steinle is dead. Law-abiding Americans of all ethnic backgrounds are becoming increasingly incensed by the crimes and gang violence committed by illegals, many repeat offenders, which emphasizes why we need comprehensive legislation dealing with immigration reform. Done correctly, we won't need sanctuary cities any longer.

Immigration, with all of the finger pointing, will be a hot topic for the 2016 elections. If this is a partisan issue, and we know it is, then the Democrats have trumped the Republicans, as most voters fault Republicans for not acting on immigration reform. Little mention is usually made as to why immigration reform wasn't passed in 2009 when it would have sailed through a democratically controlled Congress, both the Senate and the House.

While I would personally like to see comprehensive immigration reform as one piece of legislation, it may have to be done in two segments: securing the border first and then addressing those 11+ million illegals already here. Either way, it needs to get done. According to polls, most Americans want less immigration overall, but are sympathetic to those already here, particularly the American-Dreamers. Immigration has been the foundation of our country, but it involved new immigrants embracing the culture, learning the language, and fully assimilating into the larger American society. This is the kind of good immigration we need as a nation, and it is way past time for our lawmakers to get bipartisan legislation to the President's desk.

CHAPTER 6

AMERICA'S VETERANS

There should be no greater issue that we can all agree on than that of taking care of our military veterans, yet so much remains to be done. Although there were many warning signs, studies and articles that highlighted various aspects of inadequate care, this all culminated in the headline news stories that accompanied the Veterans Affairs (VA) Inspector General's report in May of 2014 which documented over 1700 veterans who were never scheduled for an appointment at the VA medical center in Phoenix, and an apparent cover-up to falsify wait times to avoid scrutiny (the goal was a 14-day wait time from request to appointment). There were other management problems uncovered at Phoenix, to include sexual harassment and bullying behavior; 42 other VA medical centers were also under investigation for scheduling problems. The VA has acknowledged 23 deaths nationwide due to delayed care, and the problems uncovered at Phoenix eventually led to a series of congressional hearings, legislation, and the resignation of the VA director, Eric Shinseki. He was replaced by former Proctor and Gamble CEO, Bob McDonald.

To those inside the Washington D.C. Beltway or close to the military community, these issues were hardly a surprise. Backlogs and complaints of access have been going on for years. If anything, it is surprising it took this long for the issue to burst into the public domain. Back in 2004 the Commanding General of Walter Reed Army Hospital was relieved following a Washington Post article that documented squalid living conditions and bureaucratic red tape that prevented some outpatients from receiving the care they needed. As Secretary of Defense Robert Gates then stated, "When the standard is not met, I will insist on swift and direct corrective action and, where appropriate, accountability up the chain of command." That was over 10 years ago. In March 2007, the President's Commission on Care for America's Returning Wounded Warriors (also called the Dole-Shalala Commission), made six actionable recommendations, which included the need to address the shortage of mental health professionals to aggressively treat Post-Traumatic Stress Syndrome (PTSD) and Traumatic Brain Injury (TBI) and strengthen support for families.

While the focus has rightly been on the veterans returning from over a decade of fighting in Afghanistan and Iraq, there are many veterans of other foreign wars that also continue to need our support. As former Chairman of the Joint Chiefs stated *"... the soldier is the servant of the state, not the maker of policy, and that sacrifice, though painful, is the price we pay for freedom."*[137] Those veterans returning from Vietnam were meant with scorn and disdain in many instances, hardly the deserved thanks of a grateful nation. Fortunately, support for our veterans since the attacks of 9/11/2011 has been markedly different. Still, as discussed in the Defense chapter, only 1 % of Americans volunteer to serve in the Armed Forces, while the 99% go about business as usual, many unconcerned or untouched by the wars and the heavy tolls incurred by those in combat roles. To editorialize Adm. Mullen's observation, this is also the price we pay for freedom and the AVF. Of this 1%, half came from military backgrounds and many are southerners, possibly troubling statistics for the long-term viability of the AVF. Here are some approximate numbers of veterans in the U.S.; your neighbors, and fellow countrymen, who live in every state:

- Over 21 million living veterans (almost 10 million over 65)
- 8.2 million from Vietnam era (2.6 million who fought in Vietnam)
- 2..6 million veterans who have fought in the Iraq or Afghanistan wars
- 2.3 million from the Korean War
- 1.6 million who served in WWII (dying at a rate of over 600/day, or over 200,000/year)

The issues veterans face are numerous. Statistics surrounding veteran issues vary significantly by survey and how data is accumulated. For example, suicide statistics is generally not considered for veterans after they leave active service or retire. Still the trends are clear: According to one survey, half of the 2.6 million veterans who fought in Afghanistan or Iraq suffer from some mental or physical disability, feel disconnected, suffer from relationship problems, and feel the government is failing to meet veteran needs.[138] The same survey found that half still saw that the Defense Department as lagging in transition assistance and that 60% feel the VA is doing an only fair to poor job meeting veterans needs. Here are just a few facts to consider:[139]

- Killed or wounded in Afghanistan or Iraq: over 6800. Physically or psychologically wounded: more than 600,000 that are receiving lifelong government support.[140]
- Suicide: the VA estimates that between 19 and 22 veterans take their lives each day, significantly above the national average. For veterans age 18-24, the rate has risen from 46 per 100,000 in 1999 to 80 per 100,000 in 2011; it continues to escalate. The Veterans Crisis Line has received about a million calls since inception in 2007 and credits 32,000 rescues over that period. One recent study of all

veterans found the suicide rates to be about 5000/year; Being in the military essentially doubles your suicide rate. Interestingly, an Army study found that being in combat did not directly correlate to higher suicide rates among military members, and that roughly a third of soldiers who attempted suicide between 2004 and 2009 had mental health problems before they joined the Army.[141]

- Post-Traumatic Stress Syndrome (PTSD): studies indicate that at least 20% of Iraq and Afghanistan Vets suffer from PTSD, and 50% of those do not seek treatment. (Of the 50% who do, only half of those get minimally adequate treatment.) Other studies of Vietnam Vets years after service support rates higher than 50%. The VA estimates that about 1000 veterans of Iraq and Afghanistan are diagnosed with PTSD each week, and another 800 with depression.[142]

- Mental Health: In 2014, more than 1.2 million veterans were treated by the VA for mental health problems, including 408,000 with PTSD.[143]

- Traumatic Brain Injury (TBI): roughly 19% of veterans suffer from TBI and 7% of recent veterans have both PTSD and TBI.

- Alcohol Abuse: 39% of veterans from Afghanistan and Iraq suffer from alcohol abuse.[144]

- Homelessness: one in ten homeless Americans are veterans. There are over 100,000 homeless veterans.[145]

- Unemployment: at least 1% higher than the general population and up to 7% higher for those under 24.[146] Enlisted members face bigger hurdles with 43% reporting they have had to take a second job or work extra hours to make ends meet.[147]

The VA department is made up of three major components: The Veterans Benefit Administration, the National Cemetery and the Veterans Health Administration (VHA). The latter has been the center of the latest controversy and is made up of around 1700 hospitals, clinics and counseling centers around the country, which annually serve about nine million of the country's nearly 22 million veterans.[148]

According to a 2005 RAND study and more recent studies, a high percentage of veterans like their VA administered care; the problem has always been access versus standards of care. There is a shortage of doctors, a case load of around 2000 (versus a goal of 1200) creating backlogs, and evidence of a cover-up of waiting times, as discussed.

Another alarming statistic is the growing impact on the 2.3 million women veterans, over 280,000 of whom have served in the wars in Iraq and Afghanistan, who face these challenges according to multiple sources: higher disability rates, earnings typically $6000 less than male counterparts, unemployment 1.4% higher (8.3% versus 6.9%), triple the likelihood of being a single parent and 2-3 times the divorce rate as compared to male counterparts[149] while serving (estimates show that only 20% actually speak out). Women veterans make up the fastest-growing segment of the homeless veteran population and have more mental health problems than their male counterparts by percentage, and 40% report difficulty re-adjusting once they return.[150] Female veterans commit suicide at six times the rate of female non-veterans.[151] Like male veterans, many don't seek the help they need. The evidence is overwhelming! Four Senator's in 2015 co-sponsored bipartisan legislation requiring Access to Quality Care at VA Hospitals for women, something you would have hoped wouldn't have been necessary, but very clearly was!

Caring for our veterans is one of the most important issues facing the nation. It is a statement of who we are and our values. It's our duty and moral obligation as citizens and as a country to do everything necessary to support our returning veterans, their families, their surviving spouses, and children. The bill will be expensive, but must be paid, and we have yet to see the full impact. The government can't do it all and there are many (hundreds) support organizations. The Wounded Warrior Project, maybe the best known of the veteran charities, was criticized early on for exorbitant executive salaries, but is now highly rated.[152]

Before donating, it is suggested you check independent sources such as Charity Watch or Charity Navigator. Hiring for Heroes campaign by Medal of Honor recipient Dakota Meyer, The Mission Continues (from the book Charlie Mike), Boulder Crest Retreat, The Elizabeth Dole Foundation, Salute to America's Heroes, Bull Run Warrior Retreat, and Safe Harbor Foundation are just a few of the hundreds of support organizations doing extraordinary work. Another, Michael Meade's Seattle-based non-profit "Mosaic Voices" sponsors 4-day retreats based on mythology with some remarkable results.

Another related and challenging issue is that of spouses, family members, or others providing care for the returning wounded. According to one study, 59% of caregivers have stopped working, and another 19-37 % have taken a reduction in pay to meet caregiving demands.[153]

The Caregivers and Veterans Omnibus Health Services Act of 2010 expanded VA services available to veterans and their Family Caregivers. In addition to a monthly stipend for designated caregivers, travel expenses, access to health insurance and caregiver training were expanded. However, this support covers only a small portion of the caregivers nationwide.

According to a RAND study, "Hidden Heroes: America's Military Caregivers", there are 1.1 million Americans providing care to post 9/11 veterans, often without a support network and with their own well-being compromised. They tend to be younger than other caregivers, resulting in lost workdays and other incurred hardships. The Elizabeth Dole Foundation was established to provide support to American military caregivers and to 'elevate this critical issue to national attention.' The Rehabilitation Act of 1973 requires that we provide therapeutic and supportive housing for returning veterans, something that is required to receive the mental and rehabilitative care that many need. More needs to be done.

Following the VA controversy and the resignation of the VA Director, a 14-member bipartisan panel worked through what was finally passed as the Veterans Access and Accountability Act of 2014. The three significant elements of the Bill authorized veterans to receive care outside the VA system by establishing a $10B Veterans Choice Fund and issuing choice cards, provided funding to improve VA hospitals and clinics and hire more medical and support staff, and improved VA oversight and accountability. Veterans who live more than 40 miles from a VA facility, or who are facing lengthy waits, will be able to seek medical care from a private doctor. The bill also allowed for firings of incompetent senior officials, leasing of 37 new VA facilities, and expedited hiring of doctors, nurses, and medical staff. It also improved the Montgomery GI Bill and Webb Post- 9/11 GI Bill by requiring all states to apply in-state tuition rates for veterans, regardless of residency, and improved access to health care for military sexual-assault victims.

There is some good news. Many veterans, who are in the system, say it works very well. Veterans who need care receive one-stop service, seeing the specialists they need, with coordinated scheduling rather than a series of return visits that they would experience in private care. As one resident at a VA hospital stated, "The VA system (of coordinated scheduling and patient-centered/team-based care) could be a model."[154] Most veterans' groups did not support the 2014 Veterans Access Bill for the reason that care would be dispersed and uncoordinated and require the veteran to make all the appointments. The CBO, in estimating costs, projected that 'VA health costs could double within 5 years,' partially as a result of sending veterans into private sector care. For reasons of cost and coordination-of-care, hopefully, the provisions in the 2014 Act are only a temporary patch until the VHA system is sufficiently robust and capable of meeting the demand. There is merit to the recommendations of the Fixing Veterans Task Force, co-chaired by former Senator Bill Frist and former Congressman Jim Marshall which include making VHA an independent agency, allowing veterans the choice of private care and focusing direct VA care on those who are neediest. I can support any reform that ensures those who have fought in combat and need our help are cared for, in whatever way that is best (and efficiently) achieved.

Still, even in light of all the recent focus, I worry about who is left behind, be it a wounded veteran, a wounded veteran's family, a surviving spouse and children, or a caregiver with insufficient support. It was a shock to me on 11 November 2013 that the 2013 Veterans Parade was carried only on one local channel, while Days of our Lives, TMZ Live, The Chew, and The Young and Restless aired as usual. I felt the same remorse when the 71st anniversary of the Normandy landing on 6 June 2015 received little local coverage, but American Pharaoh, a racehorse, dominated the front page. This reaffirmed in my mind that we still have a long way to go in honoring and providing for those who served our nation so honorably, and sacrificed so much.

CHAPTER 7

THE ENVIRONMENT AND ENERGY

I generally tend to think of the Republicans as the more analytic and scientific of the two major parties. Which is why I find it difficult to comprehend the tendency of some to downplay or dismiss the dangers of climate change, even in the face of nearly unanimous and overwhelming scientific evidence.

Senator James Inhofe (R—OK), the current Chairman of the Senate Energy Committee has called climate change the "greatest hoax ever played on mankind," and wrote a book about it, which doesn't bode well for enlightened legislation. We've all heard the arguments that climate change is merely cyclical and that global warming is a political scam and is now on the wane anyway. That we're in a long-term cycle that will repeat, that any impacts are overstated and the mitigation efforts now underway will be sufficient to address our future.

While emotions and passions run high on all sides of the global warming issue, I think that science, not politics or economic considerations, should frame the argument. Even the Pope has voiced concern. Some years ago I met with the Oceanographer of the Navy who told me he took no great interest in the debate as to what was causing climate change; rather his job was simply to measure the data and assess the impact on the Navy. The data surrounding sea level rise, he continued, was both convincing and alarming. There are some good sources for understanding the data and arguments: The World Health Organization, the World Bank, and the International Panel on Climate Change (IPCC) being among well-respected organizations. The IPCC, established by the UN in 1988, is a leading scientific authority on global climate change. The IPCC's Fourth Assessment Report in 2007 stated that the evidence of climate warming was "unequivocal." In late 2014 the IPCC issued a capstone document that distilled the previous five assessments conducted since 1990. That report concluded that the world is now on an "irreversible course" for global impacts from harmful emissions into the atmosphere, unless drastic actions are taken. It further warned of increasingly violent weather patterns, rising sea levels that will continue well beyond 2100, dismissed a slowdown in warming as temporary, and cited a rapidly closing window of opportunity to cut toxic emissions sufficiently. Although I admit to having been a skeptic in the past, I find the data convincing. It is impossible for me to believe that pouring greenhouse gasses into the atmosphere can do much good. In the face of such compelling scientific evidence I think climate change is now one of our clear national and international priorities.

Closely associated with climate change, most of us are intuitively aware of the damage done by mankind to the planet, from mass destruction of animal, plant and fish species to the relentless pollution of the atmosphere and waters, all of which continues today. We all became aware of environmental issues at different times. Well, most of us. The Sierra Club was established back in 1892 by conservationist and preservationist John Muir. Greenpeace dates back to the late 1960s. Major events have triggered awareness. In 1969, the polluted Cuyahoga River in Ohio caught fire. Many of us remember the 2000 movie Erin Brockovich, starring Julia Roberts, that involved contaminated water in Hinkley, California, and resulted in a $333M settlement in 1996 against Pacific Gas & Electric (PG&E.) The nuclear incident at 3-Mile Island, and the meltdowns at Chernobyl, Russia and, more recently, Fukushima Japan, are still fresh in our memories. So too, the major oil spills by the Exon Valdez in Prince William Sound in

1989 and the BP spill in the Gulf of Mexico in April 2000, and the suffocating pollution that engulfed Beijing in January 2013 and continues throughout China.

So how does this all tie into a responsible environmental policy for the U.S. and leadership in world environmental stewardship?

Climate Change begins with a discussion of pollution, which includes everything from the release of gaseous pollutants such as carbon monoxide and chlorofluorocarbons into the atmosphere, to water pollution caused by industrial waste, to soil contamination from hazardous waste and runoff, and many other factors. Motor vehicles, coal-burning power and chemical plants, farming, heavy industry and deforestation are some of the leading causes. Although not universally accepted as a metric, many scientists state that for dangerous climate change to be avoided, parts per million (PPM) of carbon dioxide in the atmosphere must be kept below 450 PPM by 2100 (we passed 400 PPM in 2013). Likewise, global emissions of carbon dioxide should not exceed 700 billion tons between now and 2050 to ensure that global temperatures do not increase by more than two (2) degrees C (3.6 degrees F) above pre-industrial levels, a widely accepted metric. You will hear the 2-degree C. metric mentioned repeatedly in climate change conversations.

According to one World Bank study, we are now on track to hit that cap well before 2050, with China currently being the largest contributor. About 400 million tons of hazardous wastes are produced each year, with the U.S. contributing about 25%. China has grown from 10% of world's greenhouse gasses in 1990 to now about 30% and burns about 50% of the world's coal. China surpassed the U.S. in carbon dioxide emissions in 2006.[155]

In the acclaimed U.S.- China summit in late 2014, Presidents Obama, and Xi agreed to a more aggressive reduction of carbon emissions for the U.S., while the Chinese agreed to "begin" reductions in 2030, the year that their planning had anticipated peaking anyway. Nevertheless, the agreement was widely touted as a success, despite the fact that China's toxic emissions are projected to grow for the next 15 years, even as they begin improving the efficiency of their coal plants, shutting down thousands of others, and investing in renewable energy. It may well be that the Beijing smog of 2013 put China on a different course as reflected in their more aggressive closing of coal plants in favor of renewables. China now generates 20% of its energy from renewables, more than the U.S., but has been proactive in recent years, even as it remains the largest coal burner in the world.

The World Bank cites research that we are on a path to a 4 degree C (7.2 degree F) increase by the end of this century and that, even if we can hold at only 2 degrees C, it will result in widespread weather disruption, food shortages, and a huge negative impact on GDP. At 4 degrees, such widespread climate impacts become the new normal. In 1997, the Kyoto Protocol to the UN Framework Convention on Climate Change was negotiated by 160 countries and extended in 2012 to 2020. This binding agreement would require signatory nations to reduce greenhouse gasses by 5.2%, from a 1990 or 1995 baseline. These would include the three most toxic emissions: carbon dioxide, methane, and nitrous oxide, as well as other industrial gasses. Although the U.S. Senate never ratified the agreement, the U.S. has repeatedly pledged to meet or beat these goals. In 2009 the current President pledged to reduce emissions by 17%, but changed the baseline to 2005; in fact, and unfortunately, we are closer to 3% reduction according to The Washington Post's Fact Checker.[156]

A 2014 report from the Energy Department showed that carbon emissions for the first six months of 2014 were 3% higher than in 2013 and 6% higher again than 2012;[157] overall not a good record for the current Administration, despite the rhetoric. In May 2014 the government's Third National Climate Assessment, produced under the provisions of the Global Change Research Act of 1990 (the previous two were in 2000 and 2009), concluded that the global warming of the past 50 years has been caused mostly by heat-trapping gasses produced by humans. Although downplayed by some, the assessment is the credible work of hundreds of experts and scientists. Not surprising, coal, gasoline, and deforestation are all contributing causes. In what is known as the 'greenhouse effect,' radiation from the sun is trapped in the atmosphere, converted to heat that contributes to global warming.

The most visible evidence of climate change is seen in sea level rise, a scientific fact that is measurable, even if you challenge the cause. Although it varies by region and how measurements are taken, notionally the sea level has risen by 1.5 – 2 millimeters a year for the past six decades, as polar ice and mountain glaciers melt. The sea level in Virginia alone is rising 4mm per year according to a National Oceanic and Atmospheric Association (NOAA) study. Throughout the past century, the sea level has risen between 4 and 8 inches, with more than 2.3 inches occurring in the past 20 years. Even a few inches can have severe consequences. The area of the Artic covered by ice has been shrinking by 11% a decade for the past 35 years. 30 % of carbon released into the atmosphere ends up in the ocean, causing acidification and killing coral and shell life. As the oceans absorb this heat, the water expands causing a corresponding rise in sea levels.

A recent World Bank report projected that major portions of Bangkok would be under water by 2030 and that other hot spots are similarly endangered. China has about 80 million people living at sea level, and about 300 million people live in coastal areas; another 3 billion are within 100 miles of the sea. The National Assessment referred to above predicts that sea levels will rise at least a foot and maybe as much as 4 feet, by the end of the century, although the latest IPCC estimate is around 20 inches by century's end. That is still a worrisome figure.

Much of the mid-Atlantic from Norfolk, Virginia to Miami is at risk from rising sea levels and disruptive weather patterns. The Chesapeake Bay region is expected to experience an increase in coastal flooding and loss of wetlands that protect storm surge, according to the assessment. Hurricane Sandy, for instance, saw surges of almost 14 feet, well above those of Donna in 1960 (10 feet.)

Loss of wetlands in the U.S. is about 60,000 acres per year.[158] These wetlands buffer large storms and sea surges, as well as contain over half of the endangered species that depend on them. The loss of wetlands is caused principally by business development, residential building, and coastal farming, all contributing to drain-off, pollution, toxins and garbage. Although there is scientific uncertainty as to how fast global temperatures are rising, primarily because the oceans are mitigating the impact in the short-term and surface temperatures are stable, most scientists regard this current pause as temporary, as the recent IPCC report stated, and that the trend for both temperatures and sea levels rise will accelerate again.[159] The economic impact of rising sea levels is enormous, impacting infrastructure, building codes, populations near sea level and much more.

Deforestation: Most of us learned in elementary school the importance of trees. They absorb bad carbon emissions resulting in better air and cleaner water downstream. If you cut them down, more carbon is released into the atmosphere, contributing to the climate change that scientists are measuring and reporting. Deforestation accounts for somewhere around 12% of annual greenhouse gas emissions according to IPCC. It also reduces the amount of water in the soil, contributing to soil erosion and flooding. Like the loss of wetlands, population growth, conversion to farmland, and demographics all play roles in deforestation. According to the UN, subsistence farming is responsible for almost half (48%) of deforestation; commercial agriculture 32%, logging 14% and fuel wood removals 5%.[160] Deforestation also impacts animal and plant species extinctions. Studies suggest that we are losing over 100 plants, insect and animal species *each day*, with more invasive species potentially replacing them.[161]

Some good news is that of recognition and action by governments to regulate and make deforestation less profitable. In China, for years every citizen who was able and between the ages of 11 and 60 was required to plant 3-5 trees per year. Although no longer a requirement, the government claims over a billion trees were planted each year since 1982. Annual deforestation in the Brazilian Amazon has been reduced by 80% from the peak but has been reported as growing again. In all, we have managed to destroy about a third of the earth's forests and are still losing ground. Protecting the tropical forests of the Amazon, Asia, and the Congo are one of the best ways to reduce harmful gaseous emissions.

Energy and Energy Policy is closely linked to climate change and the environment, so the two discussions belong together. So too does a basic understanding of terms, which are often confused.

Our energy consumption in the U.S. can be categorized broadly as supporting four sectors that include Transportation (28%), Residential (22%), Commercial (19%) and Industrial (31%). The percentages are approximations and change over time. Just looking at transportation as one example, the U.S. with roughly 5% of the world's population has over 30% of the global automobiles.

Sources for energy are broadly talked about in two categories that also need to be understood. Renewable sources include wind, hydropower, and solar. Non-renewable sources consist of coal (28%), Petroleum (oil) (36%), natural gas (23%), in approximate numbers. Coal is a well-recognized source of carbon and other greenhouse gas emissions. Some consider the term 'clean coal' a misnomer, arguing that there can be no such thing in fact. Nonetheless, investments have been made in clean coal technology that do effectively capture and store harmful pollutants. Unfortunately, that investment has been about 10% of what is needed over the next 10 years, and clean coal is very expensive and less efficient as an energy source. Still, coal will remain a major source of energy for many years to come, especially in developing countries, but also in the U.S. despite the availability of much cheaper natural gas. Coal accounts for about 1/3 of the electrical generation in this country and over 50% of the energy generation in 15 states. (The Washington Post, "Stormy Tests for climate proposal," by Joby Warrick, 8/3/2015.)

In August of 2015, the Obama Administration released the EPA's long expected Clean Power Plan that would accelerate greenhouse gas reductions in advance of the Climate Change talks in Paris in December 2015. The new baseline for measurement is 2005, not the original Kyoto baselines—as previously mentioned. Although states are given increased flexibility to meet the goals, many will sue in court, and 26 have already done so, the new standards will be in legal flux for some time.

Crude oil that is extracted from the ground, or imported, must be refined for domestic use. Natural shale-gas that is extracted goes into a pipeline for storage and, if it is to be transported or exported, is cooled and liquefied. Although estimates vary, a recent International Energy Agency (IEA) reports states that, largely due to hydraulic fracturing (fracking) technology, the U.S. is expected to be top producer of oil in the world within five years, a net exporter of oil by 2030 and energy self-sufficient around 2035. The U.S. is already the top producer of natural gas and has a supply of nearly 100 years based on current usage rates.

On the other hand, renewable energy consists of the three major sources previously mentioned: solar, wind and hydropower, which do not depend on fossil fuels and are environmentally friendly. There are now over 30 countries that have greater than 20% of energy production from renewable sources. Sadly, the U.S. is only around 13%, with over half of that figure from hydroelectric and less than 1% solar. Currently, there are no restrictions on the export of U.S. refined oil, and about 3 million barrels of refined oil products are exported each day. In the 2016 Omnibus Funding Bill Congress lifted the 40-year ban on crude exports. Liquefied natural gas (LNG) export is restricted and requires a Department of Energy (DOE) determination.

There are any number of domestic energy issues in play, but two of the most talked about, and controversial, involve fracking and the expanded Keystone pipeline. Due to horizontal drilling and hydraulic fracking (extracting oil or gas from shale by blasting it with water), shale production has been a boost to the U.S. economy and a job creator and has moved us quickly toward energy independence. Fracking is not without controversy, however. Opponents argue that fracking pollutes the groundwater and air, but studies suggest that this impact is minimal and can be mitigated. Fracking also uses huge amounts of fresh water. To export LNG it must be cooled to minus 260 degrees Fahrenheit and then transported overseas in refrigerated tankers, which is not inexpensive. It requires port facilities both in the U.S. and at receiving destinations. The benefits of natural gas are clear, however: less domestic dependency, lower home gas bills, around 500,000 jobs created and about half the harmful carbon dioxide emissions compared to coal. There are calls for the U.S. to accelerate permits for natural gas exports, which advocates argue would reduce deficits and ease Europe's reliance on Russian oil. Counter-arguments are that exporting would drive demand for fracking even higher, and could raise U.S. prices, but a DOE study found this impact would be modest. As argued, exporting would actually keep the prices sufficient to continue to drive the boom, which has stalled temporarily with falling international oil prices.[162]

Exporting LNG remains political, and requires a DOE determination that it is in the country's best interests, and an assessment of a project's safety and environmental impact by the Federal Energy Regulatory Commission (FERC.) There are currently five export facilities under construction in the U.S. and Congress/DOE should update the existing laws and approve more projects in the queue.

The second most controversial environmental issues are whether to allow TransCanada to build the proposed $5-7B Northern Keystone expansion (XL), to the 1,179-mile pipeline from Hardisty, Canada to Steele City, Nebraska here in the U.S. Transporting 800,000 barrels of oil daily through the U.S. heartland to the Gulf Coast. Unknown to most folks is that *the Keystone pipeline already exists*! Phase I from Alberta Canada to Steele City was completed in 2010; phase II from Steele City to Cushing, Oklahoma completed in 2011, and phase III from Cushing to Port Arthur, Texas was also completed and operational in 2014. What is at issue is the 4th phase of the project, the proposed XL pipeline, which would add capacity by a shorter distance and larger pipe. Because it crosses international borders, its construction must be approved by the President, and our current one has said he would approve it only 'If wouldn't produce harmful emissions and contribute to climate change.' The Department of State completed its *draft* 'Environmental Impact Statement (EIS)' on 1 March 2014 and found that the pipeline extension would have no real impact on harmful emissions. Following the public comment period and rounds of legal challenges, the State Department will issue a final EIS, which will further inform the argument. The Department of State has also estimated that the expansion will create 42,000 jobs and add $2B to annual earnings. In the meantime, both houses of Congress passed legislation in favor of the Keystone pipeline in early 2015, which was quickly vetoed by the President in February 2015. In March of 2015, the Senate failed to override the veto, achieving 62 of the 67 votes required.

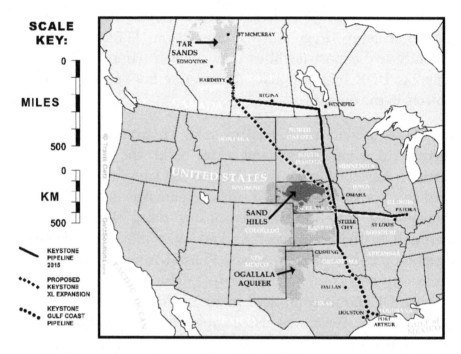

In November of 2015, President Obama announced that he would not issue a permit for the XL construction, surprising few. That decision pleased some environmentalists, although the impacts were not persuasive, angered some unions, and appeared highly political and symbolic on the eve of the Paris climate talks. While the issue is closed for now, a new Administration may take a different view if the TransCanada Corporation and new Canadian Prime Minister are even still interested in 2017.

National Security Impact: Finally, climate change fundamentally impacts National Security as populations migrate, food and water sources are disrupted and cause price spikes and economic instability, disease, and natural disasters increase and areas such as the Artic become open for maritime traffic, both commercial and military.

The DOD, the CIA and the GAO, among others, have all acknowledged climate change as a security challenge, raising further questions as to why some others remain unconvinced. The GAO states that climate change effects "will result in increased exposure for the federal government in many areas." History shows that the Mayan civilization and most Chinese dynasties fell during times of dry spells or drought.[163]

The U.S. and Russia are both viewing the strategic importance of the Artic, which is the fastest warming part of the globe. The U.S. now heads the Artic Council, a multination forum to address climate and environmental issues. Linked closely to national security is the impact of climate change and extreme climate events on the world's economy, although it is more difficult to measure. Yet there are studies that link higher temperature with lower output and unemployment. Droughts, like that in Syria, have affected food prices and water availability, and possibly contributed to the Arab Spring type of reactions, or even to the rise of ISIS, according to a couple of presidential hopefuls.

As nations increasingly compete for resources, climate change will impact the behavior of our competitors. Over-fishing is just one example. Fish stocks are being depleted worldwide, with one study supporting that marlin, tuna, and swordfish may now be 90% below 1950 levels, and 2/3 of the fish stocks over-exploited.[164] The world's fish catch increased from 19 million metric tons in 1950 to 90 million metric tons in the late 1980's, over a 4-fold increase.

Beyond the fishing and impact of deforestation mentioned above, we continue to jeopardize many of our planet's wildlife. The illegal ivory trade and the slaughter of elephants in Africa are but one of many examples of our collective lack of stewardship of the planet. The Navy's use of sonar and the impact on whale and dolphin behavior has yet to be convincingly concluded, either way. One final example is the Great Barrier Reef off of Australia's northeast coast, an ecological marvel now threatened by ocean acidification linked to climate change and discharged pesticides that are destroying the many coral and fish specifies.

A responsible way forward: Population growth, insufficient housing and water, and deteriorating health are all linked to environmental concerns. The World Bank estimates this impact at about 9% of GDP. The UN estimates that the worlds' population will rise from 7.2B to 9.6B in 2050, with a disproportionate rise in the demand for water, food, and shelter. The Montreal protocol in 1987, an agreement to eliminate dangerous chlorofluorocarbons caused by refrigerants, has been extremely successful. The 2015 Paris climate conference saw nearly 190 countries in attendance commit to reduced emissions, with developed countries agreeing to investments in undeveloped countries; most of this is voluntary.

For the future, and in particular for U.S leadership on climate change, the answers lie in many initiatives that include more environmental responsibility and energy self-sufficiency: continued investment in green technology and renewable energy (solar, wind, hydropower) where rapid technology is making returns on investment more enticing; protocols to accelerate reduction of carbon dioxide and other greenhouse emissions (such as the Obama Administration's 2015 Clean Power Plan); investments in cleaner coal in the short-term (coal is still about a third of our national electricity and the industry has invested between $100B and $200B in clean coal technologies to date);

energy efficient and net- zero buildings and residences that return energy to the grid, and slowing deforestation and better managing worldwide fish stocks. In order to manage to the 2 deg. C metric, most agree that we are going to need to reverse-engineer carbon dioxide out of the atmosphere. That will take a lot of 'geoengineering' investment,[165] new methods and subsidies for crop rotation and shifts to organic fertilizers,[166] and a whole lot of new technology not yet on the horizon. Let's hope we move that responsible direction, quickly.

CHAPTER 8

OUR YOUTH—OUR FUTURE

"If you want to invest for a hundred years, invest in people."

--Chinese Proverb

We know that we spend seven times the funding on seniors that we do on our children at the federal level, but most spending on our youth occurs at the local and state levels. Overall, the ratio is closer to 2:1. Still most would argue that we are not investing sufficiently in our greatest resource, a position I agree with. From violent video games to struggling schools to poverty to outright exploitation, we're simply not doing enough, and the consequences are far-reaching. Let's look at some of the sobering statistics and data surrounding poverty, exploitation and education in our country.

Poverty: Despite being a rich country by any standard, poverty is still relatively widespread in the United States. The Organization for Economic Development and Cooperation (OECD) defines children as 'living in poverty' if they live in households with an income less than half their country's median, adjusted for family size. That equates to a family income of about $24,000 for a family of four in the U.S. That poverty figure for U.S. children is 21.6%; just for comparison France is 8% and Japan 14.2 %.[167]

According to the census bureau, about 15% of the overall U.S. population (47 million people), are living in poverty, and includes the 22 % children's figure above. The Department of Agriculture says that 15 % of families (1 in 4 children) are "food insecure," meaning they will likely be out of food or money in any given month; a 30% increase since 2006.[168] Another 18 million are living within 130% of the poverty line or the near poor.[169]

The Food and Drug Administration runs the federal free and reduced-price school meals program, which roughly approximates the poverty definition in terms of eligibility. For a family of 4 in 2014, income below $23,850 qualified for free school meals and below $44,123 for reduced-price meals. In October 2013, the Southern Education Foundation published a stunning report based on 2011 data. It showed that a *national average of 48% of children in public school (K -12), that's 50 million kids, were low-income and eligible for free or reduced meals* (up from 38% in 2000). Seventeen states in the south and west were over 50%, led by Mississippi (a decade ago this figure was four states.) In January 2015, the study was updated with data through 2013. It revealed that over half (now 51%) of students in pre-kindergarten through 12th grade in public schools nationwide were eligible for reduced or free lunch programs. I mentioned this in the dedication because it is such a staggering figure and a sad reflection on our nation. Can it really be that over half of public school children in America are eligible for school lunch subsidies?

Recent estimates are that 1 in 30 children are homeless. Over 40 million Americans are now on food stamps, fueled by the slow economic recovery through 2014, jobs below living wages, and high birth rates among lower income families.

The impacts of poverty on children are enormous. Here are a few of the disturbing impacts that I have accumulated from a variety of sources:

- Early achievement is stagnated. Less than 1 in 5 third-graders, for example, score at or above the national average in areas of science, reading and math testing.

- Health is negatively impacted. Figures vary, but only about 50% of children are within good weight and health standards. The military has stated that about a quarter of American youth are unqualified to serve in the Armed Forces due to weight. According to the Center for Disease Control (CDC), in 1987 roughly 6 % of 18-34-year-olds were obese; in 2008 (twenty years later) that figure was 23%, almost a four-fold increase. It starts in childhood, and our current First Lady is to be commended for raising this issue to public awareness.

- Social adjustment. In 2012, the percent of single-parent families was 32% (@6% for whites, 34% for Hispanics, 59% for African Americans). Over 40 % of all American children are born out of wedlock. The lack of family structure is probably the best indicator of a child's education progress and success later in life, according to many studies. If you're African-American, there is only one chance in six you will grow up with a mother and father. From a statistics perspective, marriage remains the best way to beat poverty, child abuse, school dropout and crime. This is just data, and in no way diminishes the heroic job that many single parents are doing, some by choice and some not, some working multiple jobs, to raise their children to become responsible and accomplished citizens.

- High school dropout rates. According to the American Psychological Association (APA), there is a direct correlation between household income and dropout rates. In 2009, children from the lower 20% of income were five times as likely to drop out of high school as those from the top 20%. They were less likely to get a good job that pays a living-wage and more likely to have health issues, engage in crime and depend on public assistance in some form. A recent study by the Urban Institute found that 65% of those that quit high school are at or below the poverty line. Finally, over 60% of high school dropouts that give birth are unmarried (as opposed to 9% for college educated.)

Some 50 years ago President Lyndon Johnson launched the War on Poverty. In 2011, estimates were that federal spending was $13,000 for each person below the federal poverty line; around $600 billion to include the Earned Income Tax Credit (EITC) and Medicaid. The Head Start program and Job Corps have made some notable advances, but a 2012 federal study suggests that the benefits of the $1B Head Start program are, sadly, mostly gone by 3rd grade. EITC is credited with lifting over nine million people above the poverty line in 2012. Even though many people are better off now, the overall poverty rate of 15% is the same as it was in 1982. We talked about the impact of income disparity, and the cycle of poverty, in an earlier chapter.

In 1996, Bill Clinton signed the "Bill Emerson Good Samaritan Food Donation Act," which encourages food donation to non-profits by limiting liability. I like the program because I see food wasted all the time at large venues and wonder about the spoilage at grocery stores. The federal government runs 126 different anti-poverty programs according to the CATO Institute, many of them overlapping and confusing. Congress seems unlikely to untangle the mess. The problem of poverty has many causes and no easy solutions. I'll offer some thoughts later in the chapter.

Exploitation of children, especially young girls, is another area where the world, including the U.S., has fallen short. Sexual abuse, domestic violence, trafficking, child pornography, Internet predators, and bullying is just starting the American list. You read about new cases of deviant and criminal behavior every day in the press. In many cases, predators are actually working in the schools due to inadequate background checks, something every Parent Teacher Association (PTA) should insist upon. Local youths are abducted or killed daily. If you're in the Washington metro area, you've been touched by the disappearance of Relisha Rudd and the murders of the Peters' brothers and Genevieve Orange. Or the sad story of Joy Keo, who was shot four times by an ex-boyfriend, went on to live a challenging life in a wheelchair, and who died in 2014 at age 45. The boyfriend served only seven years in prison, was released and married, and is raising a family. Stories like these are not uncommon in other metropolitan areas and are particularly unnerving when we learn that the perpetrators had criminal records or were out of prison on parole at the time of the attack.

If you're prepared, here are some more uncomfortable statistics:

- Recent reports suggest that upwards of 50% of Internet usage is for pornography.
- The DOJ estimates that a million child pornographic images are available on the Internet at any given time and that 750,000 possible predators are online at any one time.
- The Mayo Clinic found a direct link between those who viewed child pornography and child molestation. There are 50-100 thousand child pedophile rings internationally, with about 1/3 of those in the U.S. - Read this one a second time.
- There are roughly 750,000 registered sex offenders in the U.S. Check out the web for those closest to you. Many more change locations and don't register. Research estimates that

one in six boys and one in four girls in the U.S. are sexually abused before their 18th birthday. [170] One in five women report being sexually assaulted (that's assaulted – not harassed) in college based on a 2015 survey.

- According to a 2011 FBI report, about 300,000 U.S. children are at risk of being exploited for sex, which the report called an epidemic. Most girls are 12-14 and from broken homes. Rep. Ted Poe (R—TX) made the startling observation that there are more animal shelters in the U.S. than shelters for exploited children. [171] View the documentary film "Sex + Money – a National Search for Human Worth" for more background.

- Experts state that at least 25% of students are bullied offline (traditional intimidation to include verbal abuse, questioning sexual orientation, or criticizing clothes).

If you, somehow, still believe we're doing enough for our children, then go back and read the previous couple of pages. The list goes on: violent video games (like Happy Tree Friends) protected by first amendment rights (as they should be–I guess), and 100,000 children in U.S. foster care.

Internationally the situation is much worse for children, although our record in the U.S. is pretty dismal. Virtual trafficking, denial of education for women, Female Genital Mutilation (FGM); about 10 million women between the ages of 11 and 13 are forcibly married each year, subjecting them to a life of predictable outcome.

Education is another area where we are failing our children, despite the daily efforts of many inspired and dedicated teachers in our schools. There are several good indices of student achievement; The Program for International Student Assessment (PISA) and the National Assessment of Educational Progress (NAEP) being a couple.

In 2001, Congress passed the No Child Left Behind Act (NCLB), which instituted standards-based education reform, and requires each state to develop its own standards and assess students' annual academic progress. As part of the 2009 American Recovery and Reinvestment Act, the Race to the Top (RTT), was a $4+ billion-dollar effort to spur states toward innovation and education reform through a point system. It involved improving teacher effectiveness, complying with Common Core standards, and others. So what are the results?

The 2012 PISA assessment shows the U.S. flat while countries like Poland, Ireland, Germany and Vietnam showed impressive progress. Of 65 economies (including 34 OECD countries), the U.S. ranked below average in math (26th) and about average in reading (17th) and average in science (21st).

A different study (there are many) found that only 24% of California's high school students were proficient in math. Critics have used results like these to criticize top down education direction such as NCLB (Bush) and RTT (Obama). The American Council of Trustees and Alumni (ACTA), a non-profit, found that 29% of 1000 colleges require two or fewer subjects, and only 5% require economics.[172]

Not all the news is glum, however. From 1999 to 2012 public high school graduation rate increased from 71 to 80 % according to the National Center for Education Statistics. Inside the numbers are the following: Asian 88%, White 86%, Hispanic 73% and blacks 69%; girls overall 84%, boys 77%. But that leaves over 700,000 who should have graduated with the high school class of 2012 and didn't and many more who did graduate but are unprepared for college.

College completion results are less encouraging, as again reported by the Organization for Economic Development and Cooperation (OEDC). In 2009, President Obama announced a goal for the U.S. to regain the lead in college attainment by 2020. The U.S. then ranked 12th at 39%. Most recent data shows 41% attainment, but the U.S. ranking has now slipped to 16th.

In his 2015 State of the Union, President Obama proposed federal funding for community colleges. It's not a bad idea, but with a $19 trillion-dollar debt (and growing) can we afford the bill?

I think the emphasis should be on the younger ages, particularly preschool, where early development really takes place. As the old Jesuit saying goes, 'give me a child for his first seven years and I'll give you the man.' And Bill Gates is quoted as saying "If every child had math teachers equal to those in the top quartile, the achievement gap between the U.S. and Asia would vanish in two years." Maybe not, but I accept the premise. Less than 30% of American 4-year-olds attend state-funded preschool; in China that figure is closer to 70%.[173] That's the first thing that needs to change.

> *"Many schools are in the grip of one of the most anti-meritocratic forces in America: the teacher's unions, which resist any hint that good teaching should be rewarded or bad teachers fired."*
> --The Economist, 1/24/2015

With all the data, Education is increasingly a subject of widespread discussion and heated opinions: Common Core, Charter Schools, and quality teachers rise to the top. Following the momentum of NCLB and RTT, Common Core standards were developed, which established standards for K-12 in reading and math, and was eventually adopted by 45 states and D.C. It was a bipartisan effort that was widely endorsed at the time, but is now being challenged on several fronts as being non-representative of achievement and using inappropriate measures. This despite a recent international study that showed the U.S. now ranked 21st in reading, and 31st in math. There is much misinformation regarding Common Core, which is simply a set of learning standards and does not involve curriculum development or testing. It is still up to states and local jurisdictions on how to teach to achieve those standards. Still, many on the right see a federal movement to tie these standards to federal funding, and some on the left see threats from unfair testing and impact to teachers when achievement is tied so directly to test scores. With politics of 2016 now in play, many states are walking away from Common Core, including governors who previously supported the standards. I think this should be a state decision, but I do support some federal standards as a way to measure achievement. More importantly, standardized testing shows where achievement is lacking and where remedial focus is required.

In April of 2015, the Senate began considering the bipartisan Alexander- Murray Education Reform Bill that would replace NCLB, restoring more authority to states and local boards to evaluate teachers, test academic achievement, fix failing schools and better support teachers. In July 2015, the Senate passed a bipartisan rewrite of NCLB by a vote of 81-17, almost unheard of in today's environment. As advertised, it reduced the role of the Department of Education in influencing state academic standards, reduced standardized testing and left it to the states to determine how to define and deal with failing schools. Then in early December 2015 the House passed a similar bill, subsequently passed by the Senate and signed by the President on 10 December 2015. With this bipartisan bill the role of the federal government and Department of Education is greatly reduced, with accountability for education squarely now with the states. States will still have to test in reading and math and identify the lowest 5% of schools that accept federal funds. We got what we asked for – I hope our falling international standing in education and declining test scores move in a different direction now. Time will tell if the states can do the job!

Another controversial subject is the rise of Charter schools, often with publicly supported vouchers. New York City Mayor Bill de Blasio campaigned against Charter schools, with backing from teachers' unions, but his early efforts were defeated by parents (many of whom were minorities) as well as by NY Governor Cuomo. The bottom line is that Charter schools seem to be working, and cost less. From Milwaukee to New Orleans to Chicago, Charter schools are on the rise. Rahm Emanuel, mayor of Chicago, has made a big investment in Charter schools; in New Orleans over 90% of students now attend Charter schools. Finally, rewarding and providing incentives such as merit pay for the best teachers makes sense. It would be unfair not to recognize that an overwhelming majority of teachers go to work every day with a purpose of educating our children, and most do a terrific job, with low pay and little recognition beyond self-fulfillment. The challenges are immense, as any public school teacher will relate (ask one), with increased poverty, growing violence and increased special needs. Teachers today are part counselor, part parent, hygienist, nutritionist, behavioral analyst and disciplinarian, all in a day's work. For all that responsibility, the majority deal with oversized classrooms, agitated parents, and are underpaid by any standard, and insufficiently appreciated for the herculean feat they perform daily.

Comprehensive welfare reform was last passed in 1996 (the TANF program), which limited the time that welfare recipients could receive benefits while seeking work. With the recession, it hasn't been easy for many families, some of whom lost their homes to foreclosure.

In 2013, the CATO Institute did a study that documented the 126 federal programs targeted to low-income people, of which 72 provided cash or in-kind benefits.[174] They took a single mother of two children state-by-state. In New York City, the benefits package would be worth $38,000 (and not taxed as wages.) That's about $20/hour, well above minimum wage. Considering taxes, the mother would need to find a job around $25/hour (that's about $50,000 a year) to just break even, and that doesn't include added expenses such as childcare and work transportation. While results varied by state, the report found that welfare benefits exceeded $15/hour in twelve states and in D.C., more than many administrative and many entry-level teaching jobs. So why would anyone work for $7.25, the current federal minimum wage? The issue of welfare reform splits along party lines, with Democrats usually supporting (not paid for) expansion, and Republicans more inclined to provide work incentives and reduce extended payments.

So here are some final thoughts for our kids:

(1) A new round of welfare reform should look to consolidate and simplify the 120+ existing programs. Public policy should reward work over welfare while still providing for those at the lowest income levels who need temporary assistance, and there is solid evidence that limiting welfare payments does motivate recipients to re-enter the job market.

(2) Embrace the healthier school lunches that Michele Obama has championed, modeled after Japan. Japan's child obesity rate has declined every year for the past six years; the U.S. child obesity rate has tripled over the past three decades.[175]

(3) Promote innovation in education. We know that the traditional 4-year college education will be changing with more online opportunities. The real long-term solution to hunger and poverty is living-wage laws and good jobs, complemented by a strong cultural underpinning. Our community colleges and local businesses need to continue to partner on good apprentice jobs, where a job is more certain after graduation; and let's get all 50 states to adopt student

achievement measures (not necessarily Common Core) and reward teacher effectiveness.

(4) Tax reform (also discussed in the first chapter) that gets rid of income splitting and the marriage penalty (let's encourage marriage) and encourage work to the point that those on low incomes and food stamps don't pay an enormous marginal rate when they move to the next level.

(5) Encourage Charter schools if they work, and great programs like "Teach for America" that recruit great kids right out of college to teach in some tough areas for two years. I am a fan of national service of some sort, and this one is near the top of my list, and another opportunity to reduce student debt.

(6) Re-evaluate how our funding is working. The federal government contributes about 10% to K-12 public education, with the other 90% coming from the state or localities.

(7) Accept world leadership to eliminate global hunger. The percentage of the world's population that is living in extreme poverty (defined as less than $1.25/day) has dropped to about 18%, half the rate it was 25 years ago. But there is more to be done.

(8) As for exploitation, we clearly need more shelters, tougher laws, and tougher judges for that matter. We've dumbed down the rhetoric—we need to call rape what it is, not sexual-assault. Sexual predators and pedophiles should suffer the harshest, most severe punishments that can be inflicted within the law.

(9) We can't do enough for those caregivers to children with severe handicaps, from autism to severe ADHD to mental health—across the board. Same for grandparents and other relatives raising children even as they border on poverty themselves. In November 2013, Virginia State Senator Creigh Deeds was stabbed multiple times by his son, who then took his own life. It is revealing that there had been no

hospital bed available for the treatment of his son the evening before the incident, or none that could be located.

This is only the beginning of a list of imperatives and doesn't even touch in detail on the exploitation problem. Everyone needs to be involved and initiatives like 'My Brother's Keeper' are a great place to start.

There are many other social issues we are facing. I admit to worrying about the long-term effects of the legalization of marijuana, particularly on our youth. If, as some reports indicate, it is a gateway drug for 1 in 6 new users, then the costs in human terms will be immense. In early 2015, the Center of Health Statistics reported almost a 3-fold increase in heroin deaths in the country between 2010 and 2013, and local media in the Washington metro area is talking about a heroin epidemic—it's nationwide. Unfortunately, I think this will become more common as an increased number of states legalize marijuana in the future, and the levels of addition increase dramatically. We rarely talk about the war on drugs today because we've basically lost that war. Ask any parent with a kid in middle or high school and you'll learn that drugs are available on request. It's frightening to project another 20 years into the future as this epidemic escalates.

I'll close this chapter by restating something: I do think the most important challenge for our youth is the cycle of poverty that we discussed previously. It has a direct and dramatic impact on our children. The breakdown of the family unit has been tied to income inequality, but it is increasingly difficult to determine which now is causal. Whatever more we can do to encourage responsible childbearing and parenting, strengthen the extended family, reward good teachers, improve our schools, expand preschool and provide the best opportunity for higher education to our children, is worth the investment. As has been discussed, but is also worth repeating, the importance of early preschool education and a strong social/extended family fabric are very critical elements, and are good predictors of education beyond high school and achievement post-formal schooling. For those of faith and a strong religious underpinning, those are excellent foundational building blocks as well.

CHAPTER 9

OBAMACARE

In many ways, some of the ridiculous discussions on Obamacare parallel the immigration debate, primarily in the overt hypocrisy displayed by both sides of the political aisle.

There is a long history that is conveniently overlooked. In 1989, the Heritage Foundation, a conservation Republican-leaning think tank, first proposed the individual mandate. When in 1993 Bill Clinton (an effort led by the then-First Lady, Hillary Clinton) proposed an employer mandate through regulated markets; the Republicans countered with a bill that included an individual mandate (versus employer mandate), universal coverage with a penalty for not participating, and subsidies to support state marketplaces. There was no discussion as to constitutionality at the time, and CBO considered it effectively a tax, which was not contested.

Sounds familiar? Except many have switched sides. Some of the same Republican senators who supported the Republican proposals for the individual mandate and universal coverage, now oppose Obamacare on the same grounds.[176]

In 2006, then Governor Mitt Romney signed a bill in Massachusetts that provided for universal care, an individual mandate, and a state insurance exchange. Many Republicans praised the law. In 2008, Senator John McCain ran for president on an alternative that provided everyone a refundable tax credit: $5000 for a couple and $2500 for singles, rather than employer-provided health coverage backed by tax incentives, not a bad idea. Interestingly, Obama opposed the individual mandate as a candidate for president, but was persuaded otherwise after the election.

One of the chief architects of Obamacare was none other than Jonathan Gruber, the MIT professor, and notoriously high paid consultant who modeled the new law after the Massachusetts legislation, and who in late 2014 labeled the American people "stupid" in describing the deliberate lack of transparency leading up to the bill.

It's all politics, laced with inexcusable hypocrisy.

A few years ago I was in Canada on business and one Canadian reminded me that they have free health care. Not entirely, in that coverage there only covers about 70% of costs and does not include prescription drugs, and there are plenty of stories of Canadians and others coming to the U.S. for the quality care that they cannot get at home. A few years ago the U.S. was spending more on health care as a percent of GDP ($2.7 Trillion) and per capita (@ 17.7%; $8500) than any other of the 40 countries in the OECD. Canada by comparison is 11.2% of GDP and $4500 per capita, and Britain is 9% of GDP.

The trajectory is alarming and attributable to waste, fraud, inefficiency and procedure-based costs, which encourages unnecessary tests, surgeries, and prescriptions. In 2012, about 50 million Americans were uninsured, and still health care cost was over 17% of GDP! According to the National Health Expenditure Accounts (NHEA), in 2013 those per capita U.S. figures had risen to $9255 per person.

Although we now have been through multiple rounds of sign-ups, there are surveys that show 2 in 5 Americans still do not understand what Obamacare means to them. We've all heard enough of the misquotes, like former Speaker Pelosi's comment that we should pass the law so we can "read what's in it." Some have been deliberately misleading, as the President repeatedly telling the American people that they could keep their health plan if they wanted to, or that individual health plan costs would not rise, or the Administration's placating that Jonathan Gruber was a bit player in Obamacare (his is the only name specifically mentioned on the Wikipedia site for Obamacare.) Some of this was by design, having seen why Clinton failed when citizens feared to lose their coverage, so they carefully tried to manage the message. President Obama insisted it wasn't a tax, but the Supreme Court said otherwise in upholding the individual mandate provision. It's interesting to reflect back to when Republicans were pushing health reform, and it was then commonly acknowledged as a tax.

Here are some specifics of the Patient Protection and Affordable Care Act (what everyone, except the Administration, refers to as Obamacare), and signed into law in March of 2010. In *very macro* terms (there are 10,000 pages of regulations associated with the law):

- States will operate insurance exchanges where individuals and families can shop and compare prices and coverage, and are allowed some discretion on services provided and prices. If states chose not to set up their own exchange, which 36 did not, residents will participate in a federal program run by the Department of Health and Human Services (HHS), with somewhat less discretion. Open enrollment for the second round ran through 15 February 2015, and a third round began 1 November 2015.
- Individuals must purchase insurance that meets minimum coverage standards in ten essential categories, either through their employer or otherwise, or pay a penalty, called the

individual mandate, of $95 or 1% of income (whichever is higher). Individuals are exempt if costs exceed 8% of income. (In 2015 the penalty was $325 per adult, half that for children under 18, up to a $975 ceiling – higher in 2016.) What is essential is left to the HHS to determine, thereby addressing the long-standing inadequate plans on the individual market, but also driving the plans' cost.

- Businesses with 50 or more full-time employees must offer insurance coverage, or face a tax penalty, called the *employer mandate.* Employer-sponsored coverage is tax exempt for the business.

- Insurers are required to offer coverage at comparable rates for age and location, without regard to pre-existing conditions or sex.

- Individuals and families with income between 100%-400% of the federal poverty line will receive subsidies on a graduated basis, to offset the purchase of exchange coverage. If employer coverage were offered, subsidies would only be available to those whose coverage cost exceeded 9.5% of income.

- Finally, Medicaid is expanded to individuals and families with incomes up to 133% of the FPL. However, the Supreme Court ruled the provision requiring states to expand Medicaid to be unconstitutional, and about twenty have not.

Beyond the obvious goal of expanding coverage to millions of uninsured, other objectives of the legislation were to reduce overall health care costs, or at least slow the rate of increase (sometimes referred to as bending the curve). The individual mandate, by design, would ensure that younger and healthier enrollees balanced the insurance pool, thus affording the coverage for those whose care would be costlier (in other words, the elderly and those with pre-existing conditions). Without the individual mandate (which the

Supreme Court upheld as a tax) the revenue plan and projections fall apart.

There are many other detailed elements and nuances of the law, but those are the major ones. CBO initially estimated that the legislation would reduce health care costs through 2019 by about $200 billion, but these estimates have been roundly criticized. Back in 1967 the House Ways and Means Committee estimated that by 1990 Medicare would cost $9 billion; it ended up costing $110B that year, more than ten times as much, and is now close to $500B. Many think a similar escalation will accrue to Obamacare.

Controversy: There are several overarching arguments that frame much of the current debate. First, how much government do we want in the medical aspect of our lives. In other words, should people be able to keep inadequate insurance from the individual market that they are comfortable with, or be required to buy to a higher standard? The second being, if we do want a health exchange, how do we make it work with full coverage, market-based prices through competition and transparency. Many feel, the author included, that the train has left the station on Obamacare, and efforts now should be focused on fixing the failings in the legislation. Market forces alone were not able to prevent nearly 50 million Americans from not having coverage (and many more with inadequate coverage), hence the individual mandate, a provision supported by both Democrats and Republicans at different junctures over the past three decades. Estimates vary greatly, but roughly 50 million were uninsured before Obamacare, and about 30 million will remain uninsured by 2022. These figures change often and include illegal immigrants, people who choose to pay a penalty, and those stuck in a gap between the subsidy and Medicaid and thus unable to afford coverage.

Among other controversial issues is the requirement to provide contraception coverage on all policies, except for religious organizations. In those cases, coverage is now provided by the insurer directly without additional charge, although another lawsuit is working its way to the Supreme Court.

The employer mandate has come under bipartisan fire from small businesses and unions out of concern that it will cause employers to shift to part-time workers rather than cross the 50 employee and 30-hour workweek thresholds, and incur those new costs. We've seen evidence already of precisely this impact as more employers are shifting to on-demand, part-time workers. There are two million more part-time workers now, who want to work full-time, than just prior to the recession.[177] Uber is a prime example. Their 160,000 drivers are independent contractors who are not full-time employees and, therefore, not required to have employer-provided health coverage. Uber is being challenged in court and may eventually lose, in which case it will likely limit all drivers to less than 30 hours per week, thereby avoiding Social Security taxes and mandated employer health insurance (many Uber drivers don't hit that 30-hour threshold anyway.)

Overall, I think the impact to business is overestimated as the economy has slowly improved, and employers begin to hire again. Another factor is what's called the Cadillac Tax, which is a 40% employer tax on the most generous insurance policies, now delayed two years until 1 January 2020. Politicians on both side of the aisle are now disparaging this provision over the objections of many economists.

Another frequent argument, substantiated by many actual cases, is that workers will leave better-paying jobs in order to receive expanded Medicaid benefits and subsidized health coverage.

CBO estimated that the full-time labor force would shrink by 2.5 million as a direct result.

The Administration has postponed the employer mandate twice, until sometime in 2016. Around twenty states have not voted to expand Medicaid to 133% of the poverty level, even though 90% of the additional cost would initially be provided by the federal government. Those states have argued that the additional 10% is unaffordable, a counter that is not without some merit as the Medicaid costs to states have grown substantially. By not expanding Medicaid, and being unable to attain subsidies, about six million would find (and are finding) coverage unaffordable.

Finally, the law states that only states running an exchange may receive subsidies, designed as a strong incentive for state exchanges. Although Congress expected most, if not all, states to set them up, only sixteen did so, with the other 34 leaving administrative oversight to the federal government. This interpretation of the law was challenged in the courts and, had it been held that only the sixteen states with their own exchanges could receive subsidies, much of the premise behind the legislation would have unraveled, impacting about six million people in the 34 states receiving insurance subsidies. Fortunately, in a 6-3 decision in June 2015, the Supreme Court ruled that subsidies applied to all Americans, upholding the intent (if not the letter) of the law.

Fixes needed: ACA is here to stay, but there are many changes still needed. The results vary by survey but suggest that an estimated 20 million have signed up under Obamacare and over 10 million are newly insured, helped by subsidies. The percentage of uninsured has dropped as much as 5%. Still, too many will remain unable to afford, or will otherwise remain uninsured. There are some obvious fixes and fairness issues still needed to be addressed, that we have not discussed, that include: Changing the excise tax on medical devices (now eliminated for 2016/2017); dropping the favored treatment for unions for reinsurance tax; addressing the predicted 90,000 doctor shortfall; delegating more to the states and less HHS regulation, and tort reform toward more alternate dispute resolution.

I personally favor the employer mandate and employer tax break, but struggle with how to remove the disincentive to hire the 50th worker and eliminate the full-time cutoff (30-hour) provision. That said, if employers continue to offer slimmer plans with ever-higher deductibles, of which there is growing evidence, a different approach might be needed in the future. We may yet end up with providing health care accounts for all individuals and families who can shop around for the best coverage and prices—a better market approach that McCain proposed when he ran for President, and which might be an attractive compromise and even more affordable and efficient.

We're not ready yet for a single-payer system, where one entity (presumably the HHS) would collect all the revenue and either manage or contract out the care. In some respects, reform in health started some time ago as more doctors are now salaried (meaning fewer unnecessary procedures), hospitals are consolidating, a shift to electronic records and increased physician assistant care is available.[178]

This is not all necessarily good, as doctor's risk becoming commoditized like airline pilots, spend inordinate time filling out elaborate electronic records, and lose the incentive for patient care that drove them to the profession in the first place. And we urgently need more doctors (the Association of American Medical Colleges estimates the 2025 shortfall at the 90,000 figure I just mentioned) and other health care professionals, improved cost controls (CBO predicts that by 2022 health costs will be 20% of GDP), and a plan to capture the roughly 30 million in our country that will still remain without coverage.

I mentioned this before but it bears repeating because of all the struggle and political in-fighting: Based on a recent estimate by the CBO, Obamacare should add 25 million to the ranks of the insured by 2022, still leaving approximately 30 million uninsured. That is not a very good legacy for such a hard fought for and comprehensive legislative reform. We are still a good way from universal coverage. The debate over how much government we want in our daily lives, and how to most efficiently deliver health care, will continue through the 2016 elections and well beyond.

Chapter 10

Summary

"Blessed are the peacemakers, for they shall be called the sons of God."

--Matthew 5:9

I once heard in a sermon, in matters of choice, the brain will often be trumped by the heart, which will be trumped in turn by emotions. I remember the huge emotional support for President Bush following his 9/11 speech, with promises of justice for the perpetrators. The same euphoria followed in 2008 when we elected Barack Obama, our first black president, demonstrating that we had moved beyond our racial divide. We voted our emotions; we voted for hope.

So where are we in late 2015? Let's summarize some of the data:

- The past two Administrations have increased the total national debt from around $5.8 trillion (55% of GDP) to over $18 Trillion (over 100% of GDP.)
- In a 2014 Gallup poll, 74% of Americans expressed some or a great deal of trust in the military; the presidency came in at 19% and Congress at 7%. Pew survey results have been similar, as you might recall from the Introduction.
- The economic recovery is fragile and wage growth stagnant for most Americans. The middle-class is shrinking. The

economies of our close allies are even more fragile, as are those of our competitors.

- Our foreign policy has been defined by Do No Damage, which baffles allies and adversaries alike, and is largely reactive. According to many sources, democracy and freedoms worldwide have plateaued or declined since 2006.
- Partisan politics in Washington has rendered Congress the least of the (supposedly co-equal) three branches of government, incapable of dealing with the immense problems we face. No tax reform, no immigration bill, escalating debt, and much more.

In April 2015, a Rasmussen Report showed that 63% of Americans, a staggering figure, believe that the country is headed in the wrong direction. That's worth repeating—almost 2/3 of Americans think the country is headed in the wrong direction. I don't disagree and neither do you, unless you happen to like government shutdown threats, sequestration, filibusters, political hold on nominees for key positions and general partisan rancor.

It's both sides, by the way. How we long for the old days when Bob Dole brought President Reagan and Tip O'Neill together to pass the Tax Equity and Fiscal Responsibility Act (TEFRA) in 1982. Where are the Senate barons of old like Johnson, Dirksen, Moynihan, Lugar, and Kennedy, who would battle during the day over their differences, and then have a cordial dinner with members of the other party.

So now the political season is in full swing, with all the charges and counter-charges, misleading advertising, and wasteful spending.

We'll see a lot of flip-flopping on important issues. I think there are basically three reasons why a politician changes his or her mind, and two of them are bad. First, as one becomes more informed on issues, your perspective can indeed change—this is the good one. President Obama changed his view on the Defense of Marriage Act about the same time that the national polls changed. He said his views evolved, and I take him at his word on this. Hillary Clinton changed her views as well in 2013, but she also changed her view on the Pacific Trade agreement after years of advocacy. The second reason that politicians change their views is to reflect the latest poll results; we see this all the time and it's easy to call. Thirdly, many politicians change their views because they don't know what they really believe about an issue, or even themselves, or what they stand for. This is the most serious case, and, unfortunately, we have some presidential candidates out there who fall into this category, where winning is everything at any cost.

In this book I haven't covered a lot of issues that are foremost in the minds of some voters: gun control and background checks following repeated massacres (Fort Hood 2009; Aurora, Colorado 2012; Newtown, Connecticut in 2012, and Charleston, South Carolina in 2015, to name a few—unfortunately it seems there are additions to the list every week); mandatory background checks and a ban on assault weapons won't solve the problem, but it's a good place to start; pro-choice versus pro-life; women serving in elite combat roles, race relations (in 2009 62% of Americans polled thought race relations were good; in 2015 that number is 25%), LBGT issues, genetically modified (GM) foods, urgently needed prison reform, and many others.

One that I am passionate about is cruelty to animals: the facts are staggering. I think man's inhumanity to man is only surpassed by his inhumanity to animals. I was happy to see the outrage in July of 2015 by the killing of Cecil, the sanctuary lion. All of these are important issues that require the continued attention of our leaders, and they will certainly be debated in the run up to the 2016 Presidential election, as they should.

We need to seek common ground on all these divisive issues; there is room for accommodation and compromise, each side respecting the differing views of the other, without recrimination.

> *"Where there is no enemy within, the enemies outside can't hurt you."*
>
> --Winston Churchill

Here are a few characteristics I am looking for in the next president:

- A non-polarizing leader who respects all three branches of government as equals, and has the unique ability to work across the political aisle and achieve legislative success.
- A leader of uncompromised integrity and character – trust is paramount.
- A leader who is committed to reestablishing America's primacy, prosperity and safety, for future generations.
- Moral clarity and humility with a passion for making the world a better place by reducing hunger, disease, terrorism and discrimination.
- A commitment to tackling the toughest issues first: a roadmap to balancing the budget, pass comprehensive tax and immigration reform, address income inequality, and assure our allies of our continuing commitments.

Dr. Ben Carson stated at the first Republican debate that anyone of reasonable intellect would be able to learn the issues pretty quickly. He's right, the issues aren't that hard, and the debates have become more entertainment than substance. We should not be electing a president solely because they are an eloquent speaker or great debater, or that they can name most of the current world leaders, or because they had success as a state governor, or simply because they have a great resume. The next president must be capable of great leadership and stewardship of the highest office in the world. My personal bottom line: Character counts!

I long for the day in America where the world is at relative peace and a safer place, where our economy is on a sound foundation, where meritocracy reins and political correctness has ceded way to truth, where empathy and civility are restored as American values, where American children of all races and background enjoy equal opportunity to flourish, where U.S. foreign policy is coherent and understood, where our children's future is secure, and where we are united as proud Americans and fly the flag once again from our doorsteps.

> *"If a Kingdom is divided against itself, that kingdom cannot stand. And if a house is divided against itself, that house will not be able to stand."*

> --Mark 3: 23-24

How we handle all these many challenges will define the America we leave to the next generations. Partisan politics and kicking the can won't cut it. We desperately need immigration reform to protect our borders and provide a viable path the legal status. We critically need tax reform to get billions of corporate dollars working, along with sustained infrastructure investment and a manufacturing resurgance. We need great educational institutions and more resources for STEM (science, technical, engineering and math). We need entitlement reform and balanced budgets that begin to reduce the debt. We need robust and reliable intelligence, having missed the nuclear issue with Hussein, missed the Arab Spring and re-emergence of al-Qaeda after the death of Osama bin Laden, and the rise of ISIS. To accomplish all this, we need a decisive non-partisan leader at the top, both as president and Commander-in-Chief.

"The seeds of totalitarian regimes are nurtured by misery and want. They spread and grow in the evil of poverty and strife. (They reach their full growth when the hope of a people for a better life has died. We must keep that hope alive.) The free peoples of the world look to us for support in maintaining their freedom. If we falter in our leadership, we may endanger the peace of the world – and we shall surely endanger the welfare of this nation."

--The Truman Doctrine Speech to Congress,
3/12/1947

See you at the polls in November 2016!

ABOUT THE AUTHOR

Tom Church is a retired Navy Vice Admiral, leaving active duty in 2005 after more than 36 years of service. During his career, he had the privilege of commanding warships as well as the Navy's largest Naval Station in Norfolk, Virginia. Among his staff jobs included four years as the Director of the Navy Budget and assignment as the Naval Inspector General. During the latter, he investigated the Defense Department use of harsh interrogation techniques on unlawful detainees, published in what is referred to as the *"The Church Report."* Another, often referenced 'Church Committee Report' was conducted 40 years ago by a cousin, the late Senator Frank Church (D-Idaho).

Church was born in Newport, Rhode Island into a military family and traveled as a youngster, but mostly grew up in the Northern Virginia area. He attended four different high schools in 9th and 10th grade, not unlike the experiences of other military dependents with changing duty stations. His father (Albert Church Jr.), uncle, both grandfathers, and some cousins were career military. One of his grandfathers, Albert Church of Idaho, roomed with Chester Nimitz at the US Naval Academy, graduating with the class of 1905. His other grandfather, William Hamilton of Palestine, Texas, graduated with the class of 1921. Both retired as Rear Admirals.

Following military service, Church has been in the private sector for the past 10 years. He is currently Managing Director of the Prescient Edge Federal Division. Prescient Edge, based out of Chicago, Illinois is a global operations and solutions integrator delivering full-spectrum intelligence, technology and security solutions to customers throughout the Federal Intelligence

Community, as well as corporate and international clients (www.Prescient.com).

ENDNOTES

[1] David Kotok, April 2012

[2] The Economist, 3/1/2014

[3] Mitchell F. Cannon, 7/4/ 2011, National Review

[4] U.S. Census Bureau

[5] Peter Whoriskey, The Washington Post 6/19/2011

[6] Fareed Zakaria, The Washington Post editorial, 3/7 2011

[7] The Washington Post May 2013

[8] Robert Samuelson, "The Real Medicaid problem," The Washington Post, 7/14/14

[9] Robert F. Scott, Economic Policy Institute, 2/11/2013

[10] David Kotok, 4/8/2012

[11] Steven Moore, Washington Post, "The Laffer Curve is 40 and looking pretty good," 12/28/2014

[12] Ed Leamer, UCLA Anderson School

[13] USA Today, 3/28/2012

[14] Harold Meyerson article in the The Washington Post quoting a report by Carl Benedict Frey of Oxford University's Program on the Impacts of Future Technology and Michael A. Osborn, an Oxford, engineering professor

[15] The Washington Post, Charles Lane editorial 9/18/14

[16] The Washington Post, editorial by Robert Samuelson, 2/23/15

[17] The Washington Post, Peter Whoriskey, 10/4/2011

[18] "The CEO Backlash" in The Washington Post, 6/22/15 by Robert Samuelson quoting from the Economic Policy Institute

[19] The Economist, 1/24/15

[20] "Why Nations Fail," Daron Acemoglu, and James Robinson

[21] Study by MIT professor David Autoe, reported in The Washington Post by Jim Tankersley

[22] Kathleen Parker, The Washington Post, 1/1/2014

[23] The Economist Special Report 22 February 2014

[24] Charles Krauthammer, The Washington Post, "The Cure for Inversion."

[25] The Boston Globe, 4/2/2014

[26] The Washington Post editorial by Fred Hiatt, 6/4/2012

[27] Fred Hiatt editorial in The Washington Post

[28] The Washington Post, 10/20/2011

[29] The Washington Post, 10/20/2013

[30] American Economic Review, June 2010 by Christina Romer

[31] "Thoughts from the Frontline, Half a Bubble Off Dead Center" by John Mauldin, 4/20/2015

[32] Robert Samuelson, The Washington Post, editorial

[33] From Booz and Company Forum in 2011 and printed in Strategy & Business magazine

[34] Marc Levinson of the CRS, 3/17/2015

[35] Authors Arvind Kaushal, Thomas Mayor and Patricia Riedel published in the Booz and Company Strategy & Business magazine

[36] Nathan Hodge in The Wall Street Journal, 6/9/2011
[37] Mark Helprin, The Wall Street Journal, 12/27/2010
[38] Majorie Center, The Washington Post, 5/29/2011
[39] Military Officers Association of America, MOAA, 2011
[40] Wikipedia July 2010
[41] Sonny Masso, HardBall, 4/24/2014
[42] Andrew Krepinevich, The Washington Post, editorial
[43] MOAA magazine. May 2013
[44] V.H. Krulak, "Good Luck, Secretary Cohen," in the San Diego Tribune, 12/8/1997
[45] Center for American Progress; Korb, Conley and Rothman, 2/2/2011
[46] The Washington Post, 5/29/2011
[47] The Economist, 1/25/2014
[48] "Acquisition Reform: It's Mostly Up to Congress," National Defense by Sandra Erwin, 12/4/2014
[49] ED Ross, 10/1/2012
[50] Ken Allard, Washington Times, 2/27/2014
[51] "The All-Volunteer Force is Becoming Unaffordable" by Loren Thompson, Lexington Institute, 9/22/2009
[52] Army Times magazine, 11/3/2009
[53] Speech by Deputy Secretary of Defense, Bob Work in early 2015
[54] Arms Control Association website, September 2011
[55] Reported by Douglass Hagmann, National Intelligence Network, September 2004
[56] Cal Thomas, "StopTheMadrassa," 7/17/2008
[57] Cal Thomas—same article as above
[58] IPT News, 2/10/2010
[59] Ruth Marcus, The Washington Post, editorial 3/9/2011
[60] 9/11 Commission report
[61] Wikipedia: The War on Terror
[62] Wiki, War on Terror
[63] "American Hegemony, How to Use It, How to Lose It" by General William Odom
[64] CBSNews.com 11/1/2012
[65] Wikipedia—Straits of Malacca
[66] The Economist, 11/30/2013
[67] The Economist, 12/7/2013
[68] Andrew J Bacevich, The Washington Post, 4/22/2012
[69] The Washington Post, 3/4/2015 "Petraeus admits guilt in plea" by Adam Goldman and Sari Horwitz
[70] "EX-Agency officer gave NY Times reporter classified information," The Washington Post by Matt Zapotosky
[71] The Washington Post, 3/30/2014 article by Rajiv Chandrasekaran
[72] DHS, "Implementing the 9/11 Commission Recommendations" Progress Report 2011
[73] The 9/11 Commission Report
[74] The 9/11 Commission report
[75] Reuters, 5/13/2011
[76] The 9/11 Commission Report
[77] "Implementing the 9/11 Commission Recommendations." Progress Report 2011
[78] CSIS, December 2004

[79] FoxNews.com, 5/17/2011

[80] FoxNews.com 5/17/2011

[81] FoxNews.com 5/17/2011

[82] FederalNewsradio.com, on 9/1/2011, "9/11 Panel cites unfinished business."

[83] Web memo, 11/4/2010

[84] Steven Bradbury, The Washington Post, 1/5/2014

[85] Dana Milbank, The Washington Post, 4/4/2012

[86] Congressional Record 10/25/2001

[87] NPR books review of "Cyber War: The Next Threat to National Security and What to Do About It" By Richard Clarke and Robert K. Knake

[88] The Washington Post Economy Section by Ellen Nakashima, 3/25/2014

[89] News.Discovery, "Too much hysteria over cyber-attacks." 2/16/2011

[90] Washington Post, "The Arms Race in Cyberspace" by James Lewis, 10/10/13

[91] Partnership for Public Service from data collected by OPM and reported in National Defense, February 2014

[92] "On Watch," page 319, Admiral Elmo R. Zumwalt

[93] The Economist, Special Report, 11/23/2013

[94] New York Times, 5/4/2011, by Jim Dwyer

[95] Adopted from "With all our Might: A Progressive Strategy for Defeating Jihadism and Defending Liberty," edited by Will Marshall, published in an article Grand Strategy by Kenneth Pollard in Blueprint magazine July 2006

[96] The Washington Post, article by Michael Birnbaum based on Pew poll completed 5/15/2015

[97] The Washington Post, article, 1/23/2015 by Senators (Ret.) Sam Nunn and Richard Lugar

[98] Robert Kaplan, 3/19/14, TheAtlantic.com magazine, In Defense of Empire

[99] International Monetary Fund "Globalization: A Brief Overview," May 2008

[100] Former Mexican President Ernesto Zedillo at the plenary session of the World Economic Forum in Switzerland, January 2000

[101] The World Post, 3/22/2014 and Harold Meyerson, The Washington Post, Editorial, 1/15/2014

[102] The Washington Post, Dana Milban, 4/26/2015, "Asian Trade Deal an Abomination," quoting Brandeis Professor Peter Petri

[103] About.com: "U.S. Trade Deficit" by Kimberly Amadeo

[104] The Economist, 2/22/2014

[105] The Washington Post, "A Trade Deal's Corporate Giveaway," by E. Warren

[106] The Economist, 7/5/2014

[107] MidEast Web.org 10/30/2003

[108] Yahoo News 3/3/2014

[109] Jack Matlock, former ambassador to the USSR, The Washington Post, Editorial, 3/16/2014

[110] G. Will, The Washington Post, editorial

[111] The Economist 2/21/2015, Banyan

[112] The Economist, 12/7/2013

[113] General Petraeus testimony to Congress in September 2015

[114] Clifford May, Washington Times, 3/12/2014

[115] The Washington Post, 7/29/2014, article by Anthony Faiola and Griff Witte

[116] Jack Goldstone, The Washington Post, editorial

[117] The Economist, 10/17/2015

[118] Washington Times editorial by Robert Merry 4/4/14 quoting "Asia's Cauldron: The South China Sea and the End of the Stable Pacific, by 2050"

[119] Interview with Dep. AFRICOM. Lieutenant General Hummer in The Navy Times, 2/17/2014

[120] Ben Affleck in The Washington Post on 11/29/2012

[121] Remembering Beirut, Randy Gaddo, US Naval Institute, October 2013

[122] Rajiv Shaw, USAID Administrator, "How to Keep Afghanistan on the Right Track," The Washington Post, 5/30/2014

[123] Ashish Kumar Sen, The Washington Times, 1/3/2014

[124] The Economist, 3/28/2015, "The Shia Crescendo."

[125] The Economist, 6/22/2013

[126] David Ignatius, The Washington Post, July 2014

[127] The Washington Post, "Toward a Greater Iran," by Mike Morell

[128] The Washington Post, 2/21/2014, White House Debrief by Scott Wilson

[129] Mike Kelly, The Washington Times editorial, "Remembering Who Americans Are"

[130] The Economist 5/3/2014

[131] Partially attributed to Marc Theissen, The Washington Post editorial, "Warsaw's lonely fight for liberty echoes today."

[132] The Washington Post, "A Bill that changed the face of the U.S." by Tom Gjelten 9/25/2015

[133] From FAIR website "History of Immigration Laws."

[134] President Bill Clinton, State of the Union, 1/23/1996

[135] Security Management.com, article by Lily Chapa, February 2014

[136] Judicial Watch, 5/13/2014

[137] Mullen "They did not die in vain", The Washington Post

[138] Poll conducted by The Washington Post and Kaiser Family Foundation, The Washington Post, 3/30/2014 article by Rajiv Chandrasekaran

[139] Data from Veterans and PTSD Website which acknowledges the RAND study done in cooperation with the CRS, VA, Surgeon General, unless otherwise indicated

[140] Poll conducted by The Washington Post and Kaiser Family Foundation, The Washington Post, 3/30/2014 article by Rajiv Chandrasekaran

[141] "Military Suicides," The Washington Post, 11/9/2014 by Yochi Dreazen

[142] Editor-Political News "Ancient warrior myths help veterans fight PTSD," 5/23/2014

[143] Washington Post "Mental Health needs unmet through VA, care providers say" by Steve Vogel, 10/4/2011

[144] "Mental and Physical Health Status and Alcohol and Drug Use Following Return From Deployment to Iraq or Afghanistan." By Susan V. Eisen, Ph.D.

[145] Wall Street Journal, "Why Wounded Warriors Sleep in Dumpsters" by Laurence Tribe and Bobby Shriver, 6/9/2011

[146] "Man on a Mission," Parade Magazine, 8/19/2012

[147] Poll conducted by The Washington Post and Kaiser Family Foundation, The Washington Post, 3/30/2014 article by Rajiv Chandrasekaran

[148] The Washington Post, "VA and its systemic health care problems" by Sandhya Somashekar

[149] MOAA magazine October 2014). Couple that with over 20% who report sexual trauma, sexual-assault, or repeated threatening sexual harassment

[150] Parade Magazine, 11/10/2013

[151] "High rate of suicides of female Vets alarms VA," The Federal Eye, The Washington Post, 10/12/2015

[152] Tampa Bay Times, 7/21/2013 article by Kris Hundley

[153] National Alliance for Caregiving survey 2010

[154] Yogesh Khanal, The Washington Post, 12/2/2012

[155] The Economist, 8/10/2013

[156] Glenn Kessler, The Fact Checker, The Washington Post, 9/23/2014

[157] The Washington Post, Joby Warrick, 9/27/2014

[158] Susan-Marie Stedman of NOAA and Tom Dahl of U.S. Fish and Wildlife Service

[159] NOAA, "Global Climate Change" 2013

[160] The UN Framework Convention on Climate Change, UNFCCC, from Wikipedia-Deforestation

[161] Wikipedia-Deforestation. Rainforest facts at Rain-tree.com

[162] R. Samuelson The Washington Post, "Don't Kill the Shale-Gas Boom," 12/23/2012

[163] "The Next—Security—Frontier," U.S. Naval Institute, October 2013 which references Elizabeth Landau "Climate Change May Increase Violence, Study Shows" on CNN

[164] The Economist, 2/22/2014

[165] The Economist Nov 28, 2015 Special report

[166] The Washington Post, "A Secret Weapon to fight climate change: dirt", by Debbie Barker and Michael Pollan, Dec. 6, 2015

[167] The Globalist "Child Poverty in Rich Countries."

[168] The Washington Post, "5 Myths about Hunger in America" 9/21/2010

[169] "Making the Poor Poorer" by Rubin, Altman and Kearney, The Washington Post

[170] The Washington Post, "What Joe Paterno taught me," article by J.C. Derrick, 12/12/2011

[171] "Victims, Not Prostitutes," The Washington Post, by Malika Saada Saar

[172] Kathleen Parker, The Washington Post, 10/2/2011

[173] The Economist, Leaders, 1/31/2015

[174] Michael Tanner, The New York Post online, 8/19/2013

[175] The Washington Post, "On Japan's School Lunch Menu: A Healthy Meal Made From Scratch" by Chico Harlan 1/16/2013

[176] Wikipedia: Patient Protection and Affordable Care Act

[177] The Economist, "Ways of Seeing," 7/25/2015

[178] The Washington Post, editorial by David Ignatius

CPSIA information can be obtained at www.ICGtesting.com
Printed in the USA
BVOW08*2023140616

452036BV00001B/3/P